ESSENTIALS OF
ITALIAN

WILLIAMS-SONOMA

ESSENTIALS OF
ITALIAN

RECIPES AND TECHNIQUES FOR DELICIOUS ITALIAN MEALS

GENERAL EDITOR
CHUCK WILLIAMS

PHOTOGRAPHY
BILL BETTENCOURT

RECIPES
MICHELE SCICOLONE

TEXT
STEVE SIEGELMAN

Oxmoor House®

Contents

The Italians are passionate about their food, where it comes from, and how they prepare it. From the freshest wild fish to the juiciest summer tomato, each component of a meal demands the best quality. Italians respect their ingredients, and you will find that many Italian recipes are simple, allowing those raw materials, whether just-picked artichokes from the farmers' market or a fresh ball of creamy *mozzarella di bufala,* to shine.

This book takes you on a culinary journey through the regions of Italy, each of which has its own distinctive cuisine, specialty dishes, and indigenous ingredients. In few other countries is it more apparent how geography and raw ingredients have shaped the way that people eat. This strict adherence to locality and a firm belief in seasonality are what have made Italian food one of the greatest, and most highly revered, cuisines in the world.

The authentic recipes in *Essentials of Italian* are a sampling of some of the best Italy has to offer and include a wide range of dishes—many classic and recognizable favorites—like sweet-and-sour eggplant caponata, spicy *penne alla puttanesca,* and decadent tiramisu. The richness and diversity of Italian food, from garlicky grilled prawns to slowly braised short ribs served over polenta to creamy gelato bathed in espresso, have been shaped over time, but remain true to its roots.

This book is not only an excellent collection of tried-and-true recipes that have been gathered over years of traveling throughout Italy and sampling the cuisine, but an informative reference to the specialties and dishes that define each region of Italy. The book is divided by traditional courses, from antipasti to *dolci,* and even offers suggestions for full menus from many of the regions. Whether you want to prepare a festive Italian feast or fill your table with a variety of antipasti for entertaining friends and family, *Essentials of Italian* helps set the stage for authentic Italian eating.

Michele Scicolone

One Country, Many Cuisines

Italian cooking is not a single cuisine, but a richly varied feast of regional and local cooking styles, specialties, and ingredients. This book is designed to help you master the essential foods and flavors of Italy, with recipes drawn from the country's wealth of cuisines.

THE ROLE OF REGIONALITY

The key to understanding much of what defines Italian food and culture is recognizing the importance of regionality. Italy is less than three-quarters the size of California, yet its cuisine is among the world's most diverse, due in large part to the peninsula's unusually varied geography.

Think about the differences in food and culture between Switzerland, which borders Italy to the north, and Tunisia, which lies less than a hundred miles (160 km) south of Sicily, and you will begin to grasp the scope of Italian cuisine. Fitting together like a jigsaw puzzle of flat plains, rolling hills, valleys, and mountains, bounded by rivers, lakes, and seas, Italy's twenty regions are as distinctive as individual countries. And indeed, until the

Rich, earthy Fontina is made from the milk of cows that graze on the subalpine slopes of Valle d'Aosta.

unification of the Italian republic in the 1860s, each functioned as an independent nation-state, separated from its neighbors by its dialect, the unique ethnic characteristics of its population, its traditions, and its food.

An hour's journey by car or train in Italy can mean a dramatic change of scene and climate. The boot-shaped peninsula is bounded by more than four thousand miles (6,500 km) of Mediterranean and Adriatic coastline. Yet it is the foothills and mountains of the Apennines that form the backbone of most of the peninsula, defining its landscape and delineating its regions. For centuries, the widely varying microclimates and geographic features of each region have given its cooks a unique market basket of *materie prime,* or "raw materials," with which to work.

In the flat expanses of the north, for example, ample dairy land yields a ready supply of butter, milk, cream, and cow's milk cheeses, such as Parmigiano-Reggiano and Fontina. Corn and rice grow in abundance, and until relatively recently, polenta and risotto overshadowed pasta here. In central Italy, the rolling terrain is better suited to growing olives and grazing sheep, so olive oil is the cooking fat of choice and sheep's milk cheeses, such as *pecorino romano,* are more prevalent. Some of the world's most prized tomatoes grow in abundance in the rich volcanic soil of the south, where they are featured in everything from pizza and pasta to meat and seafood.

While factors such as industrialization, education, migration, and the mass media have eroded Italy's regional diversity, the

simple reality of the lay of the land still gives the regions their distinctive identities. And when it comes to food, it is the differences, far more than the similarities, that distinguish the many microcuisines of Italy, even those of cities and towns separated by only a few miles. In restaurants and home kitchens alike, local specialties remain the pride of cooks and the preferred choice for everyday eating.

CULINARY ROOTS

In many ways, Italy is the birthplace of European cuisine. It was here that the Etruscans, as early as the twelfth century BC, turned *farro* (emmer wheat), rye, barley, and other grains into bread and pasta. The ancient Romans took full advantage of the peninsula's bounty, elevating cooking to unparalleled levels of sophistication, with seasonings and ingredients from all over the empire.

In the second century AD, the vast Trajan's Forum was Rome's supermarket, a booming food emporium stocked with everything from local produce, meat, seafood, and wine to wheat from Egypt and spices from Asia. The Romans pioneered new techniques for cultivating and foraging all things edible, a legacy that still shapes the way Italians cook. Then, as now, ingredients, gathered and prepared with exacting care, were everything. It is no accident that the word *recipe* is a Latin imperative meaning "procure."

In the ninth century, the occupation of southern Italy by the Moors brought pastries, confections, and ices and such new ingredients as almonds and spinach to the Italian menu. In subsequent centuries, the crusaders brought back sugar, buckwheat, and lemons, and Venetian and Genoese traders spiced up the mix with ingredients from Asia and the Middle East. Columbus's voyages to the New World gave Italian cooks corn, peppers, and, most important, tomatoes.

All this and more made its way to France in the 1500s, when Catherine de' Medici arrived from Florence to marry Henri II. With her came legions of expert chefs with unrivaled expertise in ingredients and culinary technique. French cooks would ultimately evolve this culinary foundation into their own highly refined haute cuisine. But in Italy, cooking would remain simpler and more direct—less about artifice and more about coaxing out and celebrating the essential flavors of *materie prime*.

A CUISINE FOR ALL SEASONS

From the 1600s until as recently as the 1960s, the agrarian economy of much of Italy was based on sharecropping. *Contadini* (peasants) ingeniously made the most of what they could grow or gather, creating a rich menu of dishes that used relatively few ingredients. Today, much of the Italian food the world reveres comes from this tradition of cooking. Dishes like *pasta e fagioli* (pasta with beans), *panzanella* (a salad made from stale bread), and *salumi* (cured meats) are examples of the Italian ability to make much from little.

Making the best of what is at hand is at the root of another pillar of Italian cooking: seasonality. The use of fresh, seasonal ingredients is a national obsession. When a locally produced food, be it artichokes, olive oil, or strawberries, comes into season, its arrival is celebrated with boisterous food fairs known as *sagre*. Italians even have a term, *scorpacciata*, for the custom of feasting on copious amounts of a single food, often for days on end, when its peak season arrives.

Seasonality is at the heart of another fundamental principle of Italian gastronomy:

foods produced together should be enjoyed together. In October, chestnuts are eaten with *mosto*, the barely fermented new wine from the recent grape harvest. Prosciutto, now available year-round, was traditionally cured from autumn until the following summer, just in time to eat with the season's first ripe figs. The earliest tender fava (broad) beans of spring are eaten raw with shavings of delicate *marzolino*, a spring sheep's milk cheese.

THE ART OF SIMPLICITY

Regionality, a rich history of diverse cultural influences, and seasonality—each of these has played an important role in shaping Italian cuisine. But they are all linked by a single overarching principle: simplicity. The true art of Italian cooking—from the refined richness of the north to the robust directness of the south—is restraint. The formula is straightforward: start with the highest-quality ingredients available, prepare them with care to bring out their best, season and taste as you go, and add only what you need. Embrace that culinary philosophy and you will enjoy the true essentials of Italian cooking.

Versions of hearty *pasta e fagioli*, a traditional bean and pasta soup, can be found throughout Italy.

SLOW FOOD

Slowly but surely, the Slow Food movement is changing the way much of the world cooks and eats. And it is no coincidence that the organization that set it in motion began in Italy, where the preservation of local food traditions has been a fundamental part of the culture for centuries.

Italian journalist Carlo Pietrini founded Slow Food in the Piedmont region in 1986, as a way to oppose the spread of fast-food restaurants and the global homogenization of food they encourage. Through international conferences and local chapters worldwide, the organization promotes biodiversity in the world's food supply, conducts educational programs, provides a networking forum for locally based food producers, and works to identify and preserve "heritage" foods, flavors, and ingredients in danger of extinction through industrialization.

Beyond the official Slow Food movement, the idea of slow food has captured the imagination of professional chefs and home cooks all over the world. More and more restaurants proudly serve locally and sustainably produced ingredients, including seasonal vegetables and fruits, artisan cheeses, hearth breads, and even wild, line-caught fish and organic, free-range meats. Local farmers' markets are thriving in greater numbers than ever. Many supermarkets and neighborhood markets are increasingly featuring organic and local foods. It appears, in other words, that when it comes to food, the world is becoming a little more Italian.

The Regions

Italy is divided into twenty administrative regions, each with its unique geographic features and its own distinctive food and wine specialties. What follows is a culinary journey through those regions, proceeding from north to south and west to east.

VALLE D'AOSTA
Capital: Aosta

Alpine Cooking

Italy's smallest and least populous region, Valle d'Aosta borders France and Switzerland and includes the Italian slopes of two of Europe's most famous mountains, Mont Blanc and the Matterhorn. The hearty and generally rustic cuisine shows influences from France and Piedmont, drawing heavily on potatoes, polenta, and cheese, especially Fontina. Wild goat, hare, veal, and pork are mainstays, whether roasted, braised, grilled, or cured in various *salumi* and sausages.

Culinary Signature: Fontina

This semisoft yellow cheese, with a rich, nutty, slightly sweet flavor, is prized for its creamy texture when melted. Fontina-style cheeses have been made in the Alps since ancient times. Today, authentic DOP Fontina, identifiable by the Matterhorn stamp of the producers' consortium, is produced exclusively in Valle d'Aosta from the milk of cows native to the region.

Regional Specialties

Tomini an antipasto of *tomini* (small, round cheeses) dressed with olive oil and lemon

Mocetta air-dried salted meat (traditionally wild goat, but now also beef and lamb) served in thin slices as an antipasto

Polenta concia a layered polenta baked with Fontina cheese and butter

Lardo d'Arnad salted, herbed pork fat

Costoletta alla valdostana a breaded veal chop stuffed with Fontina

Carbonade also *carbonada*; a stew of beef and onions braised in red wine

Caffè alla valdostana coffee with lemon zest, grappa, sugar; served in a wooden pot

PIEDMONT (PIEMONTE)
Capital: Turin (Torino)

Rich Flavors and Big Wines

Piedmont shares borders with France and Switzerland—and shares many culinary traditions with them as well, from its world-renowned wines to its famed white truffles and rich butter-and-cheese sauces. Instead of first-course pastas, locals favor soups, broths, and, because Piedmont is a leading rice-growing area, risotto, often prepared with the region's red wines. Meat and game abound in landlocked Piedmont, with fish—primarily trout—playing a lesser role. A long-standing tradition of home gardening brings an abundance of fresh vegetables to the table—from cardoons and fennel to asparagus, cabbage, and peppers—most famously in *bagna cauda*. The region's great wines include a pair of robust aged reds, Barolo and Barbaresco, both made from the Nebbiolo grape, and the sweet, sparkling Asti Spumante. Vermouth was also invented here, and Piedmont is home to the vermouth producers Martini & Rossi and Cinzano, among others. Locals love their cookies, cakes, and coffee. Famous for its cafés, Turin is renowned as a center of coffee roasting and of chocolate making, especially *gianduia*, chocolate blended with the region's prized hazelnuts (filberts).

Culinary Signature: White Truffles

Like the famous black truffles of Périgord, the *tartufi bianchi* of the Alba province and the Langhe region are among the world's most precious culinary treasures, routinely selling for thousands of dollars per kilo at the region's truffle markets. They grow underground and are harvested by truffle hunters who work with trained sniffing dogs, often late at night to avoid revealing their best locations. More refined and delicate than black truffles, white truffles are never cooked. Instead, they are shaved raw over a finished dish at the last minute, its rising heat releasing their earthy aroma and ethereal flavor. October is peak season for fresh white truffles, and they are highly perishable, but their flavor can be enjoyed year-round in preserved pastes, sauces, and infused oils.

The area around Alba, in Piedmont, is the home of the white truffle, found nowhere else in Europe.

Regional Specialties

Bagna cauda a sauce of garlic and anchovies, served hot with raw vegetables for dipping

Gnocchi alla bava potato dumplings in a creamy Fontina cheese sauce

Brasato al barolo beef or veal braised in Barolo wine

Bollito misto tender boiled beef and other meats served with *mostarda* (condiment of fruits flavored with mustard seed) or *salsa verde* (piquant herb sauce)

Grissini long, thin bread sticks

Fonduta Italian version of Swiss fondue, made with Fontina cheese

Zabaglione a dessert of whipped egg yolks, sugar, and Marsala

LOMBARDY (LOMBARDIA)
Capital: Milan (Milano)

A Golden Cuisine

If Rome is Italy's political capital, Milan is its financial center, and the food of Lombardy reflects that prosperity. It is no coincidence that many of the region's best-known dishes are golden—once a symbol of wealth—from saffron-tinged risotto and breaded veal cutlets to pale yellow panettone. The flat plains of the Po River valley extend across most of the region, affording an abundance of corn and rice. These find their way onto the menu as polenta and risotto, which are generally preferred here over pasta. Ample grazing land ensures plenty of butter, cream, and cheese, all of which are used lavishly in local kitchens, a culinary legacy of nearby France, as well as plenty of beef and veal. Cooking here tends to be low and slow, with meats more often braised and simmered than grilled or roasted. Small freshwater fish are a specialty of the region's lakes: Como, Garda, and Maggiore.

Culinary Signature: Rice

Short-grain rice, with its small, plump kernels, has a higher starch content than medium- or long-grain rice. When simmered slowly and stirred constantly, it becomes creamy and tender, with a delicate al dente firmness, making it the rice of choice for risotto. Among Italian short-grain rices sold abroad, Arborio is the best known and easiest to find, but other varieties are worth tracking down. Carnaroli, sometimes called the "caviar" of Italian rices, is prized for its creaminess and firm core, which makes it more resistant to overcooking. Vialone Nano also produces a creamy risotto and is a good choice when parcooking risotto for finishing later.

Regional Specialties

Bresaola air-cured, salted beef tenderloin, served in thin slices like prosciutto as an antipasto

Risotto alla milanese golden risotto made with saffron, butter, and Parmigiano-Reggiano

Tortelli di zucca ravioli with a pumpkin filling

Pizzocheri buckwheat pasta with potatoes, cabbage, and cheese

Minestrone classic vegetable-and-pasta soup, often served with fresh basil pesto

Osso buco veal shanks braised with wine and sometimes tomatoes, served with *gremolata,* a garnish of minced parsley, lemon zest, and garlic

Costoletta alla milanese breaded veal cutlet, often served on the bone

Mascarpone a fresh, thick cow's milk cheese similar to cream cheese and used in desserts and as a garnish for risotto

Taleggio a semisoft cow's milk cheese

Panettone a sweet yeast bread studded with candied citron and raisins, originally served at Christmas and Easter, but now available year-round

Slowly braised, tender osso buco is traditionally served with *risotto alla milanese*—golden saffron risotto—and *gremolata*, a raw citrus-herb garnish.

TRENTINO—ALTO ADIGE
Capital: Trent (Trento)

Austria Meets Italy

Even though they are joined into a single region, Trentino and Alto Adige are like two separate countries from a culinary standpoint. The food of Alto Adige (also called Südtirol) is essentially Austrian with Italian influences, while the cooking of Trentino is similar to that of neighboring Veneto. In Alto Adige, the main meat is pork, which is cooked, smoked, or cured to make *salumi,* such as *speck.* Brown rye bread, sauerkraut, goulash, and strudel are other typical Tyrolean specialties served here. In Trentino, polenta made from corn or buckwheat is a dietary mainstay and is often topped with wild mushrooms, which grow abundantly in the Dolomites. Trentino is also known for its apples, wild strawberries, and cow's milk cheeses.

Culinary Signature: Speck

Speck is the German word for bacon, but the *speck* of Alto Adige isn't bacon at all. It is made from pork leg, not pork belly, and is brined with herbs and garlic and then cold smoked and aged, resulting in a texture reminiscent of prosciutto and a flavor that recalls pancetta. Speck is eaten thinly sliced as an antipasto with figs or melon, and is also used in cooking to flavor everything from pasta sauces to pizza and dumplings.

Regional Specialties

Wild mushrooms porcini, chanterelles, and other mushrooms grow in profusion in the region

Ravioli alla pusterese wheat-and-rye pasta stuffed with cabbage or sauerkraut

Spätzle flour and egg dumplings, often served with Gorgonzola

Canederli bread dumplings made with *speck* or liver, known as *knödel* in Alto Adige

Gulasch di manzo a beef stew, similar to Hungarian goulash

VENETO
Capital: Venice (Venezia)

The Best of Land and Sea

Venice, a center of culinary and cultural refinement since the Middle Ages, was the birthplace of the fork and the napkin, and it was in Venetian kitchens that both polenta and rice were first popularized in Italy. The cooking here revolves around the bountiful fish and seafood of the Lagoon of Venice and the Adriatic Sea—from shrimp (prawns), cuttlefish, and squid to sole, bream, and mullet—as well as salt cod *(baccalà)*. Throughout the Veneto, risotto, often prepared with seafood, has traditionally been the most popular first course. Pasta turns up less frequently, with the exception of *pasta e fagioli* and *bigoli*. From Treviso, to the north, comes world-renowned red radicchio. To the west, Padua, Verona, and Vicenza have their own specialties, including squash-blossom fritters,

potato gnocchi, *pandoro* (a sweet golden bread), and *baccalà alla vicentina*. The region's best known wines are Soave, a light white; Valpolicella and Bardolino, light, fruity reds; and Amarone, a rich variety of Valpolicella made in the *passito* method, in which the grapes are dried before fermentation.

Culinary Signature: Polenta

Maize came to Italy from the New World via the port of Venice in the sixteenth century. Cooked into a mush as other grains had been before it, the golden grain—called *grano turco* because it was thought to come from Turkey—caused a sensation and became a staple of the Veneto and much of northern Italy. Slowly simmered with water or broth in a *paiolo* (hammered copper pot), it is traditionally eaten soft and warm with butter, milk, and cheese. It is also often poured into a thin sheet, cooled, cut into pieces, and fried. Although it requires more time to prepare, traditional polenta is creamier and has a more toothsome texture than quick-cooking polenta.

Regional Specialties

Pasta e fagioli a hearty, ham-based white bean soup made with pasta

Risi e bisi rice and peas with the consistency of a thick soup

Bigoli homemade thick, chewy whole-wheat (whole-grain) spaghetti

Risotto short-grain rice often made with seafood and cooked *all'onda* (wavy, or soupy)

Baccalà salt cod, served *mantecato* (pounded with olive oil and garlic until smooth and creamy) or *alla vicentina* (cooked with onions, milk, and cheese)

Seppioline cuttlefish, often served in a sauce made with their own ink

Brodetto seafood and tomato stew

Sarde in saor fried sardines layered with sweet-and-sour onions and raisins

Cicchetti the "tapas" of Venice—small-plate snacks, often seafood based, served at wine bars *(bàcari)*

Fegato alla veneziana thinly sliced calf's liver sautéed with onions and white wine

Seafood, such as fresh sardines, defines the cuisine of Venice, a city surrounded by the sea.

Creamy slow-cooked polenta, rather than pasta, is popular in the Veneto region.

Silky and tender, air-cured prosciutto is dry-salted for one month under weights, then air-dried for six months or more. It is a staple of antipasti platters.

FRIULI–VENEZIA GIULIA
Capital: Trieste

Gateway to Middle Europe

High in the northeastern corner of Italy, Friuli–Venezia Giulia borders on Austria and Slovenia, and the cuisine shows distinct middle European influences in dishes like *cotto e cren* (ham with horseradish) and goulash. For the most part, the ingredients are those of the Po River valley and the Alps—polenta, pork, potatoes, turnips, cabbage—with seafood added to the mix along the Adriatic coast. The port city of Trieste is Italy's leading coffee-roasting center. Friuli produces some of the country's best white wines, including Tocai Friulano, and the region was among the first to elevate grappa, once thought of as home-brewed firewater, to the level of a fine spirit.

Culinary Signature: *Prosciutto di San Daniele*

On a par with the famed *prosciutto di Parma*, *prosciutto di San Daniele* is somewhat sweeter and less salty. Made in the town of San Daniele at the base of the Alps, the dry-cured ham owes its distinctive flavor and meltingly soft texture to the dry mountain air of the area. Like all prosciutto, it is best enjoyed raw, in paper-thin slices, either on its own or with cheese or fresh fruit, such as figs or melon. It can also be used in cooking.

Regional Specialties

Jota a hearty soup made with beans and cabbage

Cialzons Friulian ravioli with a sweet-savory filling that can include ricotta, dried fruit, potato, and spinach

Mesta e fasoi polenta cooked with beans

Frico lacy crisps made by frying grated Montasio cheese

Stinco veal or pork shin, roasted or braised

Muset con broade pork sausages served with pickled turnips

Montasio a cow's milk cheese eaten both aged and fresh, as a grating and table cheese, respectively

LIGURIA

Capital: Genoa (Genova)

The Coastal Garden

Boomerang-shaped Liguria is a long strip of Italian Riviera, with Genoa at its center and the coastal towns of the Cinque Terre and Portofino along its coast. Just a few miles inland, the Alps and the Apennines rise steeply, and the land between the mountains and the sea is like a great kitchen garden, where the salty breeze and temperate climate are ideal for growing asparagus, artichokes, eggplants (aubergines), greens, and especially herbs, including the region's famous basil. The birthplace of Columbus, Genoa has been a center of seafaring and exploration for centuries. But unlike in Venice, where the spice trade seasoned the cuisine, the Genoese preferred to sell the spices they imported to others, relying on local herbs for seasoning, a preference that remains to this day. In the past, Ligurian sailors returning from long sea voyages yearned for fresh vegetables and greens, and local produce is still central to the cuisine, as evidenced by the region's celebrated vegetable-laden minestrone. Because the Ligurian Sea is not as rich a source of seafood as other, warmer Italian seas, fish and shellfish are not the dietary mainstays one might expect in a coastal region. But cooks here make the most of mussels, clams, eels, and such small fish as mackerel, anchovies, sardines, and mullet, as well as salt cod, a legacy of the region's seafaring heritage.

Culinary Signature: Pesto

Pesto—young basil leaves, garlic, olive oil, pine nuts, and Sardinian pecorino cheese pounded to a paste in a mortar—is Liguria's great contribution to world cuisine. It is classically tossed with *trenette* (a Ligurian pasta similar to linguine), sometimes with the addition of green beans and potatoes that have been cooked along with the pasta. It is also the crowning condiment for the region's renowned minestrone.

Regional Specialties

Olives local small black olives are cured for eating and also milled to make the region's light, delicate olive oil

Focaccia flat, yeasted bread, often baked with local sage, rosemary, and olives

Farinata chickpea (garbanzo bean) flour flatbread, often cooked in a wood-fired oven with herbs; eaten as a snack or antipasti

Minestrone classic vegetable soup, made with pasta and garnished with basil pesto

Ravioli this familiar stuffed pasta was invented in Liguria for long sea voyages

Cima alla genovese veal breast stuffed with a ground meat filling, poached, and sliced

Burrida and ciuppin Liguria's seafood stews, the latter of which was re-created in America by Genoese immigrants as cioppino

Traditionally made by hand with a mortar and pestle, vibrant green basil pesto is the epitome of summer.

Wedges of Parmigiano-Reggiano and bottles of syrupy, aged balsamic vinegar, both famous products of the Emilia-Romagna region, are now common in kitchens around the world.

EMILIA-ROMAGNA

Capital: Bologna

World-Class Gastronomy

The region made up of Emilia, which spreads across the Po River valley to the west, and Romagna, which extends eastward to the Adriatic coast, is among Italy's most famous gastronomic centers. This is the home of Parmigiano-Reggiano cheese, aged balsamic vinegar, and sweet *prosciutto di Parma*. The rich, sophisticated cuisine of the capital, Bologna, has given the city the nickname *la grassa*, "the fat one." Pork, veal, milk, cream, butter, and cheese are the hallmarks of the region's cooking, along with fresh egg-

and-flour pasta, hand-rolled with a long pin and cut into tagliatelle (the local name for fettuccine), layered in sheets as lasagne, or stuffed and folded to make tortellini. Cured meats and sausages are the pride of Emilia-Romagna, from salami and *coppa* to the famed mortadella of Bologna, from which boloney gets its name, and the stars of many antipasti platters. Along the Adriatic coast, fish and shellfish are featured in *brodetto*, the richly flavored local seafood stew, or simply grilled with olive oil and herbs. Among the Emilia-Romagna's best-known wines is Lambrusco, a young, delicately effervescent red made in the *frizzante* style, which goes well with the *salumi* and other rich, hearty foods of the region.

Culinary Signatures: Parmigiano-Reggiano

Parmigiano-Reggiano starts with milk from grass-fed cows, which is heated in copper vats with natural whey and rennet to coagulate the curds. The whey from this process was traditionally fed to pigs raised to make *prosciutto di Parma*, adding to the famed ham's distinctive flavor. Formed into giant wheels, the cheese is aged for twelve to thirty-six months. Look for the words *Parmigiano-Reggiano* stenciled on the rind. The cheese is ideal for grating and is excellent served in chunks as part of a cheese course.

Balsamic Vinegar

A world-renowned specialty of Modena, dark, sweet balsamic vinegar varies in quality and price. True *aceto balsamico tradizionale di modena* is something else altogether. Thick, syrupy, and complex, it is aged in successively smaller barrels made from a variety of woods as it evaporates and thickens in open-air lofts. It must be at least twelve years old, and is often aged for twenty-five years or more. In Emilia-Romagna, it is used sparingly as a table condiment to anoint everything from meats, fish, and salad greens to chunks of Parmigiano-Reggiano and strawberries.

Regional Specialties

Mortadella large sausages, often weighing thirty pounds (15 kg) or more, made from puréed pork, studded with bits of pork fat

Prosciutto di parma world-famous air-cured ham of Parma

Culatello among the most prized of all *salumi*, delicate, pink *culatello* is made by salting and air curing a tender section of the pig's hind leg

Piadina a griddled flatbread that is folded over prosciutto or other fillings

Gnocco fritto fried dough puff served as an antipasto, often with sliced *salumi*

Tagliatelle alla bolognese the signature pasta of the region paired with its famous meat and tomato sauce, which is often enriched with milk or cream

Tortellini stuffed pasta generally eaten in *brodo* (in broth) or *al burro* (with butter and Parmesan)

Zampone and cotechino a specialty of Modena, *zampone* is a pig's trotter stuffed with ground pork and traditionally eaten with lentils on New Year's Eve; the same filling is also made into *cotechino*, a sausage

Grana padano a hard grating cheese similar to Parmigiano-Reggiano

TUSCANY (TOSCANA)
Capital: Florence (Firenze)

Spectacular Simplicity

Of all the regional cuisines of Italy, Tuscan cooking is perhaps the least influenced by other cultures and traditions. Its foundation is good raw materials—local produce, beef (especially the prized Chianina breed), chicken, pork, beans (such as cannellini and *borlotti*)—that are generally prepared with a minimum of herbs and spices, so that their essential qualities shine through. Much of the food is homespun, and many dishes are born of poverty, like *panzanella*, a salad that turns stale bread and vegetables into a delicacy. Olive oil is the cooking fat of choice, and cheese is central to the diet, with the sheep's milk cheeses of the Pienza area among Italy's finest. Every Italian region with a coastline has its seafood stew, and Tuscany's is *cacciucco*, a spicy specialty of Livorno. Among the many celebrated Tuscan wines, standouts include Vernaccia di San Gimignano, a light, crisp white; the ruby red Brunello di Montalcino; Chianti Classico

from the Chianti zone between Florence and Siena; the complex Vino Nobile di Montepulciano; the so-called super-Tuscans, sophisticated blends created since the 1970s and produced outside the DOC system; and *vin santo*, a sweet dessert wine.

Culinary Signature: Olive Oil

Olive trees define the landscape of Tuscany, and olive oil is the common denominator of the cuisine. It is used for frying and sautéing and is drizzled over soups, pastas, vegetables, and other dishes. Tuscan olive oil is prized for its fruitiness and low acidity. Olives are harvested in the fall and pressed immediately. The bright green new oil has a peppery bite that mellows over time. Tuscan cooks prefer extra-virgin olive oil, which comes from the first pressing and has an acidity level of 1 percent or less.

Regional Specialties

Panzanella a salad made from day-old bread, tomatoes, cucumbers, and onions, moistened with olive oil and vinegar

Ribollita a bean and kale soup, layered with slices of bread and reheated

Pappardelle wide, flat pasta, often served with wild boar ragù

Bistecca alla fiorentina thick-cut grilled steak, made with meat from white Chianina cattle, a local breed

Cinghiale wild boar, prepared *in umido* (slowly braised) or simmered with tomatoes to make a robust ragù for pasta

Panforte the dense spice cake of Siena, studded with candied fruit and almonds

Pecorino sheep's milk cheese, fresh or aged, also known in Tuscany as *caciotta*

Cantucci biscotti made with almonds, often served with *vin santo,* a sweet dessert wine, for dipping

Tuscan olive oils (pictured at top) are generally full-bodied and fruity, with a pungent nose. Florentine steak (pictured at bottom) is simple and delicious.

UMBRIA

Capital: Perugia

Cooking from the Hearth

Landlocked Umbria lies at the center of Italy, with Tuscany to the west, the Marches to the east, and Lazio to the south. Often called the green heart of Italy and home to many of the country's most famous hill towns, Umbria is a rolling patchwork of olive groves, vineyards, fields, and forests. Food here is hearty and direct, and meat reigns supreme, especially pork and game, such as boar and hare. The pork butchers of Norcia are so famous for their sausages and *salumi* that *norcineria* is the name used for similar butcher shops in much of Italy. Umbrian food is a cuisine of the hearth, with meats and sausage slowly roasted or grilled over wood embers. Black truffles appear in autumn, contributing flavor to pastas and other dishes. Like Tuscans, Umbrians like their bread *sciapo*, or "unsalted," a fitting counterpoint to the often highly salted food of the region. Notable Umbrian wines include Orvieto Classico, a renowned white, and Sagrantino di Montefalco, a lush, full-bodied red.

Culinary Signature: *Porchetta*

Pork and wood-fire roasting, two hallmarks of Umbrian cooking, achieve their highest expression in *porchetta*, a regional specialty that is now found throughout central Italy. To make it, a whole pig is boned, stuffed with garlic and herbs—usually fennel and rosemary—salted liberally, and slowly roasted until the skin is golden and crisp and the meat tender and succulent. Because home ovens are not large enough to hold a whole pig, the job is left to professionals, who sell *porchetta* by the slice and in freshly made sandwiches at local markets and along roadsides.

Regional Specialties

Umbricelli flour-and-water pasta hand rolled into individual strands like thick spaghetti, often served with meat ragù or tomato sauce

Torta al testo flatbread cooked on rustic griddles, then split and stuffed with pork sausage, cooked greens, prosciutto, or other savory fillings

Bruschetta and crostini toasted bread topped with olive oil and garlic, tomatoes, or savory spreads, such as liver pâté, fava bean purée, or truffle paste

Porcini large wild mushrooms (also known outside Italy as cèpes) with a meaty consistency, often roasted or sauteéd and tossed with pasta.

Lentils Italy's most famous tiny legumes are grown in the high plains of Castelluccio

Chocolate the Perugina candy company takes its name from its hometown, Perugia, the region's capital

Bruschetta can be made with all sorts of toppings, the simplest being a rub of garlic and a drizzle of extra-virgin olive oil. Fresh summery tomatoes and basil are a classic topping for this iconic antipasto.

THE MARCHES (LE MARCHE)

Capital: Ancona

A Feast of Hidden Treasures

Bounded by the Apennines on one side and the Adriatic on the other, the Marches is unfamiliar to most visitors to Italy. Its cooking is defined by fish and seafood along the coast, and vegetables, chicken, rabbit, snails, and truffles and other wild fungi in the hills and mountains. The coastal *brodetto*, or seafood stew, is seasoned with saffron and traditionally made with thirteen kinds of fish. Verdicchio is the region's best-known white wine varietal, and Rosso Conero, produced near Ancona, its most respected red wine. Mistrà is the local anise-flavored digestive.

Culinary Signature: *Formaggio di Fossa*

This artisanal sheep's milk cheese is packed in straw and ripened in trenches (*fosse*) or caves for three months, resulting in an earthy aroma, a unique, fermented flavor, and a rich, creamy texture. It is enjoyed as a table cheese and is particularly good with honey, nuts, and fruit preserves.

Regional Specialties

Olive all'ascolana a specialty of the coastal town of Ascoli Piceno; green olives stuffed with ground meat, breaded, and fried until golden and crisp

Ciauscolo a rich, soft smoked salami, meant to be spread, not sliced

Vincisgrassi lasagne layered with prosciutto, chicken livers, sweetbreads, and white sauce

Rabbit often cooked *in porchetta* (roasted in the style of *porchetta*) with fennel and salt

Frustingolo dense fruitcake made with nuts and dried figs

LAZIO

Capital: Rome (Roma)

Capital Fare

The food of Lazio is a culinary bridge between Umbria and Tuscany to the north and Campania to the south: hearty cooking of home and farm that has centered, since the days of ancient Rome, around lamb, pork, bread, cheese, seasonal vegetables, and olive oil, with fish from Lake Bolsena and seafood from the Tyrrhenian Sea added to the mix. The cooking of the capital, much of which developed in trattorias, *osterie* (neighborhood eateries), and restaurants, is a cuisine in its own right. Roman food is bold, flavorful, and resourceful, making the most of every ingredient, from variety meats and vegetables

Artichokes are the signature vegetable of Rome, where they liven up the table in winter and spring. They are most often fried or braised, but also star in frittatas and pasta dishes.

(especially artichokes and greens) to dried pasta, including spaghetti and *bucatini*.

Culinary Signature: Variety Meats

In the nineteenth and early twentieth centuries, workers in the slaughterhouses of Rome's Testaccio district would be given, as part of their pay, the parts left over after carcasses were quartered. These parts became known as *il quinto quarto*, the fifth quarter. Neighborhood trattorias and home cooks devised all kinds of inventive uses for them, many of which have become classic Roman specialties, from oxtails and sweetbreads to *pajata* (milk-fed calf or lamb intestines, still filled with coagulated milk) and *coratella* (heart, liver, and lungs cooked together).

Regional Specialties

Guanciale salt-cured, air-dried pork jowl, used like pancetta

Pasta all'amatriciana sauce of tomatoes and *guanciale* or pancetta, tossed with *bucatini*

Tonnarelli cacio e pepe sauce of pecorino and black pepper with square-cut spaghetti

Spaghetti alla carbonara spaghetti with eggs, *pecorino romano* cheese, *guanciale* or pancetta, and pepper

Gnocchi alla romana disk-shaped dumplings made with semolina flour

Abbacchio milk-fed lamb, often served roasted or stewed

Saltimbocca veal cutlets, layered with sage and prosciutto

Coda alla vaccinara braised oxtails

Artichokes tender local specimens are prepared in a variety of ways, including *alla romana* (braised) and *alla giudia* (fried)

Puntarelle type of chicory with long, jagged, arrow-shaped leaves, served as a salad with a dressing of anchovies, garlic, and olive oil

Lamb is popular in the mountainous regions of southern Italy and is prepared in many different ways, from garlicky grilled chops to tender braised shanks.

Fresh, creamy *mozzarella di bufula* has a meltingly soft texture. It is exquisite sliced and served with tomatoes, or melted over pizzas and baked pasta dishes.

ABRUZZO AND MOLISE
Capitals: L'Aquila and Campobasso

Food of Shepherds and Fishermen

These two mountainous regions, once joined as an administrative district under the name *Abruzzi e Molise* but now separated, extend from high in the Apennines to the Adriatic coast. They are among the nation's least populated regions, with much of their land given over to national parks. This is sheepherding country, and lamb is served many different ways: roasted, stewed *alla cacciatora* with chiles, or braised with a creamy egg and lemon sauce. The region is also known for cheese making, and local specialties include sheep's milk pecorino; buffalo's milk *caciocavallo*; and cow's milk *scamorza* and mozzarella. The local *diavolillo* chile adds sweet heat to sauces, sausages, soups, and pastas. Along the coast, *brodetto*, a seafood stew of fish, mollusks, and scampi, is seasoned with chiles and served in small terra-cotta pots. Trebbiano d'Abruzzo and Montepulciano d'Abruzzo are the area's signature white and red wines, respectively.

Culinary Signature: *Maccheroni alla chitarra*

This Abruzzese egg-and-flour fresh pasta is made by rolling out sheets of dough, and then using the rolling pin to press the dough through the fine wires of a cutter called a *chitarra* (guitar). The result is long, thin strands that look like square-sided spaghetti and are often served with a hearty lamb ragù or a spicy tomato sauce.

Regional Specialties

Scamorza a cow's milk cheese similar to mozzarella, but with a firmer texture and saltier flavor; often grilled or spit roasted

Scrippelle 'mbusse delicate Abruzzese-style *crespelle,* or crêpes, stuffed with Parmigiano-Reggiano and served in rich chicken broth

Tripe principally lamb offal, prepared many ways in Molise

'Ndocca 'ndocca a stew of pork variety meats

Ventricina a spicy fennel-and-orange-scented pork sausage

Calciuni sweet fritters from Molise, filled with chestnuts and candied fruit, traditionally served at Christmastime

CAMPANIA
Capital: Naples (Napoli)

Pizza, Pasta, and Gusto

Emigrants from Campania have given the world some of the most famous and best-loved Italian foods. Two ingredients define much of the cooking of Naples and the surrounding region: fresh mozzarella, the best of which is made from buffalo's milk, and sweet, flavorful tomatoes, most notably the plum-shaped San Marzano variety grown in the fertile volcanic soil surrounding Mount Vesuvius. Pizza Margherita, topped with those two ingredients and fresh basil leaves, was a nineteenth-century Neapolitan invention, and pizza is taken so seriously here that it has been awarded a DOC designation, comparable to those granted to great wines. This is also the birthplace of dried hard-wheat pasta, and along with pizza, spaghetti is the culinary icon of Naples and the region. The Amalfi coast is famed for its large, aromatic lemons and for *limoncello*, the sweet liqueur made from their rinds. The world-famous herbal digestive Strega is produced in Benevento. Grapes grown on the slopes of Vesuvius are used to make Lachryma Christi (tears of Christ), a light white wine. Greco di Tufo is a bigger, fruitier white from Avellino, where Taurasi, a robust red often called the "Barolo of the south," is also produced.

Culinary Signature: *Mozzarella di bufala*

The herds of water buffalo raised in the area between Caserta and Salerno produce one of Italy's greatest culinary treasures, *mozzarella di bufala*. Mozzarella can also be made from cow's milk, but because buffalo's milk has two to three times the butterfat of cow's milk, buffalo mozzarella is exquisitely rich and creamy with a meltingly soft texture. The cheese is made by curdling the milk, softening the curds in hot water, and kneading them until they are elastic. The cheese maker lops off rounds of the kneaded curd (the Italian word for this action, *mozzare*, gives the cheese its name), which become individual balls or braids of cheese. *Mozzarella di bufala* is the melting cheese of choice for pizza and baked pasta and is enjoyed as a table cheese.

Regional Specialties

Pizza the two classic pizzas of the region are Margherita with buffalo mozzarella, tomato, and basil, and marinara, with tomatoes, garlic, and oregano

Dried pasta spaghetti and other dried durum-wheat pastas, including rigatoni, penne, and fusilli, prepared with a variety of sauces, most tomato based

Mozzarella in carozza fresh mozzarella sandwiched between slices of bread, dipped in an egg batter, and fried

Parmigiana di melanzane eggplant (aubergine) baked with tomato and mozzarella and Parmigiano-Reggiano cheeses

Insalata caprese a salad of mozzarella, tomatoes, basil, and olive oil

Insalata di mare mixed seafood salad

Fritto misto lightly battered and fried fish and seafood

Sfogliatelle a horn-shaped flaky pastry with a sweet ricotta and candied orange peel filling

BASILICATA

Capital: Potenza

Hearty *Cucina Povera*

Historically among Italy's least prosperous regions, with mountainous terrain, a harsh, arid climate, and limited coastal access, Basilicata (sometimes called Lucania) makes the most of its limited culinary resources, extracting intense flavors from basic ingredients in a simple, yet satisfying farm-style *cucina povera* (cuisine of the poor). The cooking draws heavily on vegetables and on legumes, including lentils and

chickpeas (garbanzo beans). Pork, much of which is cured or turned into sausages, has traditionally been the main source of meat. The hills and mountains also yield lamb, goat, and wild mushrooms, which are used in a variety of sauces, stews, and pastas. Basilicata's artisanal goat's milk and sheep's milk cheeses, including *burrata*, *caciocavallo*, and aged, salted *ricotta forte*, are known for their quality and their often intense flavor. Local chiles (of which one prominent variety is whimsically referred to as *diavolicchio*, or "little devil") are used as much for their sweet flavor as for spicy heat. Semolina flour has been a culinary staple in Basilicata since ancient times (pasta is said to have been invented here), and is used to make bread and a vast variety of handmade pastas. The region's DOC wine is Aglianico del Vulture, a rich, ruby-hued red made from a varietal introduced by the ancient Greeks (*Aglianico* means "Hellenic").

Fresh basil, a member of the mint family, is the most widely used and recognizable Italian herb, lending its peppery flavor to sauces, salads, and pizzas.

Culinary Signature: *Lucanica*

Lucania is the old Latin name for Basilicata, still used by some old-timers and still evident in the name of the region's famed *lucanica* sausage. Like its culinary cousins, Portuguese linguiça and Spanish *longaniza*, *lucanica* is a long, thin pork sausage spiced with chiles. It is made in both fresh and dried versions in Basilicata and is eaten roasted, fried, and smoked. Versions of *lucanica* are now made throughout Italy. In the north, it is known as *luganega*.

Regional Specialties

Fave e cicoria puréed fava (broad) beans served with blanched chicory

Lagane thick, fettuccine-style pasta often served with beans or lentils

'Ntruppicc tomato-based pasta sauce made with bits of chopped lamb, pork, and beef, sometimes garnished with fried chiles and *ricotta salata* cheese

Cutturiddi lamb casserole with tomatoes, celery, and chiles, cooked in a terra-cotta pot

Agnello ai funghi lamb stew with wild mushrooms

Mandorlata di peperoni sweet-and-sour peppers with almonds and raisins

PUGLIA
Capital: Bari

Mediterranean Magic

Among the regional cuisines of Italy, the food of Puglia, the "heel" and "spur" of the boot-shaped peninsula, comes closest to what the world thinks of as Mediterranean fare, Italian style. Vegetables, including tomatoes, sweet peppers, artichokes, fennel, zucchini (courgettes), and eggplants (aubergines), flourish in the temperate climate and are the mainstays of the diet, along with seafood from the region's long stretches of Adriatic and Ionian coastline. Local durum-wheat pasta is used to make outstanding, toothsome breads and countless types of pasta, including Puglia's emblematic orecchiette (little ears). Artisanal cheeses made from the milk of sheep, cows, and buffalo include mozzarella, *scamorza*, provolone, and the famed *burrata*, a delicacy made by stretching mozzarella curds into a pouch and stuffing it with more shreds of curd and cream. Olive trees cover much of the terrain, and Puglia is one of Italy's—and the world's—leading olive oil–producing areas. Along with Sicily, it also leads the nation in wine production. Locorotondo, a delicate, straw-colored white, and Salice Salentino, an intense red made primarily from Negro Amaro grapes, both pair well with the sun-drenched flavors of Pugliese cuisine.

Culinary Signature: Pugliese Bread

The bread of Puglia, especially the large, rustic loaves of the town of Altamura, is world renowned. It gets its delicate golden color and chewy texture from locally grown durum wheat (the kind used to make dried pasta), which is combined with water, salt, and a natural sourdough starter. Although much of Puglia's bread is now commercially produced, the centuries-old tradition of making dough at home (with starters passed from generation to generation) and having the loaves baked by a *fornaio* (baker) in a communal wood-fired oven continues to endure.

Orecchiette, which means "little ears," is a distinctive Pugliese pasta. It is often served tossed with broccoli rabe and spicy crumbled sausage.

Deep purple eggplant (aubergine) is a staple of the Italian kitchen, particularly in the southern regions, and can be used in many different preparations.

Melanzane alla parmigiana, thick slices of fried eggplant layered with tomato sauce and Parmigiano-Reggiano cheese, is a Calabrian favorite.

Regional Specialties

Lampascioni small, onionlike wild *muscari* (grape hyacinth bulbs), served blanched with olive oil, fried, grilled, or made into sweet onion marmalade

Orecchiette ear-shaped pasta shells dressed with broccoli rabe, tomato sauce, or meat ragù

Handmade durum-wheat pastas *strascinati* (large, flat orecchiette), *cavatieddi* (rolled shells), *lagane* (similar to fettuccine), and *minuicchi* (small gnocchi)

Tielle layered casseroles made with rice or potatoes and seafood or meat

Polipetti small octopus, often eaten raw with olive oil and lemon juice

Tarantello cured, spiced tuna belly

Friselle small, twice-baked ring-shaped breads, often dipped in water to soften and served with tomatoes and oil

Ricotta forte fermented, aged ricotta with a pungent flavor and spreadable consistency

Cotognata thick, sweet quince paste, often served with cheeses

CALABRIA
Capital: Catanzaro

Flavors of Sun and Spice

Calabria, the long, narrow toe of the Italian boot, is dominated by the Apennines at its center and bounded on both sides by coastline. As in Basilicata and Puglia, much is made here from relatively few ingredients. Lamb, local cow's milk and sheep's milk cheeses, pork *salumi*, and vegetables are the dietary staples, along with hard-wheat pastas, often handmade in a variety of shapes and dressed with sauces of vegetables and/or sausages. Along the coast, swordfish, tuna, anchovies, sardines, and salt-cured cod *(baccalà)*, are central to the menu. The sunny, dry climate produces intensely flavored tomatoes, artichokes, and sweet peppers, as well as the region's renowned eggplant (aubergine), which is prepared *alla parmigiana* and in many other ways. Chiles are everywhere, growing in gardens and hanging to dry, and their heat and flavor enliven much of the cuisine. Indeed, the term *alla calabrese* is used throughout Italy to describe spicy dishes. Calabria is famous for its wild mushrooms and chestnuts, which grow in the Sila, a high mountain plain, and for its figs and citrus fruits. It also produces some of the world's finest citron (the peel of which is candied and used in baking) and bergamot (the essential oils of which are used in Earl Grey tea and liqueurs). The region's best known wine is Cirò, produced in red, white, and rosé.

Culinary Signature: *Capocollo*

The most celebrated of Calabria's cured pork products is *capocollo*, known in other parts of the country as *coppa*. It is made from a neck muscle that connects the head *(capo)* and neck *(collo)* of the pig. After an initial salting and curing, the meat is marinated in wine and spices, stuffed into a pig's bladder, tied, lightly smoked, and air dried for about three months. The result is a cured product similar to prosciutto, with a rich, sweet flavor.

Piquant eggplant caponata is delicious served atop rustic Italian bread.

Sicily is known for its fragrant citrus, featured in many local desserts.

Regional Specialties

Licurdia an onion and potato soup, often made with the region's renowned sweet red Tropea onions

Murseddu a breakfast *ragù* made from tripe, liver, and other variety meats and chiles served in yeasted *pitta* bread

Handmade pasta *ricci di donna* (lady's curls) and *fileja*, made by rolling dough around knitting needles or rods

Pitta yeasted flatbread

Anchovies known as *alici* when served raw with oil and lemon, and called *acciughe* when packed in salt.

'Ndugghia a spicy pork sausage, related to French andouille

Soppressata a pork sausage made with large chunks of meat and fat, black pepper, chiles, and sometimes pig's blood

Scamorza and caciocavallo mild, firm cow's milk cheeses

SICILY (SICILIA)

Capital: Palermo

A Cuisine of Many Cultures

Much of the Sicilian landscape is a mix of wheat fields, fragrant citrus and almond groves, forests, and vineyards. The cooking tends to revolve around seafood (including swordfish, tuna, sardines, and lobster), vegetables (especially eggplants/aubergines and tomatoes), and pasta, which is often prepared simply and garnished with pecorino or *ricotta salata* cheese. Sicily has lived under the rule of vastly different occupying powers—Greeks, Romans, Arabs, and Normans—all of whom have left their stamp on the island's colorful, multicultural cuisine. The Arab influence is particularly evident in dishes like couscous, in the use of spices and dried fruits such as raisins, and in the island's famed sweets, pastries, and desserts. It was the Arabs who brought sugar and almonds to Sicily,

along with the art of making candied fruit, ices, and sorbets. Today, the frozen desserts and unique almond-paste confections of the region are world famous. Marsala, Sicily's renowned fortified wine made in the style of sherry, was created in the western port city of Marsala and is enjoyed throughout Italy as a cooking and dessert wine.

Culinary Signature: Almond Paste

Known in Sicily as *pasta reale* (royal dough) because it began as a delicacy served at noble tables, Sicily's version of marzipan is the base of many of the region's desserts, most notably the *frutti di Martorana*. These charming confections, sculpted to look like various fruits and vegetables, were first created in the convent of Martorana in Palermo. Shaped from a smooth paste of blanched almonds and sugar, perfumed with cinnamon, lemon, and vanilla, they are hand painted and often strikingly realistic in appearance.

Regional Specialties

Caponata sweet-and-sour eggplant (aubergine) stewed with capers and vinegar

Pasta con le sarde pasta (often *bucatini*) with sardines, fennel, raisins, and pine nuts

Pasta alla Norma pasta dressed with tomato, eggplant, basil, and *ricotta salata*, named for the heroine of the opera by Catania-born Vincenzo Bellini

Arancini bite-sized rice croquettes, often filled with meat ragù, tomato sauce, and/or cheese

Panella a deep-fried pancake made of chickpea (garbanzo bean) flour

Cannoli fried pastry shells with a sweetened ricotta filling, often dotted with candied fruit, pistachios, and chocolate

Cassata sponge cake filled with a sweet ricotta mixture similar to the filling used in cannoli, often covered with a layer of marzipan; *cassata gelata*, a frozen version, is made with ice cream

Granita crushed-ice dessert flavored with coffee, almond, lemon, or seasonal fruit

SARDINIA (SARDEGNA)
Capital: Cagliari

Hearty Shepherd's Fare

For the most part, the traditional cooking of the island of Sardinia has surprisingly little to do with the sea. Centuries of occupation by outside invaders prompted the Sardinians to retreat to the island's rugged, mountainous interior, where they herded sheep, and to this day, lamb, sheep's milk cheese, and pork remain the cornerstones of the cuisine. Shepherds would leave their homes for months at a time, carrying with them *pane carasau*, a thin, crisp durum-wheat flatbread, which they ate along with boar prosciutto or spit- or pit-roasted pork, lamb, or wild game.

Semolina pasta, particularly small gnocchi and the couscouslike *fregola*, are home-cooking staples of this region. Along the coast, seafood dishes tend toward simplicity and include the robust seafood stew, *burrida*, as well as grilled or roasted fish and lobster dressed with olive oil and lemon. Sardinian wines that pair well with the food of the region include Vermentino, a big-flavored white, and Cannonau, a dry red.

Culinary Signature: *Bottarga*

Bottarga, salted dried mullet roe, has been called the "caviar of Sardinia." To make it, the roe sac of the fish must be carefully removed so that it remains intact. It is salted, pressed, and air dried, and then coated with wax as a preservative. *Bottarga* is sliced thin and served with olive oil and lemon as an antipasto or shaved on pasta, artichokes, and other dishes to add rich, salty flavor.

Regional Specialties

Fregola also called "Sardinian couscous," toasted pellet-shaped semolina pasta, often served in broth and paired with seafood

Malloreddus small semolina gnocchi made with saffron, served with tomato sauce, lamb *ragù*, or butter and pecorino

Culingiones spinach and pecorino ravioli

Impanada a savory bread-dough turnover filled with meat or eel

Porceddu spit-roasted suckling pig

Pane carasau thin rounds of crisp flatbread, also known as *carta da musica* (music paper)

Pane frattau softened *pane carasau* topped with tomato sauce and a fried egg

Pecorino sardo prized throughout Italy as one of the country's finest sheep's milk cheeses

Miele di corbezzolo dark, bitter honey from the wild Sardinian strawberry tree

Sebadas fried sweet cheese ravioli

Simple, rustic seafood stews make the most of the abundance of fresh seafood in coastal Italy, as well as the islands of Sardinia and Sicily.

Planning an Italian Meal

At its best, a home-cooked Italian meal unfolds as a series of courses, served family style at a leisurely pace, with each one harmonizing with the others to create a pleasing whole. Here are some basic principles and menus to help you create and appreciate that harmony.

Putting Together a Menu

A traditional Italian *pranzo* (the main meal, eaten at midday) typically includes an antipasto, *primo* (first course), *secondo* (second course) with one or more *contorni* (side dishes) to accompany it, and a *dolce* (dessert) or fruit and cheese. (For more information on these courses, see the introductions to each corresponding chapter.)

In planning an authentic Italian meal, you can, of course, mix, match, and recombine any of these five courses to suit your own taste. But creating a multicourse menu in the time-honored, traditional Italian way allows you and your family and friends to experience the pleasures of the Italian table at its best, particularly if you are entertaining or celebrating a special occasion.

Rather than starting with the "main dish," consider the menu as a whole, affording equal importance to each element. One good way to choose an assortment of dishes that go well together is to think regionally, or to confine your selection to dishes from northern, central, or southern Italy. Below, you will find several regional Italian menus to get you started.

Consider the kinds of fresh ingredients that are at their seasonal best, the tastes and preferences of your guests, and the nature of the occasion. A hearty Tuscan menu might be perfect for a cozy autumn dinner, for example, while a seafood-based Sicilian menu might be just right for a midsummer alfresco supper.

REGIONAL MENUS

PIEDMONT

Fonduta with White Truffle

Lobster and Shrimp Agnolotti

Arneis

•

Barolo-Braised Pot Roast

Peperonata

Dolcetto d'Alba, Nebbiolo, Barolo

•

Zabaglione

LOMBARDY

Bresaola with Arugula and Mozzarella

Pinot Bianco, Riesling, Sylvaner

•

Osso Buco with Gremolata

Risotto alla Milanese

Nebbiolo, Lambrusco

•

Cheese Plate
(Taleggio, grana padano, and Gorgonzola)

Vin santo

TUSCANY

Field Salad with Pancetta and Walnuts

Vernaccia, Vermentino

•

Ribollita

Bistecca alla Fiorentina

Zucchini with Olive Oil, Garlic, and Basil

Brunello di Montalcino, Chianti, Carmignano

•

Olive Oil Cake with Cherry Compote

REGIONAL MENUS

VENETO

Sweet-and-Sour Sardines

Prosecco, Soave

•

Risi e Bisi

Pork Loin Braised in Milk

Warm Borlotti Bean and Radicchio Salad

Valpolicella, Refosco

•

Tiramisù

LIGURIA

Farinata with Herbs and Onions

Vermentino

•

Minestrone with Pesto

Roasted Branzino with Fennel

Cinque Terre

•

Candied fruit and walnuts

EMILIA-ROMAGNA

Prosciutto-Wrapped Figs
with Balsamic

Prosecco, Malvasia

•

Tagliatelle alla Bolognese

Balsamic Braised Chicken

Sangiovese, Lambrusco

•

Zuppa Inglese

LAZIO

Fried Ricotta-Stuffed Zucchini Blossoms

Falaghina, Verdicchio

•

Spaghetti with Pecorino
and Pepper

Saltimbocca alla Romana

Jerusalem Artichoke Gratin

Aglianico

•

Pine Nut–Orange Biscotti

Prosecco or vin santo

SICILY

Spicy Fried Chickpeas

Catarratto

•

Spaghetti alla Norma

Meatballs in Sugo

Nero d'Avola, Primitivo

•

Gelato alla Crema

Principles of Italian Cooking

The essence of Italian food is *cucina casalinga*, good everyday home cooking. The techniques used to prepare it are generally easy, and the equipment is minimal. Italian kitchens tend to be small and basic, yet they produce some of the world's most flavorful dishes.

Choose Good Ingredients

Italian cooks rely on richly flavorful artisanal ingredients to add depth and character to their cooking. In the past, many of these culinary treasures, from cheeses and cured meats to pastas and olive oil, might have been homemade, part of a family's larder of culinary treasures prepared and stored away to enhance foods all year long. Nowadays, they are more often store-bought, but they remain the products of food artisans, produced with care and attention to flavor.

As the popularity of the Mediterranean diet and the flavors of Italy continue to grow, more and more well-stocked supermarkets and specialty food stores outside Italy are carrying such artisanal foods. Seeking out these ingredients will make a huge difference as you prepare the recipes in this book, because they do much of the work of cooking for you. Good-quality pancetta or prosciutto, aged *pecorino romano* or Parmigiano-Reggiano cheese, small, delicate lentils—raw materials like these add complexity and authenticity without adding a lot of work.

Italian cooks generally shop once or twice a day to be sure they are buying the freshest fruits and vegetables, meat, poultry, seafood, and dairy available. Even if you do not have time to shop daily, the principle remains valid, especially when you are creating an Italian menu. Make frequent, small shopping trips, look for seasonal, fresh, locally produced foods, and buy them as close to the day of the meal as possible.

Cook with a Light Hand

Another hallmark of great Italian cooking is its directness. Foods are seldom obscured by complex sauces: pasta is cooked al dente and generally sauced just enough to moisten it; vegetables, though often cooked until quite soft, are usually lightly seasoned, so that their delicate flavors can be appreciated.

Resist the impulse to add more—more herbs, more garlic, more chiles. Italian cooks instinctively follow the fundamental principle of respecting their ingredients, and thus avoid masking the essential character of foods by overcooking, oversaucing, or overseasoning. That said, seasoning assertively with salt and pepper at every stage of cooking from raw ingredient to finished dish is a classic Italian way to bring out flavor.

Strive for Balance

When planning a meal, think about how the flavors, colors, and textures of the courses will contrast and complement one another. A substantial pasta can precede a light second course. If the second course is rich and hearty, you might begin the meal with a simpler pasta or soup.

Keep portions small and self-contained. A modest serving of pasta leaves room for what is ahead. Second courses in Italy are not intended to be the "main event" of the meal, served up in enormous quantities. The whole meal is the event, and serving the second course and side dishes family style allows everyone to eat as much as they want, while enjoying a variety of tastes. Pace the meal as Italians do, allowing for pauses between courses, so that everyone has time to digest and enjoy their wine and one another's company.

Prepare in Advance

At a typical Italian meal, most of the food is cooked well ahead of time. Before anyone comes to the table, the antipasto is set out on platters or multiple small plates, and the second course is usually finished and ready to be served. The side dishes, or *contorni*, are fully cooked and standing by, often to be enjoyed at room temperature. The pasta sauce is simmering gently, and the pasta water is at a rolling boil. Wine is opened and ready to pour along with still and sparkling water.

It is generally only the cooking and saucing of the pasta that are left for the last minute. This strategy works particularly well for entertaining, because it means that you can serve even a relatively complicated Italian menu with minimal stress, since almost all of the work is done before the guests arrive, and you have more time to devote to your guests.

Garlic is an essential Italian seasoning, but use it in moderation so you don't mask delicate flavors.

FOOD TYPE	WINE MATCH
Antipasti, salumi, and cheese	Sparkling wines: Prosecco, Champagne, California sparkling wine
Pasta with meat ragù or tomato sauces	Light- to medium-bodied reds: Chianti, Barbera, Bardolino, Merlot, Nebbiolo, Pinot Noir
Creamy and cheese-rich pasta sauces	Crisp, acidic whites: Vernaccia di San Gimignano, Verdicchio
Hearty vegetable soups	Medium-bodied reds: Chianti, Sangiovese, Pinot Noir
Seafood stews and pastas	Medium-bodied reds: Fiano d'Avellino, Greco di Tufo, Pinot Blanc
Risotto	Serve with the wine used in the recipe or a medium-bodied white such as Pinot Grigio
Fish and shellfish	Medium-bodied whites: Pinot Grigio, Verdicchio, Gavi, Sauvignon Blanc, Chardonnay
Roast chicken	Medium-bodied whites: Orvieto, Verdiccio, Pinot Grigio, Friulano
Steaks, chops, and roasted meats	Full-bodied reds: Amarone, Barbaresco, Barolo, Brunello di Montalcino, Vino Nobile di Montepulciano
Braised meat dishes	Serve with the same wine used in the recipe or a full-bodied red such as Barolo
Desserts	Sweet dessert or sparkling wines: Malvasia, Asti Spumante, Moscato d'Asti, vin santo

Pairing Wines with Italian Food

When choosing wines to enjoy with Italian foods, consider the regional origins of a dish and try to select a wine from the same region. Many of the regional overviews on pages 11–25 include information on noteworthy regional wines. Keep in mind the season and the recipes you are preparing when you choose a wine. In general, lighter dishes usually call for lighter wines. You can also choose a *vino da tavola* (Italian table wine), which tends to be affordable and pairs well with a variety of flavors. And, of course, many non-Italian wines make perfect matches for Italian foods. When in doubt, ask a trusted wine merchant for suggestions.

PASTA SHAPES

Bucatini	Long, hollow spaghetti-like strands
Capellini	Thin strands, also known as angel hair
Cavatappi	Hollow corkscrew spirals
Cavatelli	Shells with rolled edges
Conchiglie	Shells
Ditali	Thimbles
Ditalini	Small thimbles
Farfalle	Bow ties or butterflies
Fettuccine	Long ribbons
Fusilli	Corkscrews
Garganelli	Ribbed tubes
Gemelli	Twisted spiral tubes
Lasagne	Wide, flat noodles
Linguine	Long, flat strands
Macaroni	Elbows
Maltagliati	Flat random-cut shapes
Orecchiette	Little ears
Orzo	Barley-shaped pasta
Paccheri	Large tubes
Pappardelle	Long, wide ribbons
Penne	Quill-shaped tubes
Penne rigate	Ribbed quill-shaped tubes
Perciatelli	Long, hollow spaghetti-like strands
Rigatoni	Large, ribbed tubes
Spaghetti	Long, round strands
Spaghettini	Long, thin round strands
Tagliatelle	Long, thin ribbons
Trenette	Long, thin ribbons
Tubetti	Little tubes
Ziti	Long tubes

Pasta: Fresh Versus Dried

In Italian cooking, fresh is generally best. But when it comes to pasta, fresh is not necessarily considered better than dried. Instead, they are viewed as equals, with each having its own long-standing role. For Italian cooks, the choice to use dried or fresh pasta for a given recipe is determined by the sauce, the preparation, and the culinary tradition.

In northern and central Italy, fresh pasta is generally made from "00" flour (similar to all-purpose/plain flour but milled a bit more finely) and eggs. In the south, it is usually made from the local semolina flour, a coarse-textured, yellow flour milled from durum wheat and mixed only with water. Semolina flour and water are also used to make dried pasta.

When you have the time, making your own fresh pasta will yield the best and most delicious results. Follow the egg or spinach pasta recipe on page 274 and the pasta techniques on pages 92–95 to learn how to make fresh pasta dough and roll it and cut it or fill it. If making pasta is not an option, look for fresh pasta at upscale supermarkets and Italian delicatessens, which often prepare and cut their own sheets. When buying fresh pasta, keep in mind that it has a short shelf life, so use it as soon as possible after you buy it. You can store it for up to 2 days in an airtight container or in a zippered plastic bag.

For dried pasta, look for high-quality brands made with semolina. Artisanal Italian dried pastas are turning up with greater frequency in well-stocked grocery stores outside Italy. Check the package to see if the pasta has been extruded through bronze dies, which yields a prized, slightly rough texture that helps sauces cling to the strands. Like fresh pasta, good quality dried pasta should be used within a month or two. Older pasta becomes brittle with age and can often lose flavor.

MATCHING SAUCES AND PASTA

Italians have strong opinions about which pastas are best with which sauces. The ideal match is one that brings the sauce and pasta into a unified whole. Thus, thinner sauces tend to be served with longer pasta because they coat it evenly, and chunkier sauces go with smaller pasta shapes that trap plenty of sauce. The more substantial the sauce, the more substantial the pasta.

SAUCE	PASTA
Butter sauces	Conchiglie, farfalle, tagliatelle
Cheese sauces	Bucatini, conchiglie, farfalle, fusilli, gemelli, macaroni
Light, oil-based sauces	Capellini, farfalle, spaghetti, spaghettini
Pesto	Bucatini, linguine, penne
Ragù and meat sauces	Bucatini, conchiglie, fettuccine, fusilli, gemelli, linguine, orecchiette, pappardelle, penne, rigatoni, spaghetti, ziti
Seafood sauces	Linguine, spaghetti, spaghettini
Tomato sauces	Conchiglie, farfalle, linguine, penne, spaghetti, spaghettini, tagliatelle
Vegetable sauces	Cavatelli, gemelli, orecchiette, penne, rigatoni, ziti
Broths and soups	Small pasta shapes such as ditalini, orzo, tubetti, stelline
Baked pastas	Lasagne, penne, ziti

COOKING WITH ITALIAN CHEESES

Cheese making in Italy has long been a tradition and a great source of pride. Cheeses are produced in every style imaginable, from soft to hard, cow's milk to goat's milk. Nearly every region of Italy has its own distinct cheeses, evolving from its terrain and cuisine, designed to pair perfectly with the regional dishes. Some regions even have strict DOC laws; for example, Parmigiano-Reggiano can only be made in the region around Parma.

PURPOSE	CHEESE
Used for melting	Caciocavello, Fontina, mozzarella, provolone, scamórza, Taleggio
Used for grating	Asiago (aged), fiore sardo (aged), pecorino (aged), grana padano, Parmigiano-Reggiano, ricotta salata
Used for sauces	Fresh goat cheese, Gorgonzola, Gruyère
Used for fillings or for layering pasta	Fiore sardo, fresh ricotta, mascarpone, fresh mozzarella

Italian Pantry Essentials

Most of what makes up a typical Italian meal is fresh food, procured and cooked within hours of being eaten. However, pantry staples are used to turn these fresh ingredients into a vast array of dishes. Keep them in stock, and you will have a head start on most Italian recipes.

GRAINS, PASTAS, AND LEGUMES

Arborio, Carnaroli, or Vialone Nano rice*

Borlotti or cranberry beans, dried

Cannellini beans, dried or jarred

Chickpeas (garbanzo beans), dried or canned

Dried pastas, an assortment (see page 30)*

*Farro**

Polenta, coarse ground

DRIED HERBS AND SPICES

Bay leaves

Black peppercorns

Cayenne pepper

Red pepper flakes

Sea salt, fine and coarse

FRESH STAPLES

Cheeses for grating and cooking (see left)*

Garlic*

Onions, yellow and red*

Potatoes*

MISCELLANEOUS

Anchovy fillets

Bread crumbs

Capers

Espresso-roast coffee, ground or beans

Olives*

Pine nuts*

Porcini mushrooms, dried

Plum (Roma) tomatoes, canned

Tomato paste

OILS AND VINEGARS

Balsamic vinegar

Canola or vegetable oil

Extra-virgin olive oil

Olive oil (virgin)

Red wine vinegar

White wine vinegar

WINE AND SPIRITS

Marsala

Sambuca

Red wine, dry

White wine, dry

BAKING STAPLES

Active dry yeast

All-purpose (plain) flour

Almonds*

Amaretti

Baking powder

Brown sugar

Chocolate, semisweet (plain) and milk

Cocoa powder, Dutch process

Confectioners' (icing) sugar

Cornstarch (cornflour)

Granulated sugar

Hazelnuts (filberts)*

Ladyfingers

Pistachio nuts*

Raisins

Vanilla bean and pure extract

Staples of the Italian pantry include fragrant bay leaves, imported San Marzano tomatoes, and dried cannellini beans.

* Staples marked with an asterisk should be purchased in small quantities and replaced often.

Antipasti

About Antipasti

Not every Italian meal begins with an antipasto course. But for special occasions, an antipasto—literally, "before the meal"—makes an ideal opener: a few intensely flavored bites that welcome everyone to the table, stimulate the palate, and whet the appetite for what is ahead.

Antipasti typically favor simplicity and a strong sense of place, often showcasing local culinary treasures such as cured meats, cheeses, and specialty produce.

In restaurants, these savory offerings are frequently displayed on a buffet that greets guests as they enter the dining room. This assortment of marinated vegetables, grilled and fried foods, salads, and other small bites is invariably a visual feast of fresh, seasonal ingredients and local cooking styles.

In Italian homes, antipasti are often combined with another course for a simple meal, rather than offered as a separate course. But for virtually any special gathering of friends and family, at least one antipasto is served. It might be a platter of White Bean and Arugula Crostini (page 40) or crispy Arancini (page 76), passed in the living room with drinks, or warm Fried Ricotta-Stuffed Zucchini Blossoms (page 49), eaten at the table.

SERVING STRATEGIES

When deciding on an antipasto to begin your menu, consider the season, the regional origins of the other dishes you will be serving, and the overall complexity of the meal.

If your menu will be elaborate, requiring you to spend a lot of time in the kitchen, you might begin with one of Italy's easiest and most popular antipasti, *affettati misti,* a selection of cured meats. Choose one or more varieties, such as prosciutto, *coppa,* a mild salami, or mortadella, from a good delicatessen or specialty food store. Purchase the meats

thinly sliced and arrange them on a platter, loosely folding or rolling each slice to create an attractive presentation. If you prepare the platter ahead of time and refrigerate it, allow it to come to room temperature before serving. Accompany the meats with bread sticks or sliced bread and a bowl of Marinated Olives (page 87). Alternatively, pair the meat with fruit, such as melon or figs, as in Prosciutto-Wrapped Figs with Balsamic (page 48).

An assortment of Italian cheeses, accompanied with crusty bread, also makes an easy antipasto—and a fitting companion to an *affettati* platter. Serve cheeses with contrasting characteristics. Good choices include *bocconcini* (bite-sized rounds) of fresh mozzarella; a medium-aged slicing cheese, such as a Tuscan or Sardinian pecorino; a soft, spreading cheese, such as *robiola;* and a fresh or aged *caprino,* or goat's milk cheese.

If you are serving the antipasto course on individual small plates, you can place them directly over each dinner plate just before your guests are seated. In warm weather or for an alfresco meal, a room-temperature antipasto works well and helps minimize last-minute cooking. Select a dish that sets the tone for a regional menu, such as Caponata (page 54) or Tomato, Basil, and Mozzarella Salad (page 50) for a southern Italian–inspired meal, or Farro Salad (page 44) or Panzanella (page 59) for a Tuscan feast. If your menu includes a hot antipasto, such as Fritto Misto (page 66) or Fonduta with White Truffle (page 65), do as much of the prep ahead of time as possible,

and consider serving first and second courses that require minimal last-minute cooking.

Keep portions small. The antipasto should be an exquisite taste that leaves people hungry for more, not a rich, filling first course. The recipes in this chapter will help you get a sense of appropriate portion size.

VERSATILE ANTIPASTI

Simple, direct, and bursting with flavor, antipasti are ideal for serving in a variety of nontraditional ways. An array of several made-ahead dishes creates a memorable, easily replenished buffet for an open house. Put together a selection of offerings that includes several vegetable dishes along with items featuring seafood, dairy, and meat.

Antipasto salads, such as Salt Cod Salad (page 57) and Farro Salad (page 44), are perfect for outdoor entertaining and hold up well when packed for a picnic. Vegetable antipasti, such as Grilled Vegetables (page 75) and Risotto-Stuffed Tomatoes (page 79), can be served as side dishes, or *contorni,* to accompany a second course. And more substantial antipasti, including Artichoke Tortino (page 80), Eggplant Parmesan (page 53), and Eggplant Involtini (page 72), work well as light brunch or lunch main courses.

BEVERAGE PAIRINGS

Welcome guests with a bitter *aperitivo,* such as Campari (on the rocks or with soda) or the nonalcoholic Aperol or Crodino. Mixed drinks made with gin or vodka, including martinis and negronis, are also appropriate before or with antipasto. Good wine choices include rosé, light-bodied reds such as Bardolino or Lambrusco, or light, crisp whites such as Soave or Pinot Grigio. Chilled Prosecco or other dry sparkling wines work particularly well, too.

Tomato Bruschetta

Bruschetta, at its simplest, is grilled bread rubbed with garlic and drizzled with olive oil, but it can also be prepared with a variety of toppings. This classic version, popular in both Umbria and Tuscany, demands the best-quality ingredients. Use a crusty country-style bread; ripe, red tomatoes harvested at the height of the season; freshly picked basil; and the best extra-virgin olive oil your budget will allow

Prepare a charcoal or gas grill for direct grilling over medium-high heat, or preheat a broiler (grill).

If using cherry tomatoes, stem them and cut them in half. If using large tomatoes, core and seed them and cut into ½-inch (12-mm) dice. In a bowl, combine the tomatoes, the basil, and a pinch of salt.

BY GRILL: Using tongs, place the bread slices over the hottest part of the fire or directly over the heat elements and grill, turning once, until crisp and golden on both sides, about 3 minutes total.

BY BROILER: Place the bread slices on a broiler pan and slip it in the broiler about 4 inches (10 cm) from the heat source. Broil (grill), turning once, until crisp and golden on both sides, about 3 minutes total.

Remove from the heat and immediately rub one side of each slice vigorously with a garlic clove, using 1 clove for 4 slices.

Arrange the bread slices, garlic side up, on a serving platter or divide among individual plates. Spoon the tomato mixture on the bread, dividing it evenly. Drizzle with the olive oil. Serve at once.

About 20 cherry tomatoes, or 2 large tomatoes

About 16 fresh basil leaves, torn into small pieces

Sea salt

8 slices coarse country bread, about ½ inch (12 mm) thick

2 cloves garlic, peeled and left whole

¼ cup (2 fl oz/60 ml) extra-virgin olive oil

MAKES 4 SERVINGS

White Bean and Arugula Crostini

3 tablespoons extra-virgin olive oil, plus more for brushing and drizzling

2 tablespoons finely chopped yellow onion

2 tablespoons finely chopped carrot

2 tablespoons finely chopped celery

1 can (15 oz/470 g) cannellini beans, rinsed and drained

Sea salt and freshly ground pepper

1 baguette

2 cups (2 oz/60 g) baby arugula (rocket) leaves

MAKES 6 SERVINGS

Position a rack in the middle of the oven and preheat to 375°F (190°C).

In a frying pan over medium heat, warm the 3 tablespoons olive oil. Add the onion, carrot, and celery and sauté until the onion is golden and the carrots and celery have softened, 3–4 minutes. Add the beans, season with salt and pepper, and stir well to combine. Remove from the heat and let cool to room temperature.

Meanwhile, cut the baguette on the diagonal into 18 slices each ¹/₂ inch (12 mm) thick. (You will not need the whole loaf.) Arrange the bread slices on a rimmed baking sheet and brush the tops lightly with olive oil. Bake until golden, about 5 minutes. Remove from the oven.

Arrange the toasts on a serving platter or divide among individual plates. Spoon the beans on the toasts, dividing them evenly. Drizzle generously with olive oil, then top with the arugula. Serve at once.

Like bruschetta, these rustic "little toasts" are a popular antipasto. You can use canned beans, but if you can find jars of imported Italian cannellini beans, they will deliver a more authentic flavor. Best of all, of course, is home-cooked beans (page 275), so if you prepare a pot of white beans as a side dish, cook extra beans and use about 2 cups (14 oz/440 g) to make these crostini the next day. Chopped fresh flat-leaf (Italian) parsley or diced oil-packed sun-dried tomatoes can be used in place of the arugula.

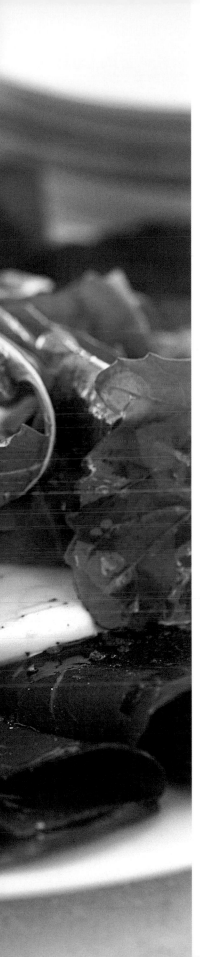

Bresaola with Arugula and Mozzarella

Bresaola, which originated in the mountains of Lombardy, is made by salting beef and allowing it to air-dry for several weeks. It is leaner than prosciutto, which is cured in much the same way, and has sweet aroma and rich flavor. It is popularly offered as an antipasto, thinly sliced in the manner of carpaccio and served with similar accompaniments. This recipe also makes a satisfying main course in summer. Franciacorta, a sparkling wine from Lombardy, pairs well with the dish.

Place the arugula in a bowl, sprinkle with salt, and drizzle with the 2 teaspoons olive oil. Toss to mix well. Add a grind or two of pepper, unless the arugula is quite peppery on its own.

Arrange the *bresaola* slices around the edge of a single platter or divide among individual plates. Arrange the slices of mozzarella around the inside edge of the *bresaola*. Mound the arugula in the middle. Sprinkle lightly with salt and pepper, drizzle with olive oil, and serve at once. Pass the lemon wedges at the table for squeezing over the *bresaola*.

2 cups (2 oz/60 g) baby arugula (rocket) leaves

Sea salt and freshly ground pepper

2 teaspoons extra-virgin olive oil, plus more for drizzling

16 paper-thin slices *bresaola*, about 4½ oz (140 g) total weight

8 slices fresh mozzarella cheese, about ¼ lb (125 g) total weight

4 lemon wedges

MAKES 4 SERVINGS

TUSCANY

Farro Salad

1 cup (6 oz/185 g) *farro*

Sea salt and freshly ground pepper

2 tablespoons extra-virgin olive oil

1 tablespoon fresh lemon juice

1 cup (6 oz/185 g) cherry or grape tomatoes, stemmed and halved

½ cup (2 oz/60 g) crumbled *ricotta salata* **cheese**

2 green (spring) onions, including tender green tops, thinly sliced

¼ cup (⅓ oz/10 g) shredded fresh basil

MAKES 4 SERVINGS

In a large saucepan, combine the *farro* and 2 qt (2 l) water and let stand for 1 hour. Place the pan over medium-high heat, bring to a boil, and add 1 teaspoon salt. Reduce the heat to medium or medium-low, so the *farro* simmers steadily, and cook, uncovered, until tender yet still slightly firm and chewy, about 25 minutes. Remove from the heat and drain well in a fine-mesh sieve.

In a serving bowl, whisk together the olive oil and lemon juice until well blended. Whisk in salt and pepper to taste. Add the *farro* and toss well. Gently stir in the tomatoes, *ricotta salata,* green onions, and basil until all the ingredients are evenly distributed. Serve at room temperature.

Farro, an ancient form of wheat, is cultivated primarily in the regions of Tuscany and Umbria. The light brown grains have a full, nutty flavor that is delicious in soups and salads. Soaking the *farro* before cooking ensures that the grains will cook evenly.

Spicy Fried Chickpeas

Here is a quick and easy antipasto made with just a few ingredients. Enjoy these full-flavored chickpeas with a glass of Prosecco *spumante* (sparkling) or *frizzante* (lightly sparkling), a fruity white wine from the Veneto. Look for a label that includes either Conegliano or Valdobbiadene as the origin, areas where Prosecco grapes yield the finest wines.

Drain the chickpeas in a colander, rinse well with cold water, and then transfer to paper towels and dry thoroughly.

Pour the olive oil to a depth of 1 inch (2.5 cm) into a deep, heavy frying pan and heat to 375°F (190°C) on a deep-frying thermometer. Line a platter or rimmed baking sheet with paper towels and set it next to the stove.

When the oil is ready, add the garlic cloves and fry until they begin to turn golden, about 1 minute. Add the chickpeas and sage and fry until crisp and browned, 4–5 minutes. Take care when adding the chickpeas as they might spit and sputter due to moisture; cook them in batches if necessary, allowing the oil to return to the original frying temperature before adding the next batch. Using a slotted spoon, transfer the chickpeas, garlic, and sage to the towel-lined platter to drain.

Sprinkle the chickpeas with salt and cayenne to taste, transfer to a serving bowl, and serve at once.

1 can (15 oz/470 g) chickpeas (garbanzo beans)

Olive or canola oil for frying

3 cloves garlic, unpeeled

6 fresh sage leaves

Sea salt

Cayenne pepper

MAKES 4–6 SERVINGS

Prosciutto-Wrapped Figs
with Balsamic

8 ripe figs such as Mission or Adriatic

4 paper-thin slices prosciutto

Aged balsamic vinegar

MAKES 4 SERVINGS

Trim the stem off each fig, then cut the fig in half lengthwise. Cut each slice of prosciutto into quarters. Wrap a piece of prosciutto around each fig half.

Arrange the wrapped figs on a serving platter. Drizzle evenly with balsamic vinegar to taste and serve.

NOTE: Fresh figs are a staple of summer antipasto platters in Italy and pair well with both meats and cheeses. Try serving the fig halves with slices of salty *ricotta salata* or chunks of Parmigiano-Reggiano. Or, trim the stems and cut each fig into quarters lengthwise, stopping about $1/4$ inch (6 mm) before the bottom so the fig remains intact. Stuff the inside with crumbled creamy blue cheese, such as Gorgonzola, or fresh goat cheese.

Fresh figs, which have a short early-summer season and a second, longer season and bigger harvest that stretches from late summer into early autumn, should be picked and purchased at their peak of ripeness, as they do not ripen further off the tree. Look for fragrant, soft fruits with tiny cracks in the skin, being careful to avoid bruised specimens.

LAZIO

Fried Ricotta-Stuffed Zucchini Blossoms

In Rome, zucchini blossoms are stuffed with mozzarella and anchovies and fried in a crisp coating. Here, herbed ricotta is tucked into the blossoms with delicious results. Try to find the best quality artisan ricotta that you can. Sheep's milk ricotta makes a particularly flavorful filling. If the ricotta is excessively moist, place it in a cheesecloth-lined fine-mesh sieve on top of a bowl, and place in the refrigerator to drain overnight. Fresh squash blossoms are highly perishable, so use them as soon as possible.

In a bowl, stir together the ricotta, parsley, and basil and season to taste with salt and pepper. Scrape the mixture into a pastry (piping) bag fitted with a large plain tip and set aside. (Or, cut off one of the bottom corners of a heavy-duty plastic bag to make a 1/2-inch/12-mm opening, and scrape the mixture into the bag.) In a small, shallow bowl, whisk the eggs until lightly beaten. Spread the flour on a plate.

Wipe the zucchini blossoms with damp paper towels, and carefully remove the stamens. One at a time, gently spread the flowers open, insert the tip of the pastry bag, and pipe about 1 tablespoon of the ricotta mixture into the blossom. Do not overfill the blossoms, or the filling may seep out as they cook. One at a time, roll the blossoms first in the flour, then in the egg, and then again in the flour, gently shaking off the excess each time.

Position a rack in the middle of the oven and preheat to 200°F (95°C). Line a platter or rimmed baking sheet with paper towels and set it next to the stove. Pour the olive oil to a depth of 1 inch (2.5 cm) into a deep, heavy frying pan and heat to 375°F (190°C) on a deep-frying thermometer.

When the oil is ready, add the blossoms a few at a time, being careful not to crowd the pan. Fry the blossoms, turning them once, until lightly golden, 3–4 minutes. Using a slotted spoon, transfer the blossoms to the paper-lined platter to drain and place in the oven to keep warm. Repeat with the remaining blossoms, allowing the oil to return to the original frying temperature before adding the next batch.

Arrange the blossoms on a warmed platter and serve at once.

1 cup (8 oz/250 g) whole-milk ricotta cheese

1/2 tablespoon chopped fresh flat-leaf (Italian) parsley

1 tablespoon chopped fresh basil leaves

Sea salt and freshly ground pepper

2 large eggs

1 cup (5 oz/155 g) all-purpose (plain) flour

12 large zucchini (courgette) or other squash blossoms

Olive or canola oil for frying

MAKES 4–6 SERVINGS

CAMPANIA

Tomato, Basil, and Mozzarella Salad

3 or 4 large, ripe tomatoes

½ lb (250 g) fresh mozzarella cheese

Sea salt and freshly ground pepper

¼ cup (2 fl oz/60 ml) extra-virgin olive oil

About 10 fresh basil leaves

MAKES 4 SERVINGS

Cut the tomatoes and mozzarella into slices ¼ inch (6 mm) thick.

On a serving platter, overlap slices of tomato and mozzarella. Sprinkle with salt and pepper. Drizzle with the olive oil. Tear the basil into small pieces and sprinkle over the salad. Serve at once.

NOTE: Tomatoes come in all sorts of shapes, sizes, and colors. For this recipe, it is essential to use the best quality, ripe, fresh tomatoes that you can find. If you can find them in season, try different heirloom varieties such as Green Zebra or Brandywine. You can also halve and scatter a handful of sweet cherry or grape tomatoes over the sliced tomatoes and mozzarella before drizzling with olive oil.

In Campania, where this salad is known as *insalata caprese* (salad in the style of the island of Capri), creamy fresh mozzarella and juicy, sun-ripened tomatoes find their way into many dishes, though none as perfect as this simple salad. This is a classic summertime dish, so don't even consider making it with out-of-season tomatoes or plastic-sheathed mozzarella.

Eggplant Parmesan

There are many versions of this dish throughout southern Italy. Some include a meat sauce, others slip hard-cooked eggs between the layers, and still others call for dipping the eggplant slices in beaten egg and bread crumbs before frying. This recipe is from Campania, where it is typically served as an antipasto, a *contorno*, or even cold as a sandwich filling. Make sure the oil is fully heated before you add the eggplant, or the slices will absorb too much oil.

Trim the eggplants, then cut crosswise into slices 1/4 inch (6 mm) thick. Layer the slices in a colander set over a plate, sprinkling each layer with salt, and let stand for 30 minutes to drain. Rinse the eggplant slices quickly under cold running water and pat dry with paper towels.

Position a rack in the middle of the oven and preheat to 350°F (180°C). Have ready a 9-by-13-inch (23-by-33-cm) baking dish.

Line a large platter or tray with paper towels and set it next to the stove. Pour the olive oil to a depth of about 1/2 inch (12 mm) into a large, heavy frying pan and place over high heat until hot. Working in batches, add the eggplant slices in a single layer, being careful not to crowd the pan. Fry, turning once, until nicely browned on both sides, about 10 minutes total. Using tongs, transfer the slices to the towel-lined platter to drain. Fry the remaining slices in the same way, adding more oil to the pan as needed.

Spread a thin layer of the tomato sauce on the bottom of the baking dish. Cover the sauce with a layer of the eggplant slices, overlapping them slightly and using about a third of the slices. Top with a third of the mozzarella, a third of the sauce, and a third of the Parmigiano-Reggiano. Repeat the layering two more times, ending with the grated cheese.

Bake until the sauce is bubbling and the cheese is lightly browned, about 45 minutes. Let stand for 5 minutes before serving.

2 eggplants (aubergines), about 1 lb (500 g) each

Sea salt

Olive oil for frying

2 1/2 cups (20 fl oz/625 ml) classic tomato sauce (page 272)

1 lb (500 g) fresh mozzarella cheese, cut into thin slices

1/2 cup (2 oz/60 g) grated Parmigiano-Reggiano cheese

MAKES 6 SERVINGS

SICILY

Caponata

Olive or canola oil for frying

2 eggplants (aubergines), about 1 lb (500 g) each, trimmed and cut into 1-inch (2.5-cm) cubes

2 red or yellow bell peppers (capsicums), seeded and cut into ½-inch (12-mm) squares

2 large yellow onions, cut into ½-inch (12-mm) cubes

3 tender inner celery stalks, sliced

3 ripe tomatoes, seeded and chopped

1 cup (5 oz/155 g) chopped pitted green olives

⅓ cup (2 oz/60 g) raisins

2 tablespoons capers, rinsed and drained

2 tablespoons sugar

2 tablespoons red wine vinegar

Sea salt

¼ cup (1 oz/30 g) sliced (flaked) almonds, toasted

Crusty Italian bread or focaccia (page 275), for serving

MAKES 8–10 SERVINGS

Pour the olive oil to a depth of ½ inch (12 mm) into a deep, heavy frying pan and place over medium heat until hot. The oil is ready when an eggplant cube dropped into it sizzles on impact. Line a large platter or tray with paper towels and set it next to the stove.

Working in batches, carefully arrange the eggplant cubes in the pan in a single layer, being careful not to crowd them. Cook, stirring occasionally, until the eggplant is tender and browned, 7–8 minutes. Using a slotted spoon, transfer to the towel-lined platter to drain. Repeat with the remaining eggplant.

When all of the eggplant has been cooked, fry the bell peppers in the same way until tender and lightly browned, 4–6 minutes, and then drain on paper towels as well. Finally, fry the onions and celery together in the same way until tender and golden, 7–8 minutes, and drain on paper towels.

In a large saucepan over low heat, combine the tomatoes, olives, raisins, capers, sugar, and vinegar. Stir well and add the fried vegetables and a pinch of salt. Cover partially and cook, stirring occasionally, until the mixture thickens, about 20 minutes. Add a little water if the mixture begins to dry out. Remove from the heat, transfer to a serving dish, and let cool to room temperature. If time permits, cover and refrigerate overnight to allow the flavors to marry; bring to room temperature before serving.

Just before serving, sprinkle the almonds over the top. Serve with slices of crusty bread or focaccia.

Caponata, an iconic antipasto of Sicily, has Arabic origins, as evidenced by its use of eggplant, almonds, and sweet-and-sour seasoning. Such influences are not uncommon in Sicily, once a crossroads of many cultures. This is a good make-ahead dish for entertaining, as the flavors improve if allowed to meld overnight. Although traditionally served at room temperature, it can also be served warm as a side dish to grilled fish or poultry.

Salt Cod Salad

Salt cod, known as *baccalà* in Italian, originated in Scandinavia. It gained popularity in Italy at a time when fresh fish was costly and difficult to transport, solving the problem of what to eat on the many fast days of the Catholic calendar. Today, of course, fresh fish is readily available, but the Italians still enjoy *baccalà* prepared in a variety ways, including in this antipasto salad.

Rinse the fish under cool running water, then cut into 4 pieces. Place the pieces in a nonreactive bowl and add cold water to cover. Cover the bowl and refrigerate for at least 24 hours, changing the water 4 or 5 times. When ready, the cod will have lightened in color and look slightly puffy.

The next day, in a saucepan, combine the potatoes with salted cold water to cover generously and bring to a boil over high heat. Reduce the heat to medium and cook until tender, about 20 minutes. Drain the potatoes, let cool slightly, and then peel and cut into slices.

Meanwhile, drain the salt cod. Pour water to a depth of about 2 inches (5 cm) into a large frying pan and bring to a boil over high heat. Reduce the heat to low, add the salt cod, and simmer until tender when tested with a fork, 5–7 minutes. Using a slotted spoon, remove the cod from the pan and briefly pat dry on paper towels.

Remove any errant bits of skin from the cod and arrange the pieces on a serving platter, breaking up the fish into large chunks. Scatter the potato and onion slices and the olives over the fish. In a small bowl, whisk together the olive oil and lemon juice, and then whisk in the garlic and red pepper flakes. Drizzle the dressing over the salad. Taste and adjust the seasoning with salt and red pepper flakes. Garnish with the parsley and serve warm or at room temperature with the lemon wedges.

1 lb (500 g) salt cod fillet

1 lb (500 g) Yukon gold or other boiling potatoes

Sea salt

1 small red onion, halved and thinly sliced

1/2 cup (2 1/2 oz/75 g) pitted brine-cured black olives, coarsely chopped

1/4 cup (2 fl oz/60 ml) extra-virgin olive oil

3 tablespoons fresh lemon juice

1 teaspoon minced garlic

1/4 teaspoon red pepper flakes, or to taste

1/4 cup (1/4 oz/7 g) coarsely chopped fresh flat-leaf (Italian) parsley leaves

Lemon wedges

MAKES 4 SERVINGS

Fava Beans with Pecorino

3 lb (1.5 kg) fava (broad) beans in their pods

6 oz (185 g) pecorino cheese, cut into ½-inch (12-cm) cubes

¼ cup (2 fl oz/60 ml) extra-virgin olive oil

Sea salt and freshly ground pepper

MAKES 4 SERVINGS

To shell the beans, press along the seam of each pod with your thumb to split it open. Bring a saucepan three-fourths full of water to a boil. Add the beans and blanch for 1–2 minutes. Drain and let cool slightly. Pinch the edge of each bean where it was attached to the pod to slip it from its skin. Discard the skins and transfer the beans to a salad bowl.

Add the cheese to the beans, then drizzle with the olive oil and season with salt and pepper. Toss to mix well and serve.

NOTE: Fava beans are often seen on antipasti platters, served atop garlicky crostini. Follow the instructions on page 40 to prepare the crostini. Blanch and peel the fava beans as directed above. In a bowl, lightly smash the beans with the back of a fork. Spread the beans on the crostini and serve with a drizzle of olive oil. Or, for a more elaborate presentation, top with a small, thin slice of prosciutto.

In Italy, fava beans are one of the first vegetables of the spring garden. Early in the season, the young beans are so crisp and tender that they are eaten raw, straight out of their bright green pods. Look for a medium-aged pecorino, which will hold its shape better when cut.

Panzanella

This hearty salad originated as a way to use up stale bread. Traditionally, the bland, salt-free bread of Tuscany is used, but you can use any day-old country-style bread. The drier the bread, the more absorbent it is, which means it will soak up more of the delicious tomato juices and dressing. As the salad sits, the bread will soften and the flavors will blend together. Serve this salad on a warm evening in late summer, when tomatoes are at their peak of ripeness.

In a large mixing bowl, combine the tomatoes, cucumber, onion, and torn basil. Drizzle with the ½ cup olive oil and the 3 tablespoons vinegar and season with salt and pepper. Toss well to coat evenly.

Cut or tear the bread into bite-sized pieces. Place half of the bread in a wide, shallow serving bowl. Spoon on half of the tomato mixture. Layer the remaining bread on top and then the remaining tomato mixture. Cover and refrigerate for 1 hour.

Toss the salad, then taste and adjust the seasoning with salt, pepper, and vinegar. If the bread is dry, add a little more olive oil. Garnish the salad with a few basil leaves just before serving.

2 large ripe tomatoes, cut into bite-sized pieces

1 small English (hothouse) cucumber, peeled, halved lengthwise, and sliced

1 small red onion, halved and very thinly sliced

1 cup (1 oz/30 g) fresh basil leaves, torn into small pieces, plus whole leaves for garnish

½ cup (4 fl oz/125 ml) extra-virgin olive oil, or to taste

3 tablespoons red wine vinegar, or to taste

Sea salt and freshly ground pepper

6–8 slices day-old coarse country bread

MAKES 6 SERVINGS

TUSCANY

Field Salad with Pancetta and Walnuts

Springtime in Italy brings the familiar sight of people walking through fields gathering tender wild greens for making *insalata del campo*, or "salad of the field." Choose whatever combination of greens looks best in the market, but be sure to include at least one or two strong-flavored or bitter varieties, such as dandelion, chicory (curly endive), escarole (Batavian endive), arugula (rocket), or radicchio, that will stand up to the big flavors of the nuts, cheese, and crisp pancetta.

Position a rack in the middle of the oven and preheat the oven to 325°F (165°C). Spread the walnuts in a single layer on a rimmed baking sheet and toast, stirring once or twice, until fragrant and the color deepens, about 10 minutes. Pour onto a small plate to cool, then coarsely chop and set aside.

In a frying pan over medium heat, fry the pancetta, stirring frequently, until browned and crisp, about 10 minutes. Using a slotted spoon, transfer the pancetta to paper towels to drain.

To make the vinaigrette, in a small bowl, whisk together the olive oil and vinegar until blended. Whisk in salt and pepper to taste.

Place the greens in a large serving bowl, drizzle with the vinaigrette, and toss to coat evenly. Add the pancetta and nuts and toss well. Using a vegetable peeler, shave the cheese over the salad, if desired. Serve at once.

½ cup (2 oz/60 g) walnuts

3 ounces (90 g) sliced pancetta, chopped

For the vinaigrette

¼ cup (2 fl oz/60 ml) extra-virgin olive oil

2–3 tablespoons balsamic vinegar

Sea salt and freshly ground pepper

6–8 cups (6–8 oz/185–250 g) torn salad greens, including some bitter varieties (see note)

Small wedge of Parmigiano-Reggiano cheese (optional)

MAKES 4 SERVINGS

Farinata with Herbs and Onions

1 cup (4 oz/125 g) chickpea (garbanzo bean) flour

Sea salt and coarsely ground pepper

⅓ cup (3 fl oz/80 ml) olive oil, plus 1 tablespoon for greasing the pan

½ yellow onion, very thinly sliced crosswise

1 tablespoon chopped fresh sage or rosemary

MAKES 4 SERVINGS

In a bowl, whisk together the chickpea flour, 1½ cups (12 fl oz/375 ml) water, 2 teaspoons salt, and the ⅓ cup olive oil until smooth. The batter should be fairly thin. Cover and let stand at room temperature for at least 4 hours, or refrigerate for up to overnight.

Bring 2 cups (16 fl oz/500 ml) water to a boil. Place the onion slices in a fine-mesh sieve in the sink. Pour the boiling water over the onions, then rinse the onions with cold water to remove their bitter sharpness.

Position a rack in the upper third of the oven and preheat to 400°F (200°C). Once the oven is preheated, place a 9-inch (23-cm) cast iron pan in the oven to heat about 5 minutes before baking the *farinata.*

While the pan is heating, add half of the sage to the batter and stir to mix. Squeeze any excess water from the onions. Carefully remove the pan from the oven and add the remaining 1 tablespoon olive oil, swirling to coat the bottom evenly.

Pour the batter into the prepared pan and scatter the onions and the remaining sage evenly over the top. Bake until the *farinata* is cooked through and the edges are crisp and browned, about 2 minutes.

Carefully slide the *farinata* out of the pan onto a serving plate. Sprinkle with salt and pepper, cut into wedges, and serve at once.

In Liguria, cooks make a crepelike flatbread from a simple batter of chickpea flour, water, and olive oil that echoes the *socca* made just across the border in Nice. Called *farinata* and traditionally a street food, it is eaten plain or topped with vegetables, herbs, or other ingredients. Look for chickpea flour in Italian stores or in Indian markets, where it is labeled gram flour or *besan.*

Fonduta with White Truffle

Fontina cheese, which has been made from cow's milk in Italy's small northern region of Valle d'Aosta for centuries, is fragrant with the grasses and mushrooms found where the cows graze. In the nearby region of Piedmont, Fontina is mixed with egg yolks and milk to make the creamy, ultrarich *fonduta*, similar to a Swiss fondue. Thinly shaved white truffles are strewn on top and the mixture is eaten warm with toasted bread. The *fonduta* can be prepared without the white truffle, but it adds a marvelous flavor. *Fonduta* can also be used as a sauce for poached eggs or steamed asparagus.

In a shallow bowl, combine the cheese and milk, submerging the cheese fully in the milk. Cover and let stand at room temperature for 2 hours, or refrigerate for up to overnight.

Drain off ½ cup (4 fl oz/125 ml) of the milk and place it in a bowl with the egg yolks. Whisk until blended. Put the cheese, the remaining milk, and the butter in a heatproof bowl that will fit snugly in the rim of a saucepan. Pour water to a depth of about 2 inches (5 cm) into the pan and bring to a simmer over medium heat. Adjust the heat so the water simmers gently, and place the bowl holding the cheese over (not touching) the simmering water. (Alternatively, use a double boiler.) Heat, stirring often, until the cheese is melted and smooth, about 3 minutes. Slowly add the egg yolk mixture while whisking constantly. Continue cooking, whisking constantly, until slightly thickened, about 5 minutes longer.

Arrange 2 slices of toast on each plate. Pour the *fonduta* evenly over the toast. Using a truffle shaver or a vegetable peeler, thinly shave the truffle over the *fonduta.* Serve at once.

½ lb (250 g) Valle d'Aosta Fontina cheese, rind trimmed and thinly sliced

1 cup (8 fl oz/250 ml) whole milk

3 large egg yolks

3 tablespoons unsalted butter

8 thin slices whole-wheat (wholemeal) Italian bread, toasted

1 white truffle

MAKES 4 SERVINGS

Fritto Misto

½ lb (250 g) cleaned squid

½ lb (250 g) medium
shrimp (prawns), peeled
and deveined

About 8 fresh sardines,
smelts, anchovies, whitebait,
or other small fish, cleaned
and gutted if necessary

2 lemons

1 cup (5 oz/155 g)
all-purpose (plain) flour

Sea salt

Olive or canola oil for
deep-frying

2 small zucchini (courgettes),
trimmed and cut into sticks
2 inches (5 cm) long by
¼ inch (6 mm) wide
and thick

MAKES 4–6 SERVINGS

Rinse the squid, shrimp, and sardines, drain well, and pat dry with paper towels. Cut the squid bodies into rings ½ inch (12 mm) wide and the tentacles into bite-sized pieces. Cut 1 lemon crosswise into very thin slices and remove the seeds. Cut the second lemon into wedges and set aside. In a bowl, toss together the flour and a pinch of salt.

Position a rack in the middle of the oven and preheat to 200°F (95°C). Line a large platter or rimmed baking sheet with paper towels and set it next to the stove. Pour the olive oil to a depth of 3 inches (7.5 cm) into a deep, heavy frying pan and heat to 375°F (190°C) on a deep-frying thermometer.

When the oil is ready, add about one-fourth of the seafood, lemon slices, and zucchini to the flour and toss until lightly coated. Lift from the flour, shaking off the excess, and drop the pieces a few at a time into the hot oil, being careful the oil doesn't splash. Fry until the shrimp turn pink and the other ingredients are pale gold, about 3 minutes. Using a slotted spoon, transfer the seafood, lemon slices, and zucchini to the towel-lined platter to drain and place in the oven to keep warm. Repeat with the remaining ingredients in three batches, always allowing the oil to return to the original frying temperature before adding the next batch. If the oil is not hot enough, the foods will absorb it, making them greasy.

Transfer the seafood, zucchini, and lemon slices to a warmed serving platter. Sprinkle with salt and serve at once with the lemon wedges.

A "mixed fry" is a typical main course in many regions of Italy. In Piedmont, it is made with vegetables and meats, such as baby lamb chops, cutlets, and brains, often in a light bread crumb coating. In Venice, Rome, and Naples, and along the rest of Italy's coastline, seafood is used instead of meat, and the coating is thin and sheer, often just a dusting of flour. Fry the ingredients in small batches for a crisp, light result.

Sweet-and-Sour Sardines

Sardines in a sweet-and-sour marinade with raisins and pine nuts is a classic antipasto in Venice, where it is known as *sarde in saor*. Other fish can be prepared this way, especially dark-fleshed varieties, such as bluefish or mackerel. The flavors come together as the fish marinates, so plan to begin marinating the sardines at least a day before serving.

Using a sharp knife, make a slit on the underside of each sardine from the head to the tail, and use your finger to push out the viscera. Gently press the body open, grasp the spine near the tail end, and carefully pull the bone free from the fish. Rinse the fish under cold running water, pat dry with paper towels, and set aside.

In a large, heavy frying pan over medium-low heat, warm 4 tablespoons (2 fl oz/ 60 ml) of the olive oil. Add the onions and cook, stirring frequently, until very tender but not browned, about 20 minutes. If the onions begin to brown, add a little water to the pan and lower the heat slightly.

Add the wine, vinegar, pine nuts, and raisins to the onions, bring to a simmer, and cook for 1 minute. Remove from the heat and set aside.

In another large frying pan over medium heat, warm the remaining 2 tablespoons olive oil. Working in batches if necessary to avoid crowding, add the sardines in a single layer and cook, turning once, until opaque in the center when tested with a knife, about 2 minutes on each side.

Arrange the sardines on a serving platter. Sprinkle with salt and pepper. Spoon the onion mixture evenly over the top. Cover and refrigerate for at least 24 hours or for up to 2 days. Serve at room temperature.

1½ lb (750 g) fresh sardines

6 tablespoons (3 fl oz/90 ml) olive oil

2 small yellow onions, thinly sliced

¾ cup (6 fl oz/180 ml) dry white wine

¾ cup (6 fl oz/180 ml) white wine vinegar

2 tablespoons pine nuts

2 tablespoons golden raisins (sultanas)

Sea salt and freshly ground pepper

MAKES 6 SERVINGS

Tuna, White Bean, and Radicchio Salad

1 can (7 oz/220 g) olive oil–packed tuna, preferably Italian

3 cups (21 oz/660 g) drained, cooked cannellini beans (page 275)

5 tablespoons (2½ fl oz/ 75 ml) extra-virgin olive oil, plus more for brushing

1 clove garlic, minced

Sea salt and freshly ground pepper

2 small heads radicchio, preferably Treviso, halved lengthwise

1 cup (5 oz/155 g) chopped celery

½ small red onion, chopped

Pinch of dried oregano

1–2 tablespoons fresh lemon juice

MAKES 6 SERVINGS

Prepare a charcoal or gas grill for direct grilling over medium-high heat and oil the grill rack. Alternatively, preheat the broiler (grill). Drain the tuna and break it up into chunks. Set aside.

In a saucepan over medium heat, combine the beans, 3 tablespoons of the olive oil, and the garlic and bring to a simmer. Season with salt and pepper and simmer until heated through and the flavors have blended, about 10 minutes. Remove from the heat and set aside to cool.

Brush the radicchio halves with olive oil and sprinkle with salt and pepper.

BY GRILL: Using tongs, arrange the radicchio halves over the hottest part of the fire or directly over the heat elements and grill, turning once, until wilted and lightly browned, about 5 minutes total.

BY BROILER: Arrange the radicchio halves on a broiler pan and slip it in the broiler about 4 inches (10 cm) from the heat source. Broil (grill) turning once, until wilted and lightly browned, about 5 minutes total.

Transfer the radicchio halves to a cutting board, let cool slightly, and then cut crosswise into ribbons.

Add the radicchio, celery, onion, oregano, and 1 tablespoon lemon juice to the beans and toss to combine. Taste and adjust the seasoning with lemon juice, salt, and pepper.

Divide the bean salad among individual plates, and top each serving with an equal amount of the tuna. Serve at once.

Red radicchio grows in heads with leaves that range from creamy to greenish white near the base to wine red at the tips. The Treviso variety has elongated leaves, while the Chioggia and most other varieties are round or oval. Here, smooth, creamy cannellini beans, a type of white kidney bean that is a favorite of Tuscans, are a perfect complement to the slight bitterness of the grilled radicchio. Maroon-speckled *borlotti* or cranberry beans can be substituted.

Bagna Cauda

Bagna cauda, literally "hot bath," is a Piedmontese anchovy-spiked hot dip for vegetables and crusty bread. Cardoon, a member of the thistle family that looks like an outsized bunch of celery and has a taste reminiscent of artichoke, is traditionally among the vegetables and is increasingly available outside Italy. Look for it in your local farmers' market or produce store during the cool-weather months.

In a small saucepan over low heat, combine the olive oil, garlic, and anchovies. Cook, mashing the anchovies with the back of a wooden spoon, until the anchovies have dissolved and the mixture is smooth and hot, about 5 minutes. Remove from the heat and stir in the butter.

Pour the mixture into a warmed chafing dish or fondue pot set over a warming candle or spirit lamp. Arrange the vegetables decoratively on a serving platter. Serve at once with the vegetables for dipping. Pass the bread slices at the table.

NOTE: This garlicky, savory sauce is excellent tossed with cooked fresh pasta such as fettuccine or drizzled over creamy polenta.

¾ cup (6 fl oz/180 ml) olive oil

8 cloves garlic, minced

12 olive oil–packed anchovy fillets

4 tablespoons (2 oz/60 g) unsalted butter

About 8 cups (2½ lb/1.25 kg) trimmed, cut-up vegetables such as raw bell pepper (capsicum), carrot, Jerusalem artichoke, celery, or green (spring) onion; cooked beet, potato, cardoon, or onion; and blanched cauliflower or broccoli

Coarse country bread slices for serving

MAKES 6–8 SERVINGS

Eggplant Involtini

1 large eggplant (aubergine), about 1½ lb (750 g)

Sea salt and freshly ground pepper

1 cup (8 oz/250 g) whole-milk ricotta cheese

¼ lb (125 g) fresh mozzarella cheese, shredded

4 tablespoons (1 oz/30 g) grated Parmigiano-Reggiano cheese

1 tablespoon chopped fresh flat-leaf (Italian) parsley

Olive oil for brushing

2½ cups (20 fl oz/625 ml) classic tomato sauce (page 272)

MAKES 4 SERVINGS

Trim the eggplant, then cut crosswise on the diagonal (so the slices are as wide as possible) ¼ inch (6 mm) thick. Layer the slices in a colander set over a plate, sprinkling each layer with salt, and let stand for 30 minutes to drain.

Meanwhile, in a bowl, stir together the ricotta, mozzarella, 2 tablespoons of the Parmigiano-Reggiano, the parsley, and pepper to taste.

Position a rack in the middle of the oven and preheat to 450°F (230°C).

Rinse the eggplant slices quickly under cold running water and pat dry with paper towels. Brush the slices on both sides with olive oil, and arrange them in a single layer on a rimmed baking sheet.

Bake the slices until lightly browned on the bottom, about 10 minutes. Turn the slices and continue to bake until browned on the second side and tender, 5–10 minutes longer. Remove the eggplant from the oven. Reduce the oven temperature to 350°F (180°C).

Spoon a thin layer of the tomato sauce into a 9-inch (23-cm) square baking dish. To make each eggplant roll, place a spoonful of the cheese mixture near one end of a slice and roll up the slice. As it each roll is formed, place it seam side down in the dish. Spoon the remaining sauce over the rolls, then sprinkle evenly with the remaining 2 tablespoons Parmigiano-Reggiano.

Bake the rolls until the sauce is bubbling hot and the rolls are heated through, about 25 minutes. Divide the rolls among individual plates and serve at once.

Eggplants are prepared in a variety of ways in southern Italy, especially in Sicily, where they turn up in pasta sauces, layered with tomatoes and cheese, and in this simple antipasto of *involtini* (stuffed rolls), which can also be served as a meatless main course in larger portions. Cooks salt eggplant for two reasons: it contains a lot of moisture and it can have bitter juices, and salt draws out both of them.

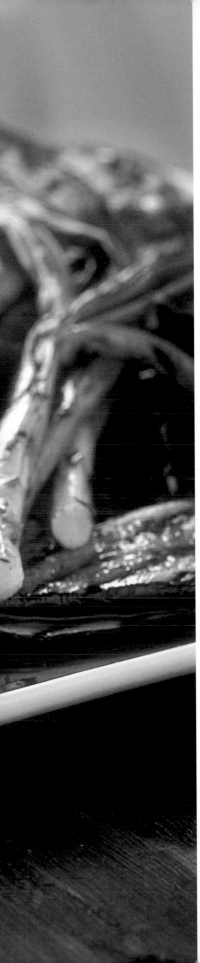

Grilled Vegetables

The vegetables in this classic antipasto signal the arrival of midsummer. The dish is unequaled in its delicious simplicity: meaty vegetables cooked over a hot fire, peeled, and drizzled with olive oil and seasonings. Enjoy this dish in the garden with soft *burrata* (a buttery fresh cheese made from mozzarella curds and cream) or fresh mozzarella, crusty country bread, and a dark pink rosé.

Prepare a charcoal or gas grill for direct grilling over medium-high heat. Oil the grill rack. Using a chef's knife, mince together the garlic and parsley. Transfer to a small bowl, add the ½ cup olive oil and the vinegar, and mix well. Set aside.

Brush the vegetables with the 2 tablespoons olive oil. Using tongs, lay the eggplant and zucchini slices, the peppers, and the green onions over the hottest part of the fire or directly over the heat elements. Cook the eggplant and zucchini slices, turning once, until both sides have grill marks and the slices are tender, about 6 minutes total for the eggplant and about 3 minutes total for the zucchini. Grill the green onions, turning as needed, until slightly charred and tender, about 4 minutes total. Grill the peppers, turning as needed, until the skin is blackened and evenly blistered on all sides, about 10 minutes total.

As the vegetables finish cooking, transfer the eggplant, zucchini, and onions to a platter. Place the peppers in a paper bag and fold over the top so they will steam. Set aside until cool enough to handle, then remove from the bag, remove and discard the stems, and slit the peppers open lengthwise and remove and discard the seeds and ribs. Peel away the blackened skin, and cut the peppers lengthwise into strips about ½ inch (12 mm) wide. Add the pepper strips to the platter.

Drizzle the olive oil–parsley mixture evenly over the vegetables, and then sprinkle with salt and red pepper flakes (if using). Serve at once.

2 cloves garlic

About ½ cup (½ oz/15 g) fresh flat-leaf (Italian) parsley leaves

½ cup (4 fl oz/125 ml) extra-virgin olive oil plus 2 tablespoons for brushing

2 teaspoons red wine vinegar

1 eggplant (aubergine), 1–1¼ lb (500–625 g), trimmed and cut crosswise into slices ½ inch (12 mm) thick

2 zucchini (courgettes), trimmed and thickly sliced lengthwise

2 red or yellow bell peppers (capsicums)

6 green (spring) onions, including tender green tops, trimmed

Sea salt

½ teaspoon red pepper flakes (optional)

MAKES 6 SERVINGS

SICILY

Arancini

2½ cups (20 fl oz/625 ml) chicken stock (page 274)

1 cup (7 oz/220 g) medium-grain white rice such as Arborio

1 tablespoon unsalted butter

Sea salt

½ cup (2 oz/60 g) grated Parmigiano-Reggiano cheese

1 large whole egg, plus 1 large egg yolk

1 cup (5 oz/155 g) all-purpose (plain) flour

2 cups (8 oz/250 g) plain fine dried bread crumbs

3 large egg whites

2 oz (60 g) prosciutto, chopped

2 oz (60 g) fresh mozzarella cheese, chopped

Olive or canola oil for deep-frying

MAKES 4–6 SERVINGS

In a saucepan over high heat, bring the stock to a boil. Stir in the rice, butter, and a pinch of salt. Cover, reduce the heat to low, and cook until the liquid is absorbed and the rice is tender, 18–20 minutes.

Transfer the rice to a bowl and stir in the Parmigiano-Reggiano. Let cool slightly, then stir in the whole egg and egg yolk. Let cool completely.

Spread the flour on a dinner plate, and then spread the bread crumbs on a separate dinner plate. In a shallow bowl, lightly beat the egg whites until blended.

In a small bowl, mix together the prosciutto and mozzarella, and then divide the mixture into 12 equal portions. Moisten your hands with water. Scoop up ¼ cup (1¾ oz/50 g) of the rice mixture and place it in the cupped palm of one hand. Flatten out the mixture slightly and place 1 portion of the prosciutto-mozzarella mixture in the center. Mold the rice over the filling, adding a bit more rice if needed to cover it completely. Shape the rice into a ball. Roll the ball in the flour, and then in the egg whites to coat completely. Finally, roll the ball in the bread crumbs and place on a rack. Continue with the remaining ingredients to make 12 balls total. Rinse your hands frequently to prevent the rice from sticking to them. Let the balls dry on the rack for at least 15 minutes before frying, or refrigerate the balls for up to 1 hour.

Position a rack in the middle of the oven and preheat to 200°F (95°C). Line a large platter or baking sheet with paper towels and set it next to the stove. Pour the olive oil to a depth of 3 inches (7.5 cm) into a deep, heavy frying pan and heat to 375°F (190°C) on a deep-frying thermometer. The oil must cover the balls by at least 1 inch (2.5 cm) so they will cook evenly and not burst. Using a slotted spoon or wire skimmer, gently lower a few of the rice balls into the hot oil, being careful not to crowd the pan. Fry until golden brown and crisp all over, about 2 minutes. Using the slotted spoon, transfer the *arancini* to the towel-lined platter to drain and place in the oven to keep warm. Fry the remaining *arancini* in the same way, allowing the oil to return to the original frying temperature before adding the next batch.

Arrange the *arancini* on a warmed platter and serve at once, or hold in the oven for up to 1 hour before serving.

Arancini means "little oranges," which is exactly what these round, deep-fried rice croquettes look like when they are lifted from the hot oil. They are served as snack food in bars and cafés all over Sicily, and their filling can vary—meat and tomato sauce with peas, chopped vegetables and white sauce, cheese and prosciutto—depending on the cook. In Lazio, Roman cooks make similar rice croquettes known as *suppli al telefono*, or "telephone wires," named for the melting strands of mozzarella that are revealed when you bite into the croquette.

Risotto-Stuffed Tomatoes

Here is an excellent use for leftover risotto in summertime when tomatoes are at their best. You can use other tender fresh herbs, such as summer savory, mint, or tarragon, in place of the basil and oregano.

Position a rack in the middle of the oven and preheat to 300°F (150°C). Lightly oil a shallow, 8-inch (20-cm) square or round baking dish.

Cut a thin slice off of the top of each tomato. Using a small spoon, carefully scoop out the pulp and seeds, leaving walls thick enough for the tomato to hold its shape. Place a wire rack on a large, flat plate. Lightly salt the inside of each tomato, and then invert the tomatoes on the rack to drain for 5–10 minutes.

In a bowl, stir together the risotto, cheese, basil, oregano, parsley, and olive oil. Season to taste with salt and pepper. Fill the tomatoes with the rice mixture, dividing it evenly. Arrange the tomatoes in the prepared dish.

Bake the tomatoes until they have softened and the tops are golden brown, 25–30 minutes. Transfer to a platter or individual plates and serve at once.

6 ripe but firm medium tomatoes

Sea salt and freshly ground pepper

1 cup (5 oz/155 g) leftover Risotto alla Milanese (page 144) or other plain risotto, at room temperature

¼ cup (1 oz/30 g) grated Parmigiano-Reggiano cheese

3 tablespoons chopped fresh basil

2 teaspoons minced fresh oregano

1 tablespoon minced fresh flat-leaf (Italian) parsley

2 tablespoons olive oil

MAKES 6 SERVINGS

SICILY

Artichoke Tortino

½ lemon

2 large artichokes

¼ cup (2 fl oz/60 ml) olive oil

1 clove garlic, minced

Sea salt and freshly ground pepper

8 large eggs

½ cup (2 oz/60 g) grated Parmigiano-Reggiano cheese

MAKES 4 SERVINGS

Fill a bowl three-fourths full with cold water. Squeeze in the juice of the lemon half. Working with 1 artichoke at a time, cut off the top ¾ inch (2 cm) of the leaves with a serrated knife to remove the prickly tips. Trim the stem even with the bottom. Pull off the tough, dark green outer leaves until you reach the tenderest, pale green inner leaves. Peel off the tough, dark outer flesh around the base of the leaves. Cut the artichoke in half lengthwise, and then scoop out the fuzzy choke at the base of the leaves. Cut each half lengthwise into slices ¼ inch (6 mm) thick. Drop the slices into the lemon water. Repeat with the remaining artichoke. Let stand for 20 minutes.

Drain the artichoke slices and pat dry with paper towels. In a 9- or 10-inch (23- or 25-cm) flameproof frying pan over medium heat, warm the olive oil with the garlic. Sauté until the garlic begins to turn golden, about 1 minute. Add the artichoke slices and season with salt and pepper. Cover and cook, stirring occasionally, until the artichokes are tender, about 10 minutes.

Preheat the broiler (grill). In a bowl, whisk the eggs until blended, and then whisk in the cheese and a little salt and pepper. Uncover the pan, spread the artichokes evenly over the bottom, and slowly pour the eggs over the artichokes, trying not to dislodge them. Reduce the heat to medium-low and cook, uncovered, until the eggs begin to set, 1–2 minutes. Then, using a spatula, lift the edges of the egg to allow the uncooked egg to flow underneath. Continue to cook until the edges and bottom are set but the center is moist, about 3 minutes.

Transfer the pan to the broiler about 4 inches (10 cm) from the heat source and broil (grill) until the top sets and browns lightly, about 2 minutes. Watch carefully so that it does not overbrown. Slide the *tortino* onto a serving plate, cut into wedges, and serve.

In Sicily in the spring, artichokes seem to be growing everywhere, wild in the fields and carefully tended in backyard gardens. The bumper crop is used in dozens of ways—deep-fried, stuffed, roasted over hot coals, tossed with pasta, braised with other spring vegetables—but this *tortino di carciofi*, a simple omelet, is a seasonal favorite.

Fried Artichokes with Lemon

In spring and again in fall, artichokes fill the markets in Lazio, and Romans eat them every chance they get. Here, small, tender artichokes are lightly cloaked in bread crumbs before they are fried, yielding a crisp result. A squeeze of fresh lemon juice lifts the sweet artichoke flavor.

Fill a large bowl three-fourths full with cold water. Cut 1 lemon in half and squeeze the juice of both halves into the water. Working with 1 artichoke at a time, cut off the top ¹/₂–³/₄ inch (12 mm–2 cm) of the leaves with a paring knife to remove the prickly tips. Pull off all the tough, dark green outer leaves until you reach the tender, pale inner leaves. Cut a thin slice off the base of the stem, then peel off the tough, dark outer flesh around the base of the leaves and along the length of the stem, leaving the stem attached. Cut the artichoke in half or quarters lengthwise, and then cut out the fuzzy choke, if any, at the base of the leaves. Drop the wedges into the lemon water. Repeat with the remaining artichokes. Let stand for about 10 minutes.

Drain the artichokes and pat dry on paper towels. In a shallow bowl, beat together the eggs and cheese until blended, and season with salt and pepper. Spread the bread crumbs on a plate. One at a time, dip the artichoke pieces into the egg mixture, and then roll them in the bread crumbs. As the pieces are coated, place them on a wire rack. When all the pieces are coated, let them dry for 15 minutes.

Position a rack in the middle of the oven and preheat to 200°F (95°C). Pour the olive oil to a depth of 1 inch (2.5 cm) into a deep, heavy frying pan and heat to 375°F (190°C) on a deep-frying thermometer. Line a platter or baking sheet with paper towels and set it next to the stove.

When the oil is ready, add a few artichoke pieces, being careful not to crowd the pan. Fry the pieces, turning them once or twice, until golden brown, about 4 minutes. Using a slotted spoon, transfer the artichokes to the towel-lined platter to drain and place in the oven to keep warm. Fry the remaining artichoke pieces in the same way, allowing the oil to return to the original frying temperature before adding the next batch.

Cut the remaining lemon into wedges. Arrange the artichokes on a platter, sprinkle with additional salt and pepper, and serve at once with the lemon wedges.

2 lemons

12 baby artichokes with stems

3 large eggs

¼ cup (1 oz/30 g) grated *pecorino romano* cheese

Sea salt and freshly ground pepper

2 cups (8 oz/250 g) plain fine dried bread crumbs

Olive oil for frying

MAKES 4–6 SERVINGS

Cipolline in Agrodolce

1 lb (500 g) *cipolline* onions, about 1½ inches (4 cm) in diameter

2 cups (16 fl oz/500 ml) white wine vinegar

2 cups (16 fl oz/500 ml) balsamic vinegar

3 tablespoons granulated sugar

3 tablespoons firmly packed brown sugar

¼ teaspoon salt

MAKES 6–8 SERVINGS

Agrodolce means "sweet and sour," a flavoring particularly popular in southern Italy and usually achieved by mixing vinegar and sugar. For this recipe, an inexpensive young balsamic vinegar should be used in place of a more expensive aged vinegar. *Cipolline* are small, flat Italian onions. They are available in some supermarkets and farmers' markets. Pearl onions or small boiling onions may be substituted. Serve these piquant onions alongside a platter of cheeses and sliced cured meats, such as prosciutto and *coppa*.

Bring a large saucepan three-fourths full of water to a boil. Add the onions and cook for 30 seconds. Drain, place under cold running water to stop the cooking, and drain again. Using a small, sharp knife, trim off the root end of each onion and slip off the skin. Do not cut too deeply into the onions or they will fall apart.

In a nonreactive saucepan, combine the white wine and balsamic vinegars, granulated and brown sugars, and salt. Bring to a boil over medium-high heat, stirring to dissolve the sugars. Add the onions and cook until softened when pierced with the tip of a knife, 2–3 minutes. Remove from the heat and let cool for about 1 hour.

Transfer the onions and liquid to a nonreactive container, making sure that the onions are submerged in the liquid. Cover and let stand for 1 week at room temperature before using, to allow the onions to mellow and absorb the flavors. The onions will keep for up to 6 months in the refrigerator.

Marinated Olives

Nothing could be simpler than mixing up a dish of these flavorful olives, whether you are serving them as part of an antipasto platter for a party or as a small bite with chilled white wine for a afternoon get-together in the garden.

If the olives are in brine, drain them. In a nonreactive bowl, combine the olives, garlic, red pepper flakes, orange zest, and olive oil and toss well.

Cover the bowl with plastic wrap and marinate the olives at room temperature for at least 2 hours or for up to 24 hours before serving. Store the olives in an airtight container in the refrigerator for up to 2 weeks.

NOTE: Choose a mixture of colors and textures, such as green Cerignola or Picholine olives, black Gaetas or Kalamatas, purplish black niçoise olives, and wrinkled Moroccan dry-cured black olives. These are just a few of the many choices now widely available at most supermarket olive bars.

2 cups (10 oz/315 g) mixed unpitted olives

2 cloves garlic, minced

½ teaspoon red pepper flakes

Grated zest of 1 orange

¼ cup (2 fl oz/60 ml) extra-virgin olive oil

MAKES 2 CUPS (10 OZ/315 G)

Primi

About Primi

From soup and pasta to risotto, gnocchi, and polenta, first courses are the pride of the Italian kitchen, transforming a handful of ingredients into culinary works of art. Light or hearty, casual or elegant, the *primo piatto* sets the tone for the entire meal.

Italian *primi* are the ambassadors of the cuisine. Dishes like Spaghetti alla Carbonara (page 117), Tagliatelle alla Bolognese (page 131), and Risotto alla Milanese (page 144) have become popular menu mainstays throughout the world. Yet outside Italy, these classic *primi* tend to be served as main courses, often accompanied by a salad. Even in Italian homes and restaurants, the old rules are bending, and people often make a light meal of a *primo piatto,* with or without a simple accompaniment. Indeed, many of the recipes in this chapter can, and should, be enjoyed as main dishes.

But to experience an Italian meal at its traditional best, it helps to understand both the function of the *primo piatto* in the context of the entire menu and the importance of pacing. A full Italian meal is meant to be savored slowly, and a well-made first course, served with good wine, ensures this. If two courses seem like too much food, remember that the secret of the *primo* is to keep portions small.

CHOOSING A PRIMO

While the first and second courses are never served together, you should think of them as a complementary pair, just as you do when you order two courses from an Italian restaurant menu. If the *secondo* will be rich or hearty, start with a lighter *primo,* such as Minestrone with Pesto (page 104). Simple, straightforward *secondi,* like Herb-Roasted Pork Loin (page 186) or Grilled Marinated Lamb Chops (page 205), can be preceded by a richer, more substantial

primo, such as Crespelle with Prosciutto and Fontina (page 153), Lasagne alla Bolognese (page 143), or Potato Gnocchi with Chanterelles and Pancetta (page 149). Pair seafood *secondi* with seafood-based *primi,* such as Linguine with Clams (page 111) or Lobster and Shrimp Agnolotti (page 136), or with a meatless *primo,* such as Risotto with Spring Vegetables (page 146) or Penne alla Vodka (page 129).

SERVING OPTIONS

For more formal suppers, *primi* can be plated in the kitchen on dinner plates or soup bowls. This is a particularly good idea for delicate filled pastas, such as Pumpkin Tortelli with Brown Butter and Sage (page 135). Plating also allows the cook to distribute the sauce evenly among the portions, an advantage when serving a pasta with lots of solid ingredients, such as Pasta alla Puttanesca (page 107) or Seafood Spaghetti (page 125). Use tongs to mound a small amount of pasta and sauce on each plate, then spoon additional sauce and ingredients evenly over each serving.

For casual meals, soups and such simple pastas as Linguine Aglio e Olio (page 114) or Spaghetti with Pecorino and Pepper (page 115) can be served family style from a tureen, large bowl, or platter. Gratins and baked dishes, including Spinach and Cheese Cannelloni (page 140), Crespelle with Prosciutto and Fontina (page 153), and Lasagne alla Bolognese (page 143), can be served at the table directly from the pan in which they are baked.

For special occasions, Italians sometimes serve two or three *primi piatti.* These are usually offered in sequence, rather than all at once, so that they can each be perfectly cooked and served piping hot, and so that their flavors and textures can be individually appreciated. If you plan to serve more than one *primo,* keep portions small (this custom is called an *assagio di primi,* a "taste of first courses"). You may want to include at least one recipe that is prepared completely in advance, such as Wedding Soup (page 98) or Gratinéed Ricotta and Spinach Gnocchi (page 150).

Pizza is neither a *primo* nor a *secondo* in Italy, but rather a quick all-in-one meal. Yet simple pizzas, such as Pizza alla Margherita (page 156), Pizza Bianca (page 154), and Sausage Calzone with Peppers (page 155), work well as casual starters, so they have been included in this chapter. Serve them piping hot and whole at the table for the best effect.

ACCOMPANIMENTS

If your *primo* calls for grated cheese as a garnish, you can pass the cheese and a grater at the table, or, for a more refined presentation, you can grate the cheese just before the meal and pass it in a small bowl with a spoon for serving. For pastas with olive oil–based sauces and some soups, Italians often add a *filo d'olio*— a light drizzle of extra-virgin olive oil—at the table. Set out an attractive bottle, fitted with a slow-pouring stopper, for the purpose.

Pass a basket of artisan bread for sopping up the sauce from the *primo piatto,* and replenish it when you serve the *secondo.* Choose a bread that reflects the regional origins of the food you are serving, such as Pugliese with southern Italian food or focaccia with Penne with Pesto, Potatoes, and Green Beans (page 122).

Pasta Techniques

ROLLING WITH A PASTA MACHINE

1 Follow the manufacturer's instructions to anchor the pasta machine to the counter. Turn the dial to set the rollers at the widest setting and attach the crank.

2 Cut the dough into 4 pieces and flatten each into a disk ½ inch (12 mm) thick. Run 1 disk through the widest setting on the machine 2 or 3 times. Flour the dough lightly if it starts to stick.

3 Fold the dough lengthwise into thirds, turn the dial to the next narrower setting, and run the dough through again. Repeat this twice, lightly flouring as needed.

4 Fold, flour, and run the sheet of dough 2 or 3 times through each progressively narrower setting until the pasta is ¹/₁₆ inch (2 mm) thick, then cut as directed in individual recipes. Repeat with the remaining disks of dough.

ROLLING BY HAND

1 Cut the dough into 4 pieces and place 3 pieces back under the bowl. Dust a large work surface with flour and flatten the dough piece into a disk about ½ inch (12 mm) thick.

2 Place a rolling pin in the middle of the dough and start rolling out toward the edge. Pick up the dough and give it a quarter turn. Keep rolling out toward the edge and turning the dough until it is about ¹/₁₆ inch (2 cm) thick, then cut as directed in individual recipes.

CUTTING PASTA STRANDS

1 Cut the pasta sheet into 4 sections 10 inches (25 cm) long. Lay the sections on a lightly floured rimmed baking sheet, layering them and separating the layers with floured kitchen towels.

2 Secure the strand-cutting attachment and crank onto the pasta machine. One at a time, insert the dough sections into the blades and turn the crank to create strands.

3 Spread the strands out on a lightly floured baking sheet, separating them so they have room, and let them dry for 10–20 minutes. They should feel slightly leathery, but not be brittle.

Pasta Techniques

FILLING RAVIOLI

1 Place one pasta sheet on a lightly floured work surface. Using a chef's knife or pastry wheel, trim the dough into strips 4 inches (10 cm) wide. Layer the strips on a floured baking sheet as directed in the recipe, and roll out and trim the remaining dough pieces.

2 Lightly flour 3 more baking sheets. Lay 1 dough strip on the work surface. Fold the dough in half lengthwise to mark the center and then unfold it.

3 Beginning about 1 inch (2.5 cm) from one of the short ends, place teaspoonfuls of the filling about 1 inch apart in a straight row down the center of one side of the fold.

4 Dip a pastry brush or your fingertip in cool water. Lightly brush around the filling.

5 Fold the dough over the filling, molding it around the filling to press out any air pockets. With your fingertips, firmly press the edges of the dough together to seal.

6 Using a fluted pastry wheel or a sharp knife, cut between the mounds of filling. Separate the squares and place, not touching, in a single layer on the prepared baking sheets.

FORMING TORTELLINI

1 Place one pasta sheet on a lightly floured work surface. Lightly flour a large baking sheet. Using a knife or pastry wheel, cut the dough into 2-inch (5-cm) squares.

2 Layer the squares flat on the prepared baking sheet, spacing them so they don't touch and separating each layer with a lightly floured kitchen towel. Roll out and cut the remaining dough sheets.

3 Lightly flour 3 more baking sheets. Place about ½ teaspoon of the filling in the center half of each square. Dip a pastry brush in cool water and lightly brush around the filling.

4 Fold a corner of the dough over the filling to form a triangle. Using your fingers, mold the dough around the filling to eliminate any air pockets. Firmly press the edges together to seal.

5 Bring the 2 opposite points of the triangle together to form a circle, and pinch the points together to seal. The third point forms a peaked top; curl it back slightly.

6 Place the tortellini, not touching, in a single layer on the prepared baking sheets.

Pasta e Fagioli

Here, beans and pasta are combined in a classic soup of southern Italy. *Borlotti* beans, which are ivory-beige with maroon speckles, are known as cranberry beans or French horticultural beans in the United States. If you can find fresh *borlotti* shell beans, which are in season in late summer and early autumn, you can substitute 2 cups (14 oz/440 g) of them for the dried beans. Cook them in boiling water until tender, about 30 minutes.

Pick over the beans and discard any misshapen beans or stones. Rinse the beans under cold running water and drain. Place in a large bowl with cold water to cover generously and let soak for at least 4 hours or for up to overnight. Drain the beans, rinse well, and transfer to a large saucepan. Add 8 cups (64 fl oz/2 l) cold water and the garlic cloves and bring to a boil over high heat, skimming off the foam that rises to the surface. Reduce the heat to low and simmer, uncovered, until the beans are tender, about 1 1/2 hours. Drain and set aside.

In another large saucepan over medium heat, warm the olive oil. Add the onion, carrot, and celery and sauté until the onion is golden, 6–8 minutes. Add the tomato, stock, and beans and bring to a boil. Reduce the heat to medium-low and simmer, stirring occasionally, until the vegetables are tender, about 10 minutes. If desired, to thicken the soup, remove 1 cup (8 fl oz/250 ml) and purée in a food processor or blender. Add the puréed soup back to the saucepan and stir to combine. Raise the heat to medium, add the pasta, and cook until al dente, 8–10 minutes.

Season the soup to taste with salt and pepper. Ladle into warmed soup bowls and serve at once.

1 cup (7 oz/220 g) dried *borlotti* or cranberry beans

2 cloves garlic

3 tablespoons olive oil

1 yellow onion, finely chopped

1 carrot, finely chopped

1 celery stalk, thinly sliced

1 large tomato, peeled, seeded, and finely chopped

8 cups (64 fl oz/2 l) beef stock (page 273) or chicken stock (page 274)

2 cups (7 oz/220 g) *ditalini*, *tubetti*, or other small hollow pasta

Sea salt and freshly ground pepper

MAKES 6 SERVINGS

Wedding Soup

3 qt (3 l) chicken stock (page 274)

1 lb (500 g) *cavolo nero*, dinosaur kale, escarole, or other greens, trimmed and cut into bite-sized pieces

3 large carrots, chopped

1 celery stalk, chopped

For the meatballs

1 lb (500 g) ground (minced) pork

2 large eggs, lightly beaten

½ cup (2½ oz/75 g) minced yellow onion

½ cup (2 oz/60 g) plain fine dried bread crumbs

½ cup (2 oz/60 g) grated *pecorino romano* cheese

Sea salt and freshly ground pepper

3 tablespoons olive oil

Grated *pecorino romano* cheese for serving

MAKES 6 SERVINGS

Good enough to serve at any celebratory meal, *minestra maritata*, or "wedding soup," traditionally included different cuts of pork and a big variety of vegetables, which were slowly simmered together until the ingredients were pronounced "married." Here, in a streamlined version of this classic southern soup, pork meatballs are cooked with a handful of fresh, hearty vegetables.

In a large soup pot, bring the stock to a boil over high heat. Add the *cavolo nero,* carrots, and celery, reduce the heat to low, and simmer, uncovered, until the vegetables are tender, about 30 minutes.

Meanwhile, make the meatballs. In a large bowl, combine the pork, eggs, onion, bread crumbs, cheese, 1 teaspoon salt, and several grinds of pepper and mix well. Moisten your hands and shape the mixture into small balls, handling them gently. As they are formed, place them on a plate.

In a large frying pan over medium-high heat, warm the olive oil. When all the meatballs are ready, gently add them to the frying pan and brown on all sides, about 5 minutes. Using a slotted spoon, carefully add them to the simmering soup and simmer gently over low heat until the meatballs are cooked through, about 10 minutes. Taste and adjust the seasoning.

Ladle the soup into warmed soup bowls and sprinkle each serving with grated cheese. Serve at once.

Chickpea, Porcini, and Farro Soup

Tuscany is filled with treasures of all kinds—art, architecture, food—and this is one of them. Every ingredient in this warming soup represents the region, from the beans and fresh herbs to the *farro* and porcini mushrooms. This hearty recipe illustrates the timeless appeal of regional peasant cooking, the source of many traditional Tuscan soups and other dishes. For the most authentic pairing, serve with a Chianti Classico.

Pick over the chickpeas and discard any misshapen beans or stones. Rinse the chickpeas under cold running water and drain. Place in a large bowl with cold water to cover generously and let soak for at least 4 hours or for up to overnight. Drain the chickpeas, rinse well, and transfer to a large saucepan. Add 8 cups (64 fl oz/ 2l) cold water and bring to a boil over high heat, skimming off the foam that rises to the surface. Reduce the heat to low and simmer, uncovered, until the chickpeas are tender, about 2 hours. Remove from the heat.

In a soup pot over medium-low heat, warm the olive oil. Add the onion, garlic, and rosemary and sauté until the onion is softened and translucent but not browned, about 6 minutes. In a small bowl, dissolve the tomato paste in 1 cup (8 fl oz/250 ml) warm water and add to the pot. Stir in the chickpeas and their cooking liquid and season with salt and pepper. Bring to a simmer over medium heat and cook for 3 minutes. Add the stock, return to a simmer, and cook, uncovered, until the flavors have melded, about 30 minutes longer. Remove and discard the rosemary sprig.

Working in batches, process the soup in a blender until smooth and creamy and return it to the pot. Alternatively, process the soup in the pot with an immersion blender. Return the soup to a simmer over medium heat, add the *farro*, and cook until the *farro* is tender yet still slightly firm and chewy, about 25 minutes.

Meanwhile, to prepare the mushrooms, cut away the tips of the mushroom stems. Thinly slice the mushrooms lengthwise. In a large, heavy-bottomed frying pan over medium heat, warm the 1½ tablespoons olive oil. Add the garlic and sauté until fragrant, about 1 minute. Add the mushrooms and cook, stirring with a wooden spoon, until they begin to soften, 3–4 minutes. (They might stick to the pan for a moment before beginning to release their juices, but it is not necessary to add more oil.) Raise the heat to high, add the wine and thyme, and cook, stirring constantly, to cook off the alcohol from the wine, about 3 minutes. Reduce the heat to low, season with salt and pepper, and continue to cook, stirring often, until the mushrooms are cooked and their juices have evaporated, about 15 minutes longer. Remove from the heat and discard the thyme sprig. Stir in the butter.

Add the mushrooms to the soup and stir to combine. Ladle the soup into warmed soup bowls, garnish with a drizzle of olive oil and a sprinkling of freshly ground pepper, and serve at once.

1½ cups (9½ oz/295 g) dried chickpeas (garbanzo beans)

⅓ cup (3 fl oz/80 ml) olive oil

1 yellow onion, finely chopped

2 cloves garlic, minced

1 small fresh rosemary sprig

1 tablespoon tomato paste

Sea salt and freshly ground pepper

4 cups (32 fl oz/1 l) vegetable stock or water

⅓ cup (2 oz/60 g) *farro*

For the mushrooms

½ lb (250 g) fresh porcini or cremini mushrooms, brushed clean

1½ tablespoons extra-virgin olive oil, plus extra for drizzling

1 clove garlic, minced

2 tablespoons dry white wine

1 fresh thyme sprig

Sea salt and freshly ground pepper

1½ teaspoons unsalted butter

MAKES 4–6 SERVINGS

Pappa al Pomodoro

4 tablespoons (2 fl oz/60 ml) extra-virgin olive oil

1 yellow onion, chopped

2 celery stalks, chopped

2 cloves garlic, minced

2 lb (1 kg) fresh tomatoes, peeled, seeded, and chopped, or 1 can (28 oz/875 g) plum (Roma) tomatoes, drained and chopped

4 slices day-old coarse country bread, crusts removed and torn into small pieces

4 fresh basil leaves, torn into small pieces

Sea salt and freshly ground pepper

MAKES 4 SERVINGS

In a large saucepan over medium heat, warm 2 tablespoons of the olive oil. Add the onion and celery and sauté until the vegetables are tender, about 7 minutes. Add the garlic and sauté until fragrant, about 1 minute longer. Add the tomatoes and 4 cups (32 fl oz/1 l) water and bring to a simmer. Cook uncovered, stirring occasionally, until the vegetables are soft, about 20 minutes.

Fit a food mill with the fine disk, place over a bowl, and pass the contents of the saucepan through the mill. Or, purée in batches in a blender or food processor. Return the soup to the pan over medium heat. Add the bread, basil, and salt and pepper to taste and bring to a simmer. Cook until the bread is soft, about 10 minutes. Stir in a little more water if the soup becomes too thick.

Serve the soup hot, warm, or at room temperature. Ladle into soup bowls and drizzle evenly with the remaining 2 tablespoons olive oil.

Tuscan cooks are frugal, as this traditional tomato and bread soup made from cubes of day-old bread illustrates. Italians typically feel that many foods, including a number of soups, taste best when they are neither too hot nor too cold. They believe that moderate temperatures don't shock the taste buds, so that all of the flavors will come through. This soup is a good candidate for testing the theory, as it is delicious fresh off the stove, at room temperature, or in between.

TUSCANY

Ribollita

When Tuscan cooks make this soup, they often serve it in two or three forms over the next few days. It starts as a hearty vegetable soup, which can be eaten as is. The soup is then layered, at the time it is made or as leftovers the next day, with stale bread to make *zuppa di pane,* or "bread soup." When the leftover bread soup is baked until hot and drizzled with olive oil, it is declared *ribollita,* or "reboiled." The version here is prepared and served the same day. The ingredient that makes the soup authentic is *cavolo nero,* or "black cabbage," a dark green, leafy vegetable. Dinosaur kale can be substituted.

In a large soup pot over medium-high heat, warm the ½ cup olive oil. Add the onion, carrots, and celery and sauté until the onion is golden, 3–4 minutes. Add the cauliflower and sauté until tender-crisp, about 5 minutes. Add the *cavolo nero,* chard, zucchini, and potato (in that order) and cook, stirring, for 5 minutes.

Add the beans and herbs to the pot, stir well, and pour in the stock. Bring to a boil over medium-high heat, and cook, uncovered, until the vegetables are tender, about 30 minutes. Season to taste with salt and pepper. Remove from the heat.

Position a rack in the middle of the oven and preheat to 425°F (220°C).

Ladle enough soup into a 9-by-13-by-2-inch (23-by-33-by-5-cm) baking dish to cover the bottom. Top with 4 or 5 bread slices, trimming them to fit if necessary. Add another layer of soup. Sprinkle evenly with one-third of the cheese. Top with a layer each of the bread slices, then the soup, and finally the cheese. Repeat for a third layer.

Bake until heated through, about 20 minutes. Remove from the oven and drizzle with olive oil. Spoon the soup into warmed soup bowls and serve at once.

½ cup (4 fl oz/125 ml) extra-virgin olive oil, plus more for drizzling

1 yellow onion, chopped

2 carrots, chopped

1 celery stalk, chopped

1 cup (3 oz/90 g) coarsely chopped cauliflower florets

4 or 5 *cavolo nero* or dinosaur kale leaves, shredded

1 cup (2 oz/60 g) shredded Swiss chard leaves

2 zucchini (courgettes), trimmed and diced

1 large boiling potato, peeled and diced

2 cups (14 oz/440 g) drained cooked cannellini beans (page 275)

¼ cup (⅓ oz/10 g) minced mixed fresh flat-leaf (Italian) parsley, rosemary, and sage, in about equal parts

2½ qt (2.5 l) chicken stock (page 274) or vegetable broth

Sea salt and freshly ground pepper

12–15 thin slices day-old coarse country bread

½ cup (2 oz/60 g) grated Parmigiano-Reggiano cheese

MAKES 6 SERVINGS

Minestrone with Pesto

1 oz (30 g) dried porcini mushrooms

¼ cup (2 fl oz/60 ml) olive oil

1 yellow onion, chopped

2 carrots, chopped

1 celery stalk, chopped

1 bunch Swiss chard, tough stems removed and chopped

3 Yukon gold or other boiling potatoes, peeled and chopped

1½ cups (8 oz/250 g) peeled, seeded, and diced butternut squash

4 fresh tomatoes, peeled, seeded, and chopped, or 2 cups (12 oz/375 g) seeded and chopped canned plum (Roma) tomatoes, with juice

2 cups (8 oz/250 g) fresh *borlotti* or other shelling beans, or 2 cups (14 oz/ 440 g) drained cooked beans (page 275)

1 piece Parmigiano-Reggiano cheese rind (optional)

Sea salt and freshly ground pepper

1 cup (3½ oz/105 g) macaroni, *tubetti,* or other small pasta shape

¼ cup (2 fl oz/60 ml) pesto, homemade (page 273) or purchased

Grated Parmigiano-Reggiano cheese for serving

MAKES 6 SERVINGS

In a bowl, combine the mushrooms and 2 cups (16 fl oz/500 ml) warm water and let soak for 30 minutes. Drain the mushrooms, reserving the liquid. Strain the liquid through a paper coffee filter or a fine-mesh sieve lined with dampened cheesecloth (muslin) and set aside. Rinse the mushrooms well under cold running water, paying special attention to the stem pieces where bits of soil sometimes cling to the base. Drain well, chop, and set aside.

In a large saucepan over medium heat, warm the olive oil. Add the onion, carrots, and celery and cook, stirring frequently, until tender and golden, 10–15 minutes. Stir in the mushrooms, chard, potatoes, squash, tomatoes, beans, and cheese rind (if using). Add the mushroom liquid and enough water to cover the vegetables by about ½ inch (12 mm), bring to a simmer, and reduce the heat to low. Season with salt and pepper and cook uncovered, stirring occasionally, until the soup has thickened and the vegetables are soft, about 1½ hours, adding water as needed if the soup becomes too thick.

Add the pasta and continue to cook, stirring frequently, until the pasta is al dente, about 15 minutes. If the cheese rind has been used, you can remove it from the pot, cut it into small pieces, and return it to the soup or discard it.

Ladle the soup into warmed soup bowls and top each serving with a dollop of the pesto. Serve at once. Pass the grated cheese at the table.

The best versions of this soup are made with fresh seasonal vegetables. Don't hesitate to add or substitute cabbage, green beans, eggplant (aubergine), cauliflower, peas, zucchini (courgette), leeks, or whatever else looks good at the market or that you might have on hand. After long, slow cooking, the soup should be thick and the vegetables soft. In Liguria, minestrone is eaten in different ways: sometimes a dollop of fragrant pesto is added to the hot soup, sometimes the soup is served at room temperature, and sometimes rice is used instead of pasta. Simmering the rind from a wedge of Parmigiano-Reggiano in the soup imparts a rich, deep flavor.

Pasta alla Puttanesca

In this classic pasta dish, popular in both Calabria and Lazio, the bold flavors of olives, anchovies, and capers are incorporated into a simple tomato sauce. *Puttanesca* means "harlot style," a reference to the spiciness and saltiness of the dish.

In a large frying pan over medium heat, warm the olive oil. Add the garlic and red pepper flakes and sauté until the garlic is lightly golden, about 2 minutes. Add the tomatoes, 1 teaspoon salt, and a pinch of black pepper and bring to a simmer. Reduce the heat to low and cook uncovered, stirring occasionally, until thickened, about 20 minutes. Add the anchovies, olives, capers, and parsley and simmer for about 1 minute longer. Taste and adjust the seasoning.

While the sauce simmers, bring a large pot three-fourths full of water to a rolling boil and add about 2 tablespoons salt. Add the penne, stir well, and cook, stirring occasionally, until al dente, according to the package directions. Scoop out and reserve about 2 ladlefuls of the cooking water, then drain the pasta.

Add the drained pasta to the sauce in the pan and stir and toss over low heat until well coated with the sauce, adjusting the consistency with some of the cooking water if needed. Transfer to a warmed serving bowl and serve at once.

¼ cup (2 fl oz/60 ml) olive oil

2 cloves garlic, minced

½ teaspoon red pepper flakes

1 can (28 oz/875 g) plum (Roma) tomatoes, drained and chopped

Sea salt and freshly ground black pepper

6–8 olive oil–packed anchovy fillets, chopped

¼ cup (1½ oz/45 g) chopped pitted Gaeta or other Mediterranean-style black olives

2 tablespoons chopped, rinsed capers

2 tablespoons chopped fresh flat-leaf (Italian) parsley

1 lb (500 g) penne or other pasta

MAKES 4–6 SERVINGS

Spaghetti with Salsa di Pomodoro

5 tablespoons (2½ oz/75 g) unsalted butter

2 carrots, finely chopped

1 small celery stalk, finely chopped

1 small yellow onion, finely chopped

2 lb (1 kg) fresh plum (Roma) tomatoes, peeled, seeded, and chopped, or 1 can (28 oz/875 g) plum (Roma) tomatoes, drained and chopped

Sea salt and freshly ground pepper

1 lb (500 g) spaghetti

10 fresh basil leaves, torn into small pieces

½ cup (2 oz/60 g) grated Parmigiano-Reggiano cheese, plus more for serving

MAKES 4–6 SERVINGS

In a large frying pan over medium heat, melt 4 tablespoons (2 oz/60 g) of the butter. Add the carrots, celery, and onion and cook, stirring frequently, until the onion has softened and the carrots and celery are tender, about 15 minutes.

Add the tomatoes, 1 teaspoon salt, and ⅛ teaspoon pepper and cook until the sauce begins to bubble. Reduce the heat to low and cook, stirring occasionally, until the sauce has thickened, about 20 minutes. Season to taste with salt and pepper.

While the sauce simmers, bring a large pot three-fourths full of water to a rolling boil and add about 2 tablespoons salt. Add the spaghetti, stir well, and cook, stirring occasionally, until al dente, according to the package directions. Scoop out and reserve about 2 ladlefuls of the cooking water, then drain the pasta.

Add the drained pasta to the sauce in the pan and stir and toss over low heat until well coated with the sauce, adjusting the consistency with some of the cooking water if needed. Add the basil and the remaining 1 tablespoon butter and toss to distribute evenly. Remove from the heat, add the ½ cup cheese, and toss again. Transfer to a warmed serving bowl and serve at once, passing additional cheese at the table.

Cooking the carrots, onion, and celery in butter, a mixture known as a *soffritto*, imparts a mild, sweet flavor to this simple sauce. But the primary component is still tomato, which means using vine-ripened plum tomatoes in summer and the best-quality canned tomatoes, such as Italy's superb San Marzano variety, the rest of the year. To make a creamy tomato sauce, stir in ½ cup (4 fl oz/125 ml) heavy (double) cream once the sauce has thickened and simmer for 5 minutes longer.

Linguine with Clams

The best clams for this pasta are Manila or littlenecks. Choose the smallest ones you can find, as they are the most tender. Tiny New Zealand cockles, now widely available in many fish markets, are another excellent choice, though they result in a more delicately flavored sauce.

Bring a large pot three-fourths full of water to a rolling boil. Meanwhile, put the clams in a separate large saucepan or pot, discarding any that do not close to the touch. Pour in the wine, place over medium-high heat, and cook, stirring the clams occasionally, until they start to open, 2–3 minutes. Pull each clam from the pot as it opens and place in a large bowl (some take longer than others; if you leave them all in the pot, the early openers will be overcooked). Discard any clams that fail to open. Strain the clam broth through a paper coffee filter or a fine-mesh sieve lined with dampened cheesecloth (muslin) into a bowl and set aside.

When the water is boiling, add about 2 tablespoons salt. Add the linguine, stir well, and cook, stirring occasionally, until al dente, according to package directions.

Meanwhile, in a large frying pan, warm the olive oil over medium-low heat. Add the garlic and sauté until lightly golden, about 30 seconds. Add the reserved clam broth and the lemon juice and simmer over low heat until slightly reduced, about 4 minutes. Add the red pepper flakes and black pepper to taste. Taste and adjust the seasoning with a pinch of salt, if necessary.

Drain the linguine well and add it to the sauce in the pan. Add the clams in their shells and any juices that have accumulated. Stir and toss well over low heat for about 1 minute to coat the pasta. Transfer to a warmed serving bowl, add the parsley, and toss gently. Serve at once.

2 lb (1 kg) Manila or other small clams or cockles, scrubbed

½ cup (4 fl oz/125 ml) dry white wine

Sea salt and freshly ground black pepper

1 lb (500 g) linguine or spaghetti

½ cup (4 fl oz/125 ml) extra-virgin olive oil

4 cloves garlic, thinly sliced

Juice of 1 lemon

Generous pinch of red pepper flakes

Large handful of fresh flat-leaf (Italian) parsley leaves, coarsely chopped

MAKES 4 SERVINGS

Orecchiette with Broccoli Rabe and Sausage

⅓ cup (3 fl oz/80 ml) plus 1 tablespoon extra-virgin olive oil

½ cup (2 oz/60 g) plain fine dried bread crumbs

Sea salt

1½ lb (750 g) broccoli rabe, trimmed

1 lb (500 g) dried orecchiette

½ lb (250 g) Italian sweet fennel sausages, casings discarded and meat coarsely chopped

4 large cloves garlic, minced

Pinch of red pepper flakes

½ cup (2 oz /60 g) *pecorino romano* or Parmigiano-Reggiano cheese

MAKES 4–6 SERVINGS

In a frying pan over medium-low heat, warm the 1 tablespoon olive oil. Add the bread crumbs and stir to coat them with the oil. Season lightly with salt and cook, stirring often, until the crumbs are an even, deep golden brown, about 10 minutes. Pour onto a plate and set aside to cool.

Bring a large pot three-fourths full of water to a rolling boil and add 2 tablespoons salt. Add the broccoli rabe and cook, testing often, until the stems are just tender, 2–3 minutes. Using tongs or a wire-mesh skimmer, lift out the broccoli rabe into a sieve and cool it quickly under cold running water. Drain and squeeze gently to remove excess moisture. Chop coarsely and set aside.

Add the orecchiette to the boiling water, stir well, and cook, stirring occasionally, until al dente, according to the package directions.

Meanwhile, warm the remaining olive oil in the frying pan over medium-low heat. Add the sausage, garlic, and red pepper flakes and cook, stirring and breaking up the sausage meat with a wooden spoon, until the sausage is browned, about 7 minutes. Add the broccoli rabe and stir to combine with the sausage. Cook until the broccoli rabe is hot throughout, about 2 minutes. Season to taste with salt.

When the orecchiette is ready, scoop out and reserve about 2 ladlefuls of the cooking water, then drain the pasta and return it to the pot. Add the sausage mixture and the cheese and stir and toss well over low heat to combine, adjusting the consistency with some of the cooking water if needed.

Divide among warmed plates, top each portion with a sprinkle of the toasted bread crumbs, and serve at once. Pass the remaining bread crumbs at the table.

Broccoli rabe, also known as *rapini* and *cime di rapa*, has a pleasantly bitter flavor that is an appealing contrast to the sweet pork sausages in the sauce. As you toss, both ingredients become trapped in the hollows of the ear-shaped pasta, making every bite wonderfully flavorful. Prepare this dish in cool-weather months, when broccoli rabe is in season.

Linguine Aglio e Olio

⅓ cup (3 fl oz/80 ml)
extra–virgin olive oil

6 large cloves garlic, thinly
sliced

½ teaspoon red pepper flakes

⅓ cup (½ oz/15 g) minced
fresh flat–leaf (Italian) parsley

Sea salt

1 lb (500 g) linguine or
spaghetti

MAKES 4–6 SERVINGS

In a large frying pan, warm the olive oil over medium-low heat. Add the garlic and red pepper flakes and sauté until the garlic is golden and fragrant, about 2 minutes. Stir in the parsley and remove the pan from the heat.

Bring a large pot three-fourths full of water to a rolling boil and add about 2 tablespoons salt. Add the linguine, stir well, and cook, stirring occasionally, until al dente, according to the package directions.

Just before the linguine is cooked, reheat the sauce over medium-low heat. When the pasta is ready, scoop out and reserve about 2 ladlefuls of the cooking water, then drain the pasta. Add to the sauce in the pan and stir and toss over low heat until well coated with the sauce, adjusting the consistency with some of the cooking water if needed. Transfer to a warmed serving bowl and serve at once.

Named after its primary ingredients, *aglio* (garlic) and *olio* (oil), this simple pasta dish depends on using a good-quality, flavorful extra-virgin olive oil. Without it, the naturally bold flavors of the garlic and red pepper flakes will dominate the sauce, rather than blend with the oil that forms its base.

Spaghetti with Pecorino and Pepper

Pasta, grated cheese, and black pepper—it sounds simple. And it is, but that simplicity demands excellent ingredients: freshly grated *pecorino romano* cheese, freshly cracked black pepper, a superb extra-virgin olive oil, and, if you have time, freshly made pasta. In Lazio, the sauce is tossed with *tonnarelli*, a fresh square-cut strand pasta, but spaghetti can be substituted.

Bring a large pot three-fourths full of water to a rolling boil. While the water is heating, begin making the sauce. Put the peppercorns in a small frying pan over low heat and heat, shaking the pan occasionally, until fragrant, about 5 minutes. Remove from the heat, pour into a cloth napkin or on a piece of waxed paper, and crush with a meat mallet or the bottom of a heavy frying pan.

When the water is boiling, add about 2 tablespoons salt. Add the spaghetti, stir well, and cook, stirring occasionally, until almost al dente, according to the package directions.

While the spaghetti cooks, scoop out a ladleful of the cooking water and add it and the olive oil to a large frying pan. Add a small handful of the cheese and mix vigorously with a fork or whisk. When the pasta is ready, scoop out and reserve 1½ cups (12 fl oz/375 ml) of the cooking water, then drain the pasta.

Add the drained pasta to the frying pan and place over low heat. Gradually add the remaining cheese, the crushed pepper, and spoonfuls of the cooking water as needed to make a creamy sauce, stirring and tossing for about 3 minutes to finish cooking the pasta and to coat the strands evenly with the sauce. Divide among warmed bowls and serve at once.

2 teaspoons peppercorns

Sea salt

1 lb (500 g) spaghetti

1 tablespoon extra-virgin olive oil

1½ cups (6 oz/185 g) grated *pecorino romano* cheese

MAKES 4–6 SERVINGS

Spaghetti alla Carbonara

The origin of this Roman dish has long been in dispute. Was it invented by local *carbonari* (charcoal makers)? Or was it a practical way to use bacon and egg rations during World War II? Whatever its origin, the success of this simple dish is all about technique: you must mix the raw eggs into the hot spaghetti until they are no longer liquid but have not yet formed curds.

In a large frying pan over medium-low heat, combine the pancetta and olive oil and heat slowly until much of the fat is rendered and the meat has browned a little, about 15 minutes. Leave the meat and fat in the pan and cover to keep warm.

Bring a large pot three-fourths full of water to a rolling boil and add about 2 tablespoons salt. Add the spaghetti, stir well, and cook, stirring occasionally, until al dente, according to the package directions.

Meanwhile, in a bowl, mix together the cheeses. In another bowl, whisk together the whole eggs and egg yolk until well blended. Stir the cheese mixture and several grinds of pepper into the eggs.

From this point on, timing and temperature are crucial. Put a large serving bowl in the sink and set a colander in the serving bowl. When the spaghetti is ready, pour it into the colander, so that its cooking water will warm the serving bowl. Grab the colander quickly out of the water and shake a couple of times. Toss the drained spaghetti into the pan with the pancetta and stir a couple of times to coat the pasta with the fat. Being careful not to burn your fingers, empty the hot water from the serving bowl, reserving about 2 ladlefuls. Transfer the pasta to the warmed bowl, add the egg mixture, and stir and toss vigorously with a wooden spoon to coat the pasta evenly. Adjust the consistency of the sauce with some of the cooking water if needed. Divide among warmed plates and serve at once.

6 oz (185 g) pancetta or bacon, preferably at least ¼ inch (6 mm) thick, chopped

1 tablespoon olive oil

Sea salt and freshly ground pepper

1 lb (500 g) spaghetti

¼ cup (1 oz/30 g) grated *pecorino romano* cheese

¼ cup (1 oz/30 g) grated Parmigiano-Reggiano cheese

2 large whole eggs, plus 1 large egg yolk, at room temperature

MAKES 4–6 SERVINGS

Pappardelle with Pork Ragù

1½ lb (750 g) meaty pork
spareribs, cut into individual
ribs

Sea salt and freshly ground
pepper

2 tablespoons olive oil

1 yellow onion, chopped

1 carrot, chopped

1 celery stalk, chopped

½ cup (4 fl oz/125 ml)
dry red wine

2½ lb (1.25 kg) fresh plum
(Roma) tomatoes, peeled,
seeded, and chopped, or
1 can (28 oz/875 g) plum
(Roma) tomatoes, chopped

1 lb fresh egg pasta dough
(page 274)

½ cup (2 oz/60 g) grated
pecorino romano cheese,
plus more for serving

MAKES 6–8 SERVINGS

Meaty pork ribs add hearty flavor to this *ragù*, which marries perfectly with homemade *pappardelle*, wide ribbons of egg pasta. The pasta is topped with freshly grated *pecorino romano* cheese, an aged sheep's milk cheese made in the countryside around Rome. Aged *pecorino sardo* or *pecorino siciliano*, from Sardinia and Sicily, respectively, is a good substitute.

Pat the ribs dry with paper towels and sprinkle them with salt and pepper. In a nonreactive Dutch oven or other large, heavy pot over medium-high heat, warm the olive oil. Add the ribs and cook, turning as needed, until nicely browned on all sides, about 20 minutes. Using a slotted spoon, transfer the ribs to a plate.

Add the onion, carrot, and celery to the pot, reduce the heat to medium, and cook, stirring frequently, until tender and golden, 10–15 minutes. Add the wine, bring to a simmer, and deglaze the pot, scraping up the browned bits from the pot bottom. Cook for 1 minute to cook off some of the alcohol. Add the tomatoes, 1 cup (8 fl oz/250 ml) water, and a pinch each of salt and pepper, and bring the mixture to a simmer. Return the ribs to the pan, cover, reduce the heat to low, and cook until the ribs are very tender and the meat comes away easily from the bone, about 2½ hours.

While the ribs simmer in the sauce, make the pasta dough, then divide and roll out each piece into a sheet ¹⁄₁₆ inch (2 mm) thick as directed on pages 92–93. Lightly flour a rimmed baking sheet. Lay 1 pasta sheet on a lightly floured work surface and, using a chef's knife or pastry wheel, cut it into strips 4 inches (10 cm) long by 1 inch (2.5 cm) wide. Lay the strips flat on the prepared baking sheet, spacing them so they don't touch and separating each layer with a lightly floured kitchen towel. Repeat with the remaining 3 dough pieces. Let the pasta dry for 10–20 minutes.

Using a slotted spoon, remove the ribs from the sauce and let cool slightly. Remove the meat from the bones and shred it. Return the meat to the pan and cook, uncovered, over low heat until the sauce has thickened, about 15 minutes.

Meanwhile, bring a large pot three-fourths full of water to a rolling boil and add about 2 tablespoons salt. Add the *pappardelle*, stir well, and cook, stirring occasionally, until al dente, 1–2 minutes. Drain and add to the sauce, tossing gently to coat evenly. Sprinkle with the ½ cup cheese and toss again. Serve at once. Pass additional cheese at the table.

Bucatini all'Amatriciana

Guanciale, pork cheek that resembles unsmoked bacon and is cured with salt, pepper, and sometimes garlic, is traditionally used in this dish from Amatrice, a small town near Rome known for its excellent pork products. Pancetta, rolled pork belly cured in a similar manner and more widely available outside Italy, can be substituted. Tomatoes, onion, garlic, and chile complete the sauce, which is usually served over *bucatini*, a thick strand pasta with a hole in the center.

In a frying pan over medium heat, cook the *guanciale* in the olive oil, stirring often, until golden, about 10 minutes. Add the onion and sauté until tender and golden, about 5 minutes. Add the garlic and red pepper flakes and sauté until the garlic is golden, about 1 minute longer.

Pass the chopped tomatoes through a food mill fitted with the medium disk or a medium-mesh sieve directly into the pan. Add a pinch of salt, bring to a simmer, and cook uncovered, stirring occasionally, until the sauce has thickened, about 15 minutes.

Meanwhile, bring a large pot three-fourths full of water to a rolling boil and add about 2 tablespoons salt. Add the *bucatini,* stir well, and cook, stirring occasionally, until al dente, according to the package directions. Scoop out and reserve about 2 ladlefuls of the cooking water, then drain the pasta. Return it to the pot.

Add the sauce to the drained pasta and stir and toss over low heat until well coated with the sauce, adjusting the consistency with some of the cooking water if needed. Sprinkle with the ⅓ cup cheese and toss again. Transfer to a warmed serving bowl and serve at once. Pass additional cheese at the table.

¼ lb (125 g) *guanciale* or pancetta, chopped

2 tablespoons olive oil

1 small yellow onion, chopped

2 cloves garlic, minced

Pinch of red pepper flakes

2½ cups (15 oz/470 g) peeled, seeded, and chopped fresh or canned tomatoes

Sea salt

1 lb (500 g) *bucatini*, spaghetti, or rigatoni

⅓ cup (1½ oz/45 g) grated *pecorino romano* cheese, plus more for serving

MAKES 4–6 SERVINGS

Penne with Pesto, Potatoes, and Green Beans

For the pesto

1½ cups (1½ oz/45 g) lightly packed fresh basil leaves

3 tablespoons pine nuts

1 clove garlic, coarsely chopped

Salt

⅓ cup (3 fl oz/80 ml) extra-virgin olive oil

¼ lb (125 g) Parmigiano-Reggiano cheese, grated

½ lb (250 g) small red potatoes, peeled and cut into slices about ¼ inch (6 mm) thick

½ lb (250 g) young, slender green beans, stem ends trimmed

1 lb (500 g) penne, ziti, or *trenette*

1 tablespoon unsalted butter, at room temperature

MAKES 4–6 SERVINGS

To make the pesto, in a large mortar, combine the basil, pine nuts, garlic, and ½ teaspoon salt. Using a pestle, and working in a circular motion, grind the ingredients together until a dense, thick green paste forms. This can take several minutes. Slowly drizzle in the olive oil while stirring continuously with the pestle until a thick, flowing sauce forms. Transfer to a bowl and stir in the cheese. Taste and adjust the seasoning. Alternatively, in a food processor or blender, combine the basil, pine nuts, garlic, and ½ teaspoon salt and process until finely chopped. Then, with the motor running, pour in the oil in a slow, steady stream and process until a smooth, flowing sauce forms. Transfer to a bowl and stir in the cheese. Taste and adjust the seasoning. Set aside.

Bring a large pot three-fourths full of water to a rolling boil and add about 2 tablespoons salt. Add the potatoes and green beans and cook until tender, about 5 minutes. Using a large slotted spoon, transfer the potatoes and beans to a large, warmed serving bowl. Cover the bowl lightly with aluminum foil to keep the vegetables warm.

Bring the water back to a rolling boil, add the penne, stir well, and cook, stirring occasionally, until al dente, according to the package directions. Scoop out and reserve about 2 ladlefuls of the cooking water, then drain the pasta.

Add the drained pasta to the bowl with the vegetables and then add the pesto. Stir and toss until the pasta and vegetables are evenly coated with the sauce, adjusting the consistency with some of the cooking water if needed. Add the butter and toss to coat evenly. Serve at once.

At its best, pesto is a beautiful emerald green and still has a bit of texture. In Liguria, it is traditionally paired with *trenette*, a strand pasta available fresh or dried, but it also goes well with dried pasta in other shapes, such as penne or ziti. Green beans and new potatoes are classic partners, making this a perfect dish for early summer when the vegetables and basil are at their peak.

Seafood Spaghetti

Neapolitan cooks use small, sweet tomatoes called *ciliegini* for this seafood pasta, believing that the bolder flavor of larger tomatoes would compete with the delicate taste of the seafood. The pasta can be made with just one or two varieties of seafood, increasing their amounts accordingly. Italians never serve grated cheese with seafood pasta. Toasted bread crumbs make a delicious, crunchy garnish that is perfect with seafood.

Place the clams and mussels in a large pot, discarding any that do not close to the touch. Add ¼ cup (2 fl oz/60 ml) water, place over medium heat, cover, and cook until the shells open, 3–5 minutes. Lift out the clams and mussels with a slotted spoon and place in a large bowl, discarding any that fail to open.

Pour the liquid from the pot into a separate bowl. Remove the clams and mussels from their shells, discard the shells, and place in a clean bowl. If they seem sandy, rinse them in their cooking liquid. Strain the liquid through a paper coffee filter or a fine-mesh sieve lined with dampened cheesecloth (muslin) into the bowl with the clams and mussels and set aside.

In a large frying pan, warm the olive oil over medium heat. Add the garlic and red pepper flakes and sauté until the garlic is golden, about 2 minutes. Add the tomatoes and cook, stirring often, until they begin to collapse and release their juices, about 5 minutes. Stir in the squid and shrimp and season with salt. Pour in the wine and simmer until the squid and shrimp are nearly tender, about 5 minutes. Stir in the clams and mussels and their liquid and cook for 5 minutes longer to heat through and blend the flavors.

While the sauce simmers, bring a large pot three-fourths full of water to a rolling boil and add about 2 tablespoons salt. Add the spaghetti, stir well, and cook, stirring occasionally, until al dente, according to the package directions. Scoop out and reserve about 2 ladlefuls of the cooking water, then drain the pasta.

Add the drained pasta to the sauce in the pan and stir and toss over low heat until well coated with the sauce, adjusting the consistency with some of the cooking water as needed. Transfer to a warmed serving bowl, sprinkle with the parsley, and serve at once.

1 lb (500 g) Manila or other small clams or cockles, scrubbed

1 lb (500 g) mussels, scrubbed and debearded

⅓ cup (3 fl oz/80 ml) extra-virgin olive oil

4 cloves garlic, thinly sliced

Pinch of red pepper flakes

2 cups (about 12 oz/375 g) cherry or grape tomatoes, stemmed and halved

½ lb (250 g) cleaned squid, bodies cut into rings ½ inch (12 mm) wide and tentacles halved through the base

12 shrimp (prawns), peeled and deveined

Sea salt

½ cup (4 fl oz/125 ml) dry white wine

1 lb (500 g) spaghetti or linguine

2 tablespoons torn fresh flat-leaf (Italian) parsley leaves

MAKES 4–6 SERVINGS

Fettuccine with Black Truffles

1 lb fresh egg pasta dough (page 274)

Sea salt

6 tablespoons (3 oz/90 g) unsalted butter, melted

½ cup (2 oz/60 g) grated Parmigiano-Reggiano cheese

1 or 2 black truffles

MAKES 4–6 SERVINGS

Make the pasta dough, then divide and roll out each piece into a sheet ¹/₁₆ inch (2 mm) thick as directed on pages 92–93. Following the directions for cutting pasta strands on page 93, cut the pasta sheets into fettuccine (the widest setting) and let dry for 10–20 minutes.

Bring a large pot three-fourths full of water to a rolling boil and add about 2 tablespoons salt. Add the fettuccine, stir well, and cook, stirring occasionally, until al dente, 1½–2 minutes. Scoop out and reserve about 2 ladlefuls of the cooking water, then drain the pasta.

Transfer the drained pasta to a warmed serving bowl. Add the butter and cheese and stir and toss well to combine, adjusting the consistency with some of the cooking water if needed. Using a truffle shaver or vegetable peeler, thinly shave the truffle over the top. Toss again and serve at once.

Black truffles, found primarily in Umbria, are neither as aromatic nor as expensive as the white truffles of Piedmont, yet their earthy flavor is still highly prized. They are best served in simple preparations such as this one, where their strong, woodsy aroma can be appreciated. Use truffles as soon as possible after purchasing them, brushing them clean with a soft, dry brush.

Spaghetti alla Norma

1 large or 2 medium eggplants (aubergines)

Olive oil for frying, plus ⅓ cup (3 fl oz/80 ml)

1 yellow onion, finely chopped

2 cloves garlic, minced

2–2½ lb (1–1.25 kg) fresh tomatoes, peeled, seeded, and chopped, or 1 can (28 oz/875 g) plum (Roma) tomatoes, seeded and chopped, with juice

Sea salt and freshly ground pepper

1 lb (500 g) spaghetti

½ cup (½ oz/15 g) fresh basil leaves, torn into small pieces

½ cup (2 oz/60 g) coarsely grated *ricotta salata* cheese, plus more for garnish

½ cup (2 oz/60 g) grated *pecorino romano* or Parmigiano-Reggiano cheese

MAKES 6 SERVINGS

Trim the eggplant, then cut crosswise into slices ½ inch (12 mm) thick. Layer the slices in a colander set over a plate, sprinkling each layer with salt, and let stand for 30 minutes to drain. Rinse the eggplant slices quickly under cold running water and pat dry with paper towels.

Line a large platter or tray with paper towels and set it next to the stove. Pour the olive oil to a depth of ½ inch (12 mm) into a large, heavy frying pan and place over medium heat until hot. Working in batches, add the eggplant slices in a single layer, being careful not to crowd the pan. Fry, turning once, until lightly browned on both sides, about 8 minutes total. Using tongs, transfer the slices to the towel-lined platter to drain. Fry the remaining slices in the same way, adding more oil to the pan as needed.

In a frying pan over medium heat, warm the ⅓ cup olive oil. Add the onion and sauté until tender, about 5 minutes. Add the garlic and sauté until fragrant, about 30 seconds. Add the tomatoes and season with salt and pepper. Reduce the heat to low and simmer, uncovered, until the sauce has thickened, about 20 minutes.

Meanwhile, bring a large pot three-fourths full of water to a rolling boil and add about 2 tablespoons salt. Add the spaghetti, stir well, and cook, stirring occasionally, until al dente, according to the package directions.

Just before the pasta is ready, remove the sauce from the heat. Cut the eggplant slices into strips and stir the strips into the tomato sauce along with the basil.

Drain the pasta and transfer it into a warmed serving bowl. Add the sauce, the ½ cup *ricotta salata,* and the *pecorino romano* and stir and toss well to combine. Garnish with more *ricotta salata* and serve at once.

Sicilians are masters of cooking eggplant, and their island home is the source of countless delicious and interesting ways to prepare it. In the past when meat was scarce, eggplant, with its meaty look and flavor, was often substituted. This recipe, named for the opera *Norma,* by Catania-born Vincenzo Bellini, is typical of Sicilian cooking. *Ricotta salata* is a salted, pressed form of ricotta. If it is unavailable, a mild feta cheese can be used instead.

Penne alla Vodka

A Roman chef reportedly invented this pasta dish in the 1980s for a vodka company that wanted to popularize its product in Italy. Although it faded from menus in Italy, it remains a perennial favorite in Italian restaurants in the United States.

Bring a large pot three-fourths full of water to a rolling boil. Meanwhile, in a large frying pan over medium heat, melt the butter. Add the garlic and sauté until lightly golden, about 2 minutes. Stir in the tomato purée, red pepper flakes, and salt to taste. Bring the sauce to a simmer and cook for 5 minutes to blend the flavors.

When the water is boiling, add about 2 tablespoons salt. Add the penne, stir well, and cook, stirring occasionally, until al dente, according to package directions.

Meanwhile, add the cream and vodka to the sauce and bring to a simmer. Cook for 2 minutes longer.

When the penne is ready, scoop out and reserve about 2 ladlefuls of the cooking water, then drain the pasta. Add the drained pasta to the sauce in the pan and stir and toss over low heat until well coated with the sauce, adjusting the consistency with some of the cooking water if needed. Remove from the heat, add the cheese, and toss again. Transfer to a warmed serving bowl and serve at once.

4 tablespoons (2 oz/60 g) unsalted butter

2 cloves garlic, minced

1 can (28 oz/875 g) plum (Roma) tomato purée

Pinch of red pepper flakes

Sea salt

1 lb (500 g) penne

½ cup (4 fl oz/125 ml) heavy (double) cream

¼ cup (2 fl oz/60 ml) vodka

½ cup (2 oz/00 g) grated Parmigiano-Reggiano cheese

MAKES 4–6 SERVINGS

EMILIA-ROMAGNA

Tagliatelle alla Bolognese

Bolognese sauce owes its rich, deep flavor to long, slow cooking and to starting with a *soffritto*, the mixture of carrot, onion, celery, and, in this case, pancetta, that forms the base of the sauce. The finished sauce should be delicate and creamy (helped, in part, by the addition of dairy, a signature of recipes from Bologna) and cling nicely to the pasta strands when tossed. This sauce is classically served with fresh tagliatelle or fettuccine, but dried pasta can be substituted. Make a double batch of sauce and you will have enough to make the lasagne on page 143.

To make the Bolognese sauce, in a Dutch oven or other large, heavy pot over medium-low heat, melt the butter. Add the carrots, celery, onion, and pancetta and cook, stirring occasionally, until the ingredients are tender and a rich golden brown, about 30 minutes. If the ingredients begin to brown too much, reduce the heat and stir in a spoonful or two of warm water.

Add the ground meats to the pot and stir well. Raise the heat to medium and cook, breaking up the meats with a wooden spoon, until lightly browned and crumbly and their juices have evaporated, about 20 minutes.

Add the wine and deglaze the pot, scraping up the browned bits from the pot bottom. Cook until the wine evaporates, about 2 minutes. Stir in the tomatoes, the tomato paste, the 2 cups stock, the milk, 1 teaspoon salt, 1/4 teaspoon pepper, and the nutmeg. Cook the mixture until it just begins to simmer, then reduce the heat to very low and continue to cook, stirring occasionally, for about 1 hour. If the sauce becomes too thick or threatens to scorch, add a little more stock.

Partially cover the pot and continue cooking the sauce on the lowest heat setting until it is thick and dark brown, 1–1 1/2 hours longer. When the sauce is ready, use a large spoon to skim off and discard any fat that floats on the surface. Cover the pan and set aside.

While the sauce is simmering, make the pasta dough, then divide and roll out each piece into a sheet 1/16 inch (2 mm) thick as directed on pages 92–93. Following the directions for cutting pasta strands on page 93, cut the pasta sheets into tagliatelle (the widest setting) and let dry for 10–20 minutes.

Bring a large pot three-fourths full of water to a rolling boil and add about 2 tablespoons salt. Add the tagliatelle, stir well, and cook, stirring occasionally, until al dente, 1 1/2–2 minutes.

While the pasta is cooking, reheat the sauce over medium-low heat. Taste and adjust the seasoning with salt, pepper, and/or nutmeg.

When the tagliatelle is ready, scoop out and reserve about 2 ladlefuls of the cooking water, then drain the pasta. Add the drained pasta to the sauce in the pot and stir and toss until well coated with the sauce, adjusting the consistency with some of the cooking water if needed. Transfer to a warmed serving bowl and serve at once. Pass the cheese at the table.

For the Bolognese sauce

2 tablespoons unsalted butter

2 small carrots chopped

1 celery stalk, chopped

1 yellow onion, chopped

2 oz (60 g) thick-cut pancetta, chopped

1/2 lb (250 g) ground (minced) pork

1/2 lb (250 g) ground (minced) beef chuck

1/2 cup (4 fl oz/125 ml) dry red wine such as Barbera

1 cup (6 oz/185 g) drained, chopped canned plum (Roma) tomatoes

1 tablespoon tomato paste

2 cups (16 fl oz/500 ml) beef stock (page 273), plus more as needed

1 cup (8 fl oz/250 ml) whole milk

Sea salt and freshly ground pepper

1/8 teaspoon freshly grated nutmeg

1 lb fresh egg pasta dough (page 274)

Grated Parmigiano-Reggiano cheese for serving

MAKES 4–6 SERVINGS

Beef Ravioli with Fresh Tomato Sauce

For the filling

2 tablespoons unsalted butter

1 small yellow onion, chopped

½ cup (2½ oz/75 g) *each* **finely chopped carrot and celery**

¾ lb (375 g) ground (minced) beef sirloin

Sea salt and freshly ground pepper

½ cup (4 fl oz/125 ml) dry red wine

2 large eggs, beaten

½ cup (2 oz/60 g) grated Parmigiano-Reggiano cheese, plus more for serving

¼ cup (1 oz/30 g) plain fine dried bread crumbs

1 lb fresh egg pasta dough (page 274)

For the sauce

¼ cup (2 fl oz/60 ml) olive oil

4 cloves garlic, minced

1½ lb (750 g) plum (Roma) tomatoes, peeled, seeded, and chopped

Sea salt and freshly ground pepper

Handful of fresh basil leaves

MAKES 6 SERVINGS

To make the filling, in a frying pan over medium heat, melt the butter. Add the onion, carrot, and celery and sauté until golden, 10–15 minutes. Add the beef, ¾ teaspoon salt, and ¼ teaspoon pepper. Cook, stirring and breaking up the meat with a wooden spoon, until the meat is no longer red and its juices have evaporated, about 10 minutes. Add the wine, bring to a simmer, and cook until the wine evaporates, about 2 minutes. Remove from the heat and let cool slightly.

Scrape the beef mixture into a food processor and pulse until chopped. Add the eggs, ½ cup cheese, and bread crumbs and pulse just until blended. Scrape the mixture into a bowl, cover, and chill for at least 1 hour or for up to overnight.

Make the pasta dough, then divide and roll out each piece into a sheet ¹⁄₁₆ inch (2 mm) thick as directed on pages 92–93. Lightly flour a rimmed baking sheet. Following the directions on page 94, cut each pasta sheet into strips 4 inches (10 cm) wide. Layer the strips flat on the prepared baking sheet, spacing them so they don't touch and separating each layer with a lightly floured kitchen towel. Fill and cut the ravioli as directed on page 94.

You can cook the ravioli immediately, or cover with a kitchen towel and refrigerate until ready to cook. They will keep for up to 3 hours; turn them several times during that time so that they do not stick.

To make the sauce, in a frying pan over medium-low heat, warm the olive oil. Add the garlic and cook, stirring frequently, until golden, about 1 minute. Add the tomatoes, raise the heat to medium, and bring to a simmer, stirring occasionally. Reduce the heat to low, season to taste with salt and pepper, add the basil leaves, and simmer until the tomatoes thicken into a light sauce, about 7 minutes. Keep warm.

Bring a large pot three-fourths full of water to a rolling boil. Add about 2 tablespoons salt, and then add the ravioli and stir gently. Cook, stirring occasionally and adjusting the heat so the water simmers gently, until the ravioli rise to the surface and are al dente, 3–4 minutes.

Using a large slotted spoon, divide the ravioli among warmed plates. Spoon the sauce over the ravioli, dividing it evenly, and serve at once. Pass the cheese at the table.

Ravioli are made all over Italy, with different fillings in every region. For example, in Liguria they are sometimes stuffed with fish and greens, in Tuscany with nettles, and in Sardinia with ricotta and mint or with eggplant (aubergine). In this recipe from Emilia-Romagna, a simple filling of beef and Parmigiano-Reggiano cheese is infused with the flavor of the local Barbera.

LOMBARDY

Pumpkin Tortelli with Brown Butter and Sage

Aromatic, velvety gray-green sage is a perennial that grows in profusion all over Italy. In Roman times, it was prized for both its medicinal properties and as a flavoring. Today, its chief use is culinary, including in such traditional recipes as chicken livers sautéed in butter and veal saltimbocca. Here, it infuses melted butter, to create a common northern Italian preparation for saucing stuffed pastas, in this case *tortelli*, a classic Lombardian ravioli.

Position a rack in the middle of the oven and preheat to 400°F (200°C). Line a rimmed baking sheet with parchment (baking) paper.

Cut the pumpkin in half lengthwise. Scoop out the seeds and discard. Peel the pumpkin halves and cut the flesh into chunks. Place on the prepared baking sheet, and bake until very soft when pierced with the tip of a knife, about 25 minutes. Let cool to the touch, then put into a food processor. Process the pumpkin until smooth. Add the egg yolk and cheese and pulse to blend. Season with salt, pepper, and nutmeg and pulse to combine. Set aside.

Make the pasta dough, then divide and roll out each piece into a sheet $1/16$ inch (2 mm) thick as directed on pages 92–93. Lightly flour a rimmed baking sheet. Trim each pasta sheet into long strips that will fit on the baking sheet. Layer the strips flat on the prepared baking sheet, spacing them so they don't touch and separating each layer with a lightly floured kitchen towel.

To make the *tortelli*, place one pasta strip on a floured work surface. Use a 2-inch (5-cm) round pastry cutter to make pasta circles. Place 1 teaspoon filling in the center of half the circles. Lightly brush a little water around the filling, top with the remaining circles, and press the edges to seal. Place in a single layer on a lightly floured rimmed baking sheet, separating each layer with a lightly floured kitchen towel. Keep the top layer covered as you prepare the *tortelli*. Repeat with the remaining strips. They will keep, refrigerated, for up to 3 hours before cooking.

To make the sauce, in a large frying pan over medium heat, melt the butter. Cook, swirling the pan, until the butter foams and begins to brown. Add the sage and cook until the leaves crisp slightly and the butter turns nut brown, about 3 minutes. Be careful not to burn the butter. Remove from the heat and cover to keep warm.

Meanwhile, bring a large pot three-fourths full of water to a rolling boil. Add about 2 tablespoons salt, and then add the *tortelli* and stir gently. Cook, stirring occasionally and adjusting the heat so the water simmers gently, until the *tortelli* rise to the surface and are al dente, 3–4 minutes.

Return the frying pan with the sauce to low heat. Using a large slotted spoon, transfer the *tortelli* to the sauce and toss gently to coat. Divide among warmed plates and serve at once.

For the filling

1 sugar pie pumpkin or butternut squash, about 1½ lb (750 g)

1 large egg yolk

¼ cup (1 oz/30 g) grated Parmigiano-Reggiano cheese

Sea salt and freshly ground pepper

Pinch of freshly grated nutmeg

1 lb fresh egg pasta dough (page 274)

For the sauce

½ cup (4 oz/125 g) unsalted butter

About 10 small fresh sage leaves

MAKES 6 SERVINGS

Lobster and Shrimp Agnolotti

For the filling

2 tablespoons unsalted butter

2 tablespoons chopped shallot

¹/₂ lb (250 g) shrimp (prawns), peeled and deveined

Sea salt and freshly ground pepper

¹/₂ lb (250 g) cooked lobster meat, roughly chopped

1 tablespoon plain fine dried bread crumbs, or as needed

1 tablespoon minced fresh flat-leaf (Italian) parsley

1 large egg white

1 lb fresh egg pasta dough (page 274)

2¹/₂ cups (20 fl oz/625 ml) tomato cream sauce (page 272)

MAKES 6 SERVINGS

To make the filling, in a large frying pan over medium heat, melt the butter. Add the shallot and sauté until tender and golden, 2–3 minutes. Add the shrimp, 1 teaspoon salt, and ¹/₈ teaspoon pepper and sauté until the shrimp are just opaque when cut into at the thickest part, about 2 minutes. Remove from the heat and let cool slightly.

Scrape the shrimp mixture into a food processor, add the lobster, and pulse just until the shrimp and lobster are coarsely chopped. Add the 1 tablespoon bread crumbs and pulse just to blend. If the mixture seems wet and soft, pulse in another 1 tablespoon bread crumbs. Add the parsley and egg white and pulse until evenly mixed. Scrape the mixture into a bowl. Cover and chill the filling for at least 1 hour or for up to overnight.

Make the pasta dough, then divide and roll out each piece into a sheet ¹/₁₆ inch (2 mm) thick as directed on pages 92–93. Lightly flour a rimmed baking sheet. Trim each pasta sheet into long strips that will fit on the baking sheet. Layer the strips flat on the prepared baking sheet, spacing them so they don't touch and separating each layer with a lightly floured kitchen towel.

To make the *agnolotti*, place one pasta strip on a floured work surface. Use a 2-inch (5-cm) round pastry cutter to make pasta circles. Place ¹/₂ teaspoon filling in the center of each circle. Lightly brush a little water around the filling, fold in half, and press the edges to seal. Place in a single layer on another lightly floured rimmed baking sheet, separating each layer with a lightly floured kitchen towel. Keep the top layer covered with a kitchen towel as you prepare the *agnolotti*. Repeat with the remaining strips. They will keep, refrigerated, for up to 3 hours before cooking.

In a wide saucepan, gently warm the tomato cream sauce over low heat. Keep it warm while you cook the *agnolotti*.

Bring a large pot three-fourths full of water to a rolling boil. Add about 2 tablespoons salt, and then add the *agnolotti* and stir gently. Cook, stirring occasionally and adjusting the heat so the water simmers gently, until the *agnolotti* rise to the surface and are al dente, 3–4 minutes.

Using a large slotted spoon, transfer the *agnolotti* to the sauce in the pan and toss gently to coat. Divide among warmed plates and serve at once.

According to legend, *agnolotti*, the typical ravioli of Piedmont, were created centuries ago by a chef named Angelotu (little angel), who lived in the town Monferrato. The most common *agnolotti* are stuffed with a filling of mixed meats and served with a meat and tomato sauce or sometimes with browned butter and sage. But here a luxurious combination of lobster and shrimp is used is to fill the small half-moons, which are then topped with a creamy tomato sauce.

Beef Tortellini in Broth

These compact pasta shapes, also called *cappelletti* (little hats) in some regions, each enclose a biteful of beef flavored with red wine and cheese. Boasting a small peaked top, tortellini are simpler to shape than they appear, and making them becomes easy with practice. Here, they are served in *brodo*, a flavorful meat broth. The recipe yields twice the amount of tortellini you will need for this *primo*. Plan to cook half of the tortellini and freeze the other half for later use. To cook the frozen tortellini, drop them into boiling water and cook until al dente.

In a large frying pan over medium heat, melt the butter. Add the carrot, celery, and onion and cook, stirring frequently, until the vegetables are tender and golden, 10–15 minutes. Add the beef, ³/₄ teaspoon salt, and a pinch of pepper. Cook, stirring and breaking up the meat with a wooden spoon, until the meat is no longer red and its juices have evaporated, about 10 minutes. Add the wine, bring to a simmer, and cook until the wine evaporates, about 2 minutes. Remove from the heat and let cool slightly.

Scrape the beef mixture into a food processor and pulse until finely chopped. Add the eggs, ¹/₂ cup cheese, and bread crumbs and pulse just until blended. Scrape the mixture into a bowl, cover, and chill for at least 1 hour or for up to overnight.

Make the pasta dough, then divide and roll out each piece into a sheet ¹/₁₆ inch (2 mm) thick as directed on pages 92–93. Lightly flour a rimmed baking sheet. Lay the pasta sheet on a lightly floured work surface and, using a knife or a pastry wheel, cut it into 2-inch (5-cm) squares. Layer the squares flat on the prepared baking sheet, spacing them so they don't touch and separating each layer with a lightly floured kitchen towel.

Fill the tortellini as directed on page 95. When you have made all of the tortellini, freeze half of them in a single layer on a baking sheet, and then transfer them to a resealable plastic bag and freeze for up to 3 months. You can cook the remaining tortellini immediately, or cover with a kitchen towel and refrigerate until ready to cook. They will keep for up to 3 hours; turn them several times during that time so that they do not stick.

In a saucepan, heat the stock over low heat until it is barely simmering. Keep warm while you cook the tortellini.

Bring a large pot three-fourths full of water to a rolling boil. Add about 2 tablespoons salt, and then add the tortellini and stir gently. Cook, stirring occasionally and adjusting the heat so the water simmers gently, until the tortellini rise to the surface and are al dente, about 2 minutes. Using a large slotted spoon, carefully transfer the tortellini to a colander to drain, then add to the broth in the saucepan. Divide evenly among warmed soup bowls and serve at once. Pass the cheese at the table.

2 tablespoons unsalted butter

1 carrot, chopped

1 large celery stalk, chopped

1 small yellow onion, chopped

³/₄ lb (375 g) ground (minced) beef sirloin

Sea salt and freshly ground pepper

¹/₂ cup (4 fl oz/125 ml) dry red wine such as Barbera

2 large eggs, beaten

¹/₂ cup (2 oz/60 g) firmly packed grated Parmigiano-Reggiano cheese, plus more for serving

¹/₄ cup (1 oz/30 g) plain fine dried bread crumbs

1 lb fresh egg pasta dough (page 274)

8 cups (54 fl oz/2 l) beef stock (page 273) or chicken stock (page 274)

MAKES 6 SERVINGS

Spinach and Cheese Cannelloni

For the sauce

2 tablespoons olive oil

1 yellow onion, chopped

2 cloves garlic, minced

½ lb (250 g) Italian sweet fennel sausages, casings discarded and meat coarsely chopped

½ lb (250 g) ground (minced) beef sirloin

Sea salt and freshly ground pepper

1 can (28 oz/875 g) plum (Roma) tomatoes, drained and chopped

1 can (28 oz/875 g) plum (Roma) tomato purée

6 fresh basil leaves, torn into pieces

For the filling

1 lb (500 g) spinach, stemmed

Sea salt and freshly ground pepper

2 lb (1 kg) whole-milk ricotta cheese

2 large eggs, lightly beaten

1¼ cups (6 oz/185 g) grated Parmigiano-Reggiano cheese

1 lb fresh egg pasta dough (page 274)

MAKES 8–10 SERVINGS

To make the sauce, in a frying pan over medium heat, warm the olive oil. Add the onion and sauté until golden, 6–8 minutes. Add the garlic and sauté until fragrant, about 1 minute. Stir in the sausage, beef, and a pinch each of salt and pepper. Cook, stirring and breaking up the meat with a wooden spoon, until the meat is browned, about 7 minutes. Add the tomatoes and tomato purée, and simmer until the sauce has thickened, about 20 minutes. Stir in the basil, remove from the heat, and set aside.

To make the filling, in a saucepan, combine the spinach, ¼ cup (2 fl oz/ 60 ml) water, and a pinch of salt. Cover, place over medium heat, and cook, stirring, until tender, 3–4 minutes. Drain the spinach and let cool, then squeeze to extract the excess liquid. Finely chop the spinach. In a bowl, stir together the spinach, ricotta, eggs, and 1 cup (4 oz/125 g) of the Parmigiano-Reggiano cheese. Season with salt and pepper. Cover and refrigerate until needed.

Make the pasta dough, then divide and roll out each piece into a sheet ¹⁄₁₆ inch (2 mm) thick as directed on pages 92–93. Lightly flour a rimmed baking sheet. Lay the pasta sheet on a lightly floured work surface and, using a knife or pastry wheel, cut into 4-inch (10-cm) squares. Layer the squares flat on the prepared baking sheet, spacing them so they don't touch and separating each layer with a lightly floured kitchen towel.

Position a rack in the middle of the oven and preheat to 375°F (190°C). Spread a thin layer of the sauce in the bottom of two 9-by-13-inch (23-by-33-cm) baking dishes. Lay a pasta square on a work surface, spoon about 3 tablespoons of the filling down one end of the square, and then roll into a tube. Place the tube, seam side down, in one of the prepared dishes. Fill the remaining pasta squares in the same way and arrange them in the dishes. Spread the remaining sauce on top of the rolls, dividing it evenly between the dishes. Sprinkle the remaining Parmigiano-Reggiano cheese over the top, again dividing it evenly.

Bake the cannelloni until they are tender and heated through and the sauce and cheese are bubbling, about 40 minutes. Serve hot.

Here, tubes of fresh pasta filled with creamy spinach and ricotta are topped with a savory meat and tomato sauce. The sauce, filling, and pasta can be made up to a day in advance, and then the dish can be assembled just before baking and serving.

Lasagne alla Bolognese

This classic lasagne is built from a hearty, slow-cooked meat sauce; a creamy, thick white sauce; tender fresh pasta; and Parmigiano-Reggiano cheese. The elements are layered in the pan, but their flavors come together as the lasagne bakes. This dish is surprisingly delicate when made with fresh spinach pasta.

Make the Bolognese sauce and the white sauce and set aside.

Make the pasta dough, then divide and roll out each piece into a sheet ¹/₁₆ inch (2 mm) thick as directed on pages 92–93. Lightly flour a rimmed baking sheet. Lay the pasta sheet on a lightly floured work surface and, using a knife or pastry wheel, cut into sections about 12 inches (30 cm) long (they will lengthen slightly as they cook). Layer the sections flat on the prepared baking sheet, spacing them so they don't touch and separating each layer with a lightly floured kitchen towel.

Position a rack in the middle of the oven and preheat to 375°F (190°C). Butter a 10-by-13-by-2-inch (25-by-33-by-5-cm) baking dish. Set aside ¹/₂ cup (4 fl oz/ 125 ml) of the white sauce and ¹/₄ cup (1 oz/30 g) of the cheese. Make a layer of pasta in the pan, overlapping the pieces slightly. Spread with a thin layer of white sauce and top with a layer of Bolognese sauce. Sprinkle with about ¹/₄ cup of the cheese. Repeat the layering, creating as many layers as you can, and ending with a pasta layer. Spread the top layer with the reserved white sauce and sprinkle with the reserved cheese. The dish can be assembled up to this point, covered, and refrigerated for up to 24 hours before baking.

Bake the lasagne for 40 minutes, then check it. If the top is browning too rapidly, cover the pan loosely with aluminum foil. Continue to bake until the sauce is bubbling around the edges and a knife inserted in the center comes out warm to the touch, about 15 minutes longer. If the dish has been refrigerated, you may need to add up to 30 minutes to the cooking time. Remove the dish from the oven, place on a wire rack, and let rest for 15 minutes before serving.

4 cups (32 fl oz/1 l) Bolognese sauce (page 272)

2 cups (16 fl oz/500 ml) white sauce (page 273)

18 oz (560 g) fresh spinach pasta dough (page 274)

1¹/₂ cups (6 oz/185 g) grated Parmigiano-Reggiano cheese

MAKES 8–10 SERVINGS

Risotto alla Milanese

7–8 cups (56–64 fl oz/ 1.75–2 l) beef stock (page 273)

¼ cup (2 fl oz/60 ml) olive oil

½ cup (2½ oz/75 g) finely chopped yellow onion

3 cups (21 oz/655 g) Arborio or Carnaroli rice

1 cup (8 fl oz/250 ml) dry white wine, at room temperature

2 pinches of saffron threads

4 tablespoons (2 oz/60 g) unsalted butter

1 cup (4 oz/125 g) grated Parmigiano-Reggiano cheese

Sea salt and freshly ground pepper

MAKES 6 SERVINGS

In a saucepan over medium heat, bring the stock just to a simmer and then keep it just below a simmer over low heat.

In a large, heavy saucepan over medium heat, warm the olive oil. Add the onion and sauté until softened, about 4 minutes. Add the rice and stir until each grain is well coated with oil and translucent with a white dot in the center, about 3 minutes. Add the wine and stir until completely absorbed.

Add the warm stock a ladleful at a time, stirring frequently after each addition. Wait until the stock is almost completely absorbed (but the rice is never dry on top) before adding the next ladleful. Reserve ¼ cup (2 fl oz/60 ml) stock and add the saffron to it.

When the rice is tender to the bite but slightly firm in the center and looks creamy, after about 20 minutes, add the saffron-infused stock. You may find that you did not need all of the stock or that you need more. If more liquid is required, use hot water.

Remove from the heat and stir in the butter and cheese. Season to taste with salt and pepper. Transfer the risotto to a warmed platter and serve at once.

Saffron imparts its unique color and aromatic taste to this classic accompaniment to osso buco (page 199). For the best flavor, buy saffron threads (the stigma of a variety of crocus), rather than saffron powder, and check the date on the package to make sure that it has not been on the shelf too long. The subtle flavor of the spice dissipates after just a few months.

Risi e Bisi

Peas have long been cultivated in the Veneto, and Venetians traditionally celebrate their arrival in local markets with this creamy souplike dish of rice and peas. Some recipes call for cooking a little diced pancetta with the onion for extra flavor. Look for the youngest, sweetest peas of the season for the best result.

In a saucepan over medium heat, bring the stock just to a simmer and then keep it just below a simmer over low heat.

In a wide, heavy saucepan over medium heat, warm the olive oil. Add the onion and sauté until tender and lightly golden, about 10 minutes. Stir in the rice and cook, stirring, until the rice is hot, about 2 minutes. Add ½ cup (4 fl oz/125 ml) of the stock and stir until the stock is absorbed and the spoon leaves a wide track in the pan. Continue to add the stock ½ cup at a time, stirring and allowing it to be absorbed before adding more, for about 10 minutes. Adjust the heat as needed so that the liquid is absorbed rapidly.

Stir in the peas and parsley and season with salt and pepper. Resume adding the stock ½ cup at a time and stirring until the rice is tender yet firm to the bite, 8–10 minutes more. If you run out of stock before the rice is ready, add hot water. The finished dish should be loose and flowing.

Remove from the heat, cover, and let stand for 2 minutes. Uncover, stir in the cheese and butter, and serve at once in warmed bowls.

6 cups (48 fl oz/1.5 l) chicken stock (page 274)

¼ cup (2 fl oz/60 ml) olive oil

1 yellow onion, finely chopped

2 cups (14 oz/440 g) Arborio or Carnaroli rice

2 cups (10 oz/315 g) fresh or partially thawed frozen shelled English peas

2 tablespoons finely chopped fresh flat-leaf (Italian) parsley

Sea salt and freshly ground pepper

½ cup (2 oz/ 60 g) grated Parmigiano-Reggiano

2 tablespoons unsalted butter

MAKES 6 SERVINGS

Risotto with Spring Vegetables

1 lb (500 g) slender asparagus, tough ends removed and cut into 2-inch (5-cm) lengths

Sea salt and freshly ground pepper

7–8 cups (56–64 fl oz/ 1.75–2 l) chicken stock (page 274)

¼ cup (2 fl oz/60 ml) olive oil

1 leek, white and pale green parts only, halved lengthwise and sliced

3 cups (21 oz/655 g) Arborio or Carnaroli rice

1 cup (8 fl oz/250 ml) dry white wine, at room temperature

1 cup (5 oz/155 g) fresh or frozen shelled English peas

1 tablespoon unsalted butter

¼ cup (1 oz/30 g) grated Parmigiano-Reggiano cheese

MAKES 6 SERVINGS

Bring a large saucepan three-fourths full of water to a rolling boil. Add about 1 tablespoon salt and the asparagus and cook until nearly tender, 1–2 minutes. Drain and rinse under cold running water. Set aside.

In a saucepan over medium heat, bring the stock just to a simmer and then keep it just below a simmer over low heat.

In a large, heavy saucepan over medium heat, warm the olive oil. Add the leek and sauté until softened, 2–3 minutes. Add the rice and stir until each grain is well coated with oil and translucent with a white dot in the center, about 3 minutes. Add the wine and stir until it is completely absorbed.

Add the warm stock a ladleful at a time, stirring frequently after each addition. Wait until the stock is almost completely absorbed (but the rice is never dry on top) before adding the next ladleful. Reserve ¼ cup (2 fl oz/60 ml) stock to add at the end.

When the rice is almost tender to the bite but slightly firm in the center and looks creamy, after about 18 minutes, add the asparagus, peas, and a ladleful of stock. Cook, stirring occasionally, until the asparagus and peas are heated through and just tender and the rice is al dente, 2–3 minutes longer. You may find that you did not need all of the stock or that you need more. If more liquid is required, use hot water.

Remove the risotto from the heat and stir in the butter, the cheese, and the reserved ¼ cup stock. Season to taste with salt and pepper. Spoon onto warmed plates and serve at once.

This simple risotto showcases the flavor of fresh peas and slender asparagus, two harbingers of spring. The rice can act as a backdrop to nearly any vegetable, from sautéed artichoke hearts to roasted winter squash to earthy wild mushrooms. Cook the vegetable partway before stirring it into the nearly finished risotto to complete the cooking.

Potato Gnocchi with Chanterelles and Pancetta

Gnocchi are made primarily from potatoes or semolina, with potatoes favored in the north and semolina in the south, and the dough can be flavored with everything from spinach and pumpkin to ricotta. Here, potato gnocchi are topped with an unusual quick sauce of wild mushrooms, pancetta, and onion, but they may also be served with a simple tomato sauce, a meat ragù, or even browned butter.

To make the gnocchi, in a saucepan, combine the potatoes with water to cover, and bring to a simmer over medium heat. Cook until the potatoes are tender, about 40 minutes.

Drain the potatoes and let cool slightly. Peel the potatoes and then pass them through a ricer or a food mill fitted with the fine disk held over a rimmed baking sheet. Spread the potatoes out on the sheet and let cool. In a small bowl, lightly beat the egg with the salt. Drizzle over the potatoes, then sprinkle the ¾ cup flour over the egg. Mix together gently by hand, being careful not to overwork the dough, until the flour is incorporated. Scrape the dough onto a lightly floured work surface. Knead a few times just until smooth, adding a little more flour if needed to arrive at a dough that is not sticky yet is still moist. Set the dough aside, and scrape the work surface clean, discarding any bits of dough.

Lightly dust 2 rimmed baking sheets and the work surface. Cut the dough into 4 pieces, cover 3 pieces with an overturned bowl, and put the remaining piece on the floured surface. Using your palms, roll the dough into a long rope about ½ inch (12 mm) in diameter. Cut the rope crosswise into ½-inch (12-mm) pieces. Place the gnocchi onto the prepared pans, being careful they don't touch. Repeat with the remaining 3 dough pieces.

To make the sauce, in a large frying pan over medium heat, heat the oil and pancetta and cook, stirring occasionally, until the pancetta begins to turn golden, about 5 minutes. Add the onion and sauté until softened, about 5 minutes. Add the mushrooms, season with salt and pepper, and cook, stirring occasionally, until the mushrooms are tender, about 5 minutes longer. Remove the pan from the heat while you cook the gnocchi.

Bring a large pot three-fourths full of water to a rolling boil. Add 2 tablespoons salt, and then drop in the gnocchi a few at a time so they do not lump together. Cook, stirring once or twice, until they rise to the surface, about 3 minutes.

When the gnocchi are almost ready, return the frying pan with the sauce to medium heat, add the stock, and bring to a simmer. Using a slotted spoon, transfer the gnocchi to the sauce. Raise the heat to high and cook for 1 minute, stirring very gently. Divide the gnocchi among warmed bowls and sprinkle with the parsley, cheese, and some freshly ground pepper. Serve at once.

For the gnocchi

1 lb (500 g) small baking potatoes, unpeeled, preferably organic

1 large egg

1 teaspoon sea salt

¾ cup (4 oz/125 g) all-purpose (plain) flour, or as needed

For the sauce

2 tablespoons olive oil

2 oz (60 g) pancetta, chopped

1 small red onion, chopped

¼ lb (125 g) fresh chanterelle mushrooms, brushed clean, trimmed, and sliced

Sea salt and freshly ground pepper

2 cups (16 fl oz/500 ml) chicken stock (page 274), or as needed

1 tablespoon chopped fresh flat-leaf (Italian) parsley

½ cup (2 oz/60 g) grated *pecorino romano* cheese

MAKES 4 SERVINGS

Gratinéed Ricotta and Spinach Gnocchi

2 lb (1 kg) spinach, stemmed

Sea salt and freshly ground pepper

6 tablespoons (3 oz/90 g) unsalted butter

1 small yellow onion, finely chopped

2 cups (15 oz/470 g) whole-milk ricotta cheese

1³⁄₄ cups (7 oz/220 g) grated Parmigiano-Reggiano cheese

2 large eggs

¹⁄₄ teaspoon freshly grated nutmeg

1¹⁄₂ cups (7¹⁄₂ oz/235 g) all-purpose (plain) flour

¹⁄₂ cup (2 oz/60 g) plain fine dried bread crumbs

MAKES 6 SERVINGS

In a saucepan, combine the spinach, ¹⁄₄ cup (2 fl oz/ 60 ml) water, and a pinch of salt. Cover, place over medium heat, and cook, stirring, until tender, 3–4 minutes. Drain the spinach and let cool, then squeeze to extract the excess liquid. Finely chop the spinach and set aside.

In a small frying pan over medium heat, melt 2 tablespoons of the butter. Add the onion and sauté until tender and lightly golden, about 10 minutes. Set aside.

In a large bowl, beat together the ricotta, 1 cup (4 oz/125 g) of the Parmigiano-Reggiano, the eggs, and the nutmeg. Season with salt and pepper. Add the onion and spinach and stir well. Stir in the flour until well blended and a soft dough forms.

Line 2 rimmed baking sheets with parchment (baking) paper. Scoop up a tablespoon of the dough and, with dampened hands, lightly shape it into a ball ³⁄₄ inch (2 cm) in diameter. Place the ball on one of the prepared baking sheets. Repeat with the remaining dough, making sure the balls don't touch on the baking sheets.

Bring at large pot three-fourths full of water to a rolling boil and add 2 tablespoons salt. Position a rack in the middle of the oven and preheat to 400°F (200°C). Butter a shallow 3-qt (3-l) gratin or baking dish with 2 tablespoons of the butter.

Reduce the heat so the water is at a steady simmer. Add half of the gnocchi to the pot and cook, stirring gently once or twice, until they rise to the surface, about 3 minutes. Using a slotted spoon, transfer them to the prepared dish. Cook the remaining gnocchi in the same way and add them to the dish.

Cut the remaining 2 tablespoons butter into bits and dot the surface of the gnocchi evenly. Sprinkle with the remaining ³⁄₄ cup (3 oz/95 g) Parmigiano-Reggiano cheese and the bread crumbs. Bake until the butter is sizzling and the cheese is melted, about 15 minutes. Serve at once.

In Florence, this type of gnocchi is called *nudi*, because it is similar to ravioli filling minus the pasta. These gnocchi are particularly delicate. If you think they might not hold their shape when they are boiled, make a test gnoccho and drop it into a saucepan of boiling water. If it breaks apart, add a little more flour to the remaining mixture. You can boil the gnocchi up to 3 hours in advance, and then cover and refrigerate them until it is time to bake them. If they have been chilled, add 5 minutes or so to the baking time.

Crespelle with Prosciutto and Fontina

In Emilia-Romagna, thin, eggy crêpes, called *crespelle,* sometimes take the place of pasta. This dish is perfect for a dinner party, since both the sauce and the *crespelle* can be made up to 2 days before serving, or the entire dish can be assembled and refrigerated for up to 24 hours before you bake it.

To make the *crespelle,* in a large bowl, whisk together the flour, milk, eggs, and salt until smooth. Cover and refrigerate for at least 30 minutes or for up to overnight. Meanwhile, prepare the white sauce and set aside.

Heat a 6-inch (15-cm) crêpe pan or nonstick frying pan over medium heat. When the pan is hot, brush it very lightly with oil. Scoop up a scant ¼ cup (2 fl oz/ 60 ml) of the batter, add to the pan, and tilt and swirl the pan to spread the batter evenly over the bottom. Pour any excess batter back into the bowl. Cook the *crespelle* until the edges begin to brown and lift away from the pan sides, about 1 minute, then flip and cook until spotted with brown, about 30 seconds. Slide onto a plate, and cover with a piece of waxed paper. Repeat with the remaining batter, stacking the *crespelle* and separating them with waxed paper. You should have at least 24 *crespelle.*

Position a rack in the middle of the oven and preheat to 375°F (190°C). Butter two 9-by-13-by-2-inch (23-by-33-by-5-cm) baking dishes.

Spread a thin layer of the white sauce in the bottom of each prepared dish. Cut the prosciutto and Fontina into pieces equal to the number of *crespelle.* Stack a piece of the prosciutto and a slice of the Fontina on one-half of each *crespelle,* fold it in half, covering the prosciutto and cheese, and then fold into quarters. Place in one of the prepared dishes. Fill and fold the remaining *crespelle* in the same way and arrange them, overlapping slightly, in the dishes. Spread the remaining sauce over the *crespelle,* dividing it evenly between the dishes. Sprinkle the Parmigiano-Reggiano evenly over the top.

Bake until the sauce is lightly browned on the surface and the cheese is bubbling, about 30 minutes. Serve at once.

For the *crespelle*

1½ cups (6 oz/185 g) all-purpose (plain) flour

2 cups (16 fl oz/500 ml) whole milk

4 large eggs

1 teaspoon salt

Olive oil or canola oil

2 cups (16 fl oz/500 ml) white sauce (page 273)

6 oz (185 g) very thinly sliced *prosciutto di Parma*

½ lb (250 g) Valle d'Aosta Fontina cheese, rind trimmed

½ cup (2 oz/60) grated Parmigiano-Reggiano cheese

MAKES 10–12 SERVINGS

Pizza Bianca

2 packages active dry yeast (about 3 teaspoons)

4–4½ cups (20–22½ oz/ 625–705 g) all-purpose (plain) flour, plus more for dusting

Sea salt

Olive oil

2 cloves garlic, minced

2 tablespoons chopped fresh rosemary, oregano, or thyme leaves

MAKES 4 PIZZAS, OR 4 SERVINGS

To make the dough, pour 1½ cups (12 fl oz/375 ml) lukewarm water (100°–110°F/ 38°–43°C) into the bowl of a stand mixer. Sprinkle the yeast over the top and let stand until slightly foamy, about 5 minutes. Place the bowl on the mixer fitted with the dough hook. Add ½ cup (2½ oz/75 g) of the flour and 2 teaspoons salt; mix until combined. Add the remaining flour about ½ cup at a time, continuing to mix until all of the flour is incorporated, scraping down the sides of the bowl if necessary. Knead with the dough hook until the dough is smooth but not sticky, about 10 minutes. Transfer the dough to a lightly floured work surface, divide into 4 portions, then shape each into a ball. Rub each ball with oil, and lightly oil a rimmed baking sheet. Place the balls on the baking sheet and cover loosely with plastic wrap. Set aside in a warm place, such as on top of the stove, and let rise until doubled in bulk, about 2 hours.

Alternatively, shape the dough into a large round, coat with oil, then place in a large zippered plastic bag. Press out any excess air, and place in the refrigerator overnight. When ready to bake the pizzas, remove the dough from the refrigerator and divide into 4 equal balls. Transfer the balls to a rimmed baking sheet and allow to come to room temperature, about 1 hour.

Preheat the oven to 500°F (260°C) about 30 minutes before baking. Lightly oil a rimmed baking sheet. Lightly flour a work surface. Place 1 of the dough balls on the work surface, leaving the others under the plastic wrap. Flatten into a disk. Turn the disk over, sprinkle with additional flour, and, using your hands, stretch the dough into a thin rectangle, turning it over and dusting it regularly with flour as you work. If the dough becomes resistant, let it rest for about 5 minutes before continuing.

Transfer the dough to the baking sheet. Brush the dough gently with about 1 tablespoon olive oil. Using your fingers, dimple the dough all over, then sprinkle evenly with salt and about one-fourth of the garlic and rosemary.

Bake on the bottom rack of the oven until the crust is crisp and golden, about 7 minutes. Serve at once. Bake the remaining pizzas in the same way.

The beauty of *pizza bianca*, literally "white pizza," is in its simplicity. A staple of Roman cuisine, this sublime flatbread is soft inside and golden brown on the outside. It is found on nearly every street corner in Rome, and is often split horizontally and stuffed with fresh ripe figs and prosciutto, mortadella and fresh mozzarella, arugula (rocket) and shaved Parmigiano-Reggiano, or tuna and artichoke hearts.

Sausage Calzone with Peppers

The most classic Italian filling for calzone, essentially a stuffed folded pizza, is ricotta and mozzarella, sometimes with the addition of prosciutto. Calzone lends itself to an array of fillings, in this case a spicy blend of fennel sausage, sweet red peppers, and salty pecorino. Experiment with different meats, vegetables, and cheeses, but make sure your filling is somewhat dry or you will end up with a soggy crust.

To make the dough, pour 1 1/2 cups (12 fl oz/375 ml) lukewarm water (100°–110°F/ 38°–43°C) into the bowl of a stand mixer. Sprinkle the yeast over the top and let stand until slightly foamy, about 5 minutes. Place the bowl on the mixer fitted with the dough hook. Add 1/2 cup (2 1/2 oz/75 g) of the flour and the salt; mix until combined. Add the remaining flour about 1/2 cup at a time, continuing to mix until all of the flour is incorporated, scraping down the sides of the bowl if necessary. Knead with the dough hook until the dough is smooth but not sticky, about 10 minutes. Transfer the dough to a lightly floured work surface, divide into 6 portions, then shape each into a ball. Rub each ball with oil, and lightly oil a rimmed baking sheet. Place the balls on the baking sheet and cover loosely with plastic wrap. Set aside in a warm place, such as on top of the stove, and let rise until doubled in bulk, about 2 hours. Alternatively, shape the dough into a large round, coat with olive oil, then place in a large zippered plastic bag. Press out any excess air, and place in the refrigerator overnight. When ready to bake the pizzas, remove the dough from the refrigerator and divide into 6 balls. Transfer the balls to a rimmed baking sheet and allow to come to room temperature, about 1 hour.

Meanwhile, make the filling. In a frying pan over medium-high heat, warm the olive oil. Add the peppers and 1 teaspoon salt and cook until they begin to brown, about 5 minutes. Add 1 tablespoon water, cover, and cook until the peppers are tender, about 5 minutes longer. Add the sausage meat and the red pepper flakes and cook, stirring often, until the meat is browned. Set aside to cool slightly.

Preheat the oven to 500°F (260°C) about 30 minutes before baking. Lightly oil a rimmed baking sheet. Lightly flour a work surface. Place 1 of the dough balls on the work surface, leaving the others under the plastic wrap. Flatten into a disk. Turn the disk over, sprinkle with additional flour, and, using your hands, stretch the dough into an 8-inch (20-cm) round, turning it over and dusting it with flour as you work.

Place one-sixth of the filling in the center of the dough round and sprinkle with about one-sixth of the cheese. Lightly brush the edge of half of the dough circle with the egg mixture. Fold the dough in half over the filling and transfer to the baking sheet. Repeat with the remaining 5 dough balls. Crimp the edges with a fork and cut vents into the top of each. Brush the tops gently with the egg mixture. Bake on the bottom rack of the oven until the crust is crisp and golden, about 10 minutes. Serve at once.

For the dough

2 packages active dry yeast (about 3 teaspoons)

4–4 1/2 cups (20–22 1/2 oz/ 625–705 g) all-purpose (plain) flour, plus more for dusting

2 teaspoons sea salt

Olive oil

For the filling

3 tablespoons olive oil

2 or 3 small red bell peppers (capsicums), seeded and thinly sliced

Sea salt

1 lb (500 g) Italian sweet fennel sausages, casings discarded and meat crumbled

1/4 teaspoon red pepper flakes

1/2 cup (2 oz/60 g) grated *pecorino romano* or Parmigiano-Reggiano cheese

1 egg, beaten with 1 tablespoon water

MAKES 6 CALZONE

Pizza alla Margherita

For the dough

2 packages active dry yeast (about 3 teaspoons)

4–4½ cups (20–22½ oz/ 625–705 g) all-purpose (plain) flour, plus more for dusting

2 teaspoons salt

Olive oil

Semolina flour for dusting

For the sauce

1 can (28 oz/875 g) Italian plum (Roma) tomatoes, crushed

2 tablespoons extra-virgin olive oil

Sea salt and freshly ground pepper

1 lb (500 g) fresh mozzarella cheese, shredded or sliced, well drained, and blotted dry

½ cup (2 oz/60 g) grated *pecorino romano* or Parmigiano-Reggiano cheese

4 tablespoons extra-virgin olive oil

About 30 fresh basil leaves, torn into pieces

MAKES FOUR 12-INCH (30-CM) PIZZAS, OR 4 SERVINGS

To make the dough, pour 1½ cups (12 fl oz/375 ml) lukewarm water (100°–110°F/ 30°–43°C) into the bowl of a stand mixer. Sprinkle the yeast over the top and let stand until slightly foamy, about 5 minutes. Place the bowl on the mixer fitted with the dough hook. Add ½ cup (2½ oz/75 g) of the flour and the salt; mix until combined. Add the remaining flour about ½ cup at a time, continuing to mix until all of the flour is incorporated, scraping down the sides of the bowl if necessary. Knead with the dough hook until the dough is smooth but not sticky, about 10 minutes. Transfer the dough to a lightly floured work surface, divide into 4 portions, then shape each into a ball. Rub each ball with oil, and lightly oil a baking sheet. Place the balls on the baking sheet and cover loosely with plastic wrap. Set aside in a warm place, such as on top of the stove, and let rise until doubled in bulk, about 2 hours.

Alternatively, shape the dough into a large round, coat with olive oil, then place in a large zippered plastic bag. Press out any excess air, and place in the refrigerator overnight. When ready to bake the pizzas, remove the dough from the refrigerator and divide into 4 equal balls. Transfer the balls to a rimmed baking sheet and allow to come to room temperature, about 1 hour.

Meanwhile, make the sauce. In a blender or food processor, purée the tomatoes until smooth. Pour into a fine-mesh sieve placed over a bowl and let drain for about 30 minutes. Pour the drained tomatoes into a bowl and stir in the oil. Season to taste with salt and pepper and set aside.

Place a pizza stone or unglazed ceramic tiles on the bottom rack of the oven and preheat to 500°F (260°C) about 30 minutes before baking. Lightly flour a work surface. Place 1 of the dough balls on the work surface, leaving the others under the plastic wrap. Flatten into a disk. Turn the disk over, sprinkle with additional flour, and, using your hands, stretch the dough into a 12-inch (30-cm) round, turning it over and dusting it regularly with flour as you work.

Dust a baker's peel or rimless baking sheet with semolina flour. Gently lay the dough round on top. Cover evenly with one-fourth of the tomato sauce, one-fourth of the mozzarella, and one-fourth of the pecorino. Drizzle with 1 tablespoon of the olive oil. Bake until the crust is golden and the cheese is melted and bubbly, about 7 minutes. Remove from the oven, scatter with some of the basil leaves, and serve at once. Bake the remaining pizzas in the same way.

You will find at least one pizzeria—and usually more—in every Italian town, and the best have wood-burning ovens twice as hot as the average home oven. They also have talented *pizzaioli* (pizza makers) who pull and twirl the balls of dough to the size of a plate and to a thinness that ensures a crisp crust. Just three ingredients, tomato, mozzarella, and basil, top this Neapolitan classic, which was created in the late nineteenth century to commemorate the visit of Queen Margherita.

Secondi

About Secondi

The second course of an Italian meal usually features meat, poultry, or seafood, though a meat-less dish may sometimes be served as part of a lighter menu. In most Italian homes, *secondi* tend toward simplicity, showcasing the flavors of the main ingredient and avoiding fancy preparations.

Much of Italian home cooking has grown out of poverty and resourcefulness, and until relatively recently, meat and fish were considered special-occasion luxuries. Although they are now part of everyday eating, this legacy can still be seen in the way *secondi piatti* are served. The very fact that they are eaten second, after the first course of soup or pasta has taken the edge off the appetite, attests to the traditionally modest role of meat in the Italian diet.

The *secondo,* whether it is pork, beef, veal, lamb, poultry, game, fish, or vegetables, is not considered the "main dish," to be consumed in large portions. It is often only a slice of meat, a small fish fillet, or a modest serving of poultry, game, or vegetables—in other words, an element of the overall meal that works in concert with the equally important accompanying side dishes and the courses that precede and follow it.

REGIONAL VARIATIONS

Pork, chicken, and rabbit, all easy to raise, appear as *secondi* throughout the country, but especially in the northern and central regions of Italy where such classic dishes as Braised Rabbit Cacciatora (page 177) and Pollo alla Diavola (page 176) originated. In the south and wherever there are mountains, lamb cooked over a wood fire or slowly braised is often the meat of the day's main meal. Beef and veal are served throughout Italy as well, most famously in and around Tuscany, the home of Chianina cattle and Bistecca all Fiorentina (page 191).

Well into the twentieth century, most Italians ate fish every Friday and during Lent, in keeping with Catholic tradition, and it has remained an important part of the cuisine. Fish are enjoyed as a *secondo* all over the peninsula, even in inland regions where they are caught in lakes and rivers, rushed in fresh from the nearest seacoast, or, increasingly, purchased frozen. Shellfish and other seafood are enjoyed grilled, fried, or in stews as *secondi,* though they are as likely to be used in sauces for pasta and other first courses.

SELECTING A SECOND COURSE

When choosing a recipe to serve as a *secondo,* take into account the season, the course that will precede it, and the number of people you will be serving. Or, do as the Italians do: visit a good butcher or fishmonger and ask what is fresh and of particularly high quality with respect to price.

For warm-weather meals and casual outdoor entertaining, consider a grilled *secondo,* to keep the menu casual and the kitchen cool. You can choose a lighter preparation, such as Halibut with Salsa Verde (page 175), Grilled Shrimp with Garlic and Lemon (page 167), or Pollo alla Diavola (page 176), or you can opt for a more robust *secondo,* like Grilled Marinated Lamb Chops (page 205). A meatless *secondo,* such as Ricotta and Tomato Sformato (page 164) or Frittata with Greens (page 163), will also work well on a spring or summer menu. Any of these dishes can be preceded with a room-temperature antipasto, such as

Panzanella (page 59) or Tomato, Basil, and Mozzarella Salad (page 50), and/or a light *primo,* such as Spaghetti with Salsa di Pomodoro (page 108) or Risotto with Spring Vegetables (page 146).

During cold-weather months, you can grill indoors, using a Tuscan grill (a rack designed for cooking over embers in the fireplace) or an oven broiler (grill). Or, choose one of the many classic braises and stews in this chapter, such as Braised Rabbit Cacciatora (page 177), Osso Buco with Gremolata (page 199), or Barolo-Braised Pot Roast (page 192). Roasted foods, like Roast Chicken with Lemon and Thyme (page 178), Herb-Roasted Pork Loin (page 186), and Roasted Branzino with Fennel (page 172), are good dishes for fall and winter. These heartier *secondi* can be preceded by a soup or pasta and are particularly well matched with a *primo* of risotto.

Sautéed and panfried *secondi,* such as Saltimbocca alla Romana (page 202), Veal Piccata (page 203), and Veal Chops Milanese (page 200), are excellent year-round choices. Because these dishes must be prepared at the last minute, you may want to pair them with a *primo* that you can make in advance, such as a baked pasta or a soup.

In general, the more people you will be serving, the less labor-intensive the menu should be. Braises, roasts, and stews are ideal for feeding a large group with minimal last-minute work in the kitchen. Whatever the occasion or number of guests, Italians typically serve the *secondo* family style from a large platter or bowl, passing it, along with the side dishes, at the table. All of the recipes in this chapter are well suited to this generous, welcoming way of serving, which allows everyone to help themselves to as much or as little as they want.

Frittata with Greens

It is not unusual to drive by a meadow in Italy and see someone foraging for wild greens. Country people know just which ones are the tastiest and where to find them. If they pick more than they can use, they often bring the extra to the market to sell. In Sicily, this frittata is commonly made with wild greens, but cultivated counterparts won't disappoint.

In a large pot, combine the greens and 1 cup (8 fl oz/250 ml) water. Cover, place over medium heat, and cook, stirring occasionally, until tender, 3–4 minutes for spinach, up to 10 minutes for tougher greens. Drain the greens and let cool. Place in a kitchen towel and squeeze to extract the excess liquid. Chop the greens and set aside.

Preheat the broiler (grill).

In a bowl, beat the eggs just until blended. Season with salt and pepper.

In a 9-inch (23-cm) flameproof frying pan over low heat, warm the olive oil. Add the garlic and sauté until fragrant, about 30 seconds. Add the greens and a pinch of salt, and stir and toss to coat the greens well with the oil. Lightly stir in the eggs and arrange the cheese slices on top. Cook, using a spatula to lift the edges of the egg to allow the uncooked egg to flow underneath, until the edges and bottom are set but the center is still moist, about 5 minutes.

Transfer the pan to the broiler about 4 inches (10 cm) from the heat source and broil (grill) until the top is puffed and golden and the cheese is slightly melted, about 1 minute.

Slide the frittata onto a flat serving plate. Serve at once, cut into wedges.

About 1 lb (500 g) leafy greens such as kale, chard, broccoli rabe, or spinach, tough stems removed

8 large eggs

Sea salt and freshly ground pepper

¼ cup (2 fl oz/60 ml) olive oil

1 clove garlic, minced

¼ lb (125 g) *ricotta salata* or young pecorino cheese, thinly sliced

MAKES 4 SERVINGS

PUGLIA

Ricotta and Tomato Sformato

1 cup (6 oz/185 g) cherry tomatoes, stemmed and halved

1 tablespoon unsalted butter, at room temperature

2 tablespoons plain fine dried bread crumbs

2 cups (16 oz/500 g) whole-milk ricotta cheese

½ cup (2 oz/60 g) grated Parmigiano-Reggiano cheese

2 large eggs

2 teaspoons chopped fresh thyme

Sea salt and freshly ground pepper

MAKES 4 SERVINGS

Position a rack in the middle of the oven and preheat to 350°F (180°C). Lightly brush a rimmed baking sheet with oil.

Squeeze the tomato halves gently to extract the seeds and juice. Arrange the tomatoes, cut side up, on the prepared baking sheet. Bake the tomatoes until they are wrinkled, about 15 minutes. Remove from the oven and let cool slightly. Leave the oven on.

Generously grease an 8-inch (20-cm) baking dish with the butter. Sprinkle the dish with the bread crumbs and tap out the excess.

In a bowl, whisk together the ricotta and Parmigiano-Reggiano cheeses, eggs, and 1 teaspoon thyme. Season with salt and pepper. Stir in half of the tomatoes. Scrape the mixture into the prepared dish and smooth the top. Top with the remaining tomato halves, cut side down. Sprinkle with the remaining thyme.

Bake until the *sformato* is set around the edges but still slightly soft in the center, about 40 minutes. Remove from the oven and let cool slightly, about 10 minutes. Run a knife around the inside edge of the dish to loosen the sides of the *sformato* and serve warm.

A *sformato* is a souffle-like dish often made with vegetables. *Sformati* are often baked in ring molds and sometimes in ramekins, but here a simple ceramic baking dish is used. You can also serve this dish in smaller portions as an antipasto, or it can be the centerpiece of a light lunch, accompanied with marinated olives, salami, and a green salad.

VENETO

Grilled Shrimp with Garlic and Lemon

Fresh shellfish are one of the treasures of the Venetian kitchen, and local cooks like to prepare them simply, often grilled over a hot fire, as the shrimp are here. If you are worried about the shrimp falling through the grate as you turn them, thread them onto skewers. They can also be cooked on a stove-top grill pan in the same amount of time.

Pat the shrimp dry with paper towels. In a large bowl, toss together the shrimp, olive oil, lemon juice, parsley, garlic, a few pinches of salt, and a few grinds of pepper. Let stand for 30 minutes.

Prepare a charcoal or gas grill for direct grilling over medium-high heat. Oil the grill rack. Or, preheat a stove-top grill pan over medium-high heat and brush with oil.

BY GRILL: Using tongs, place the shrimp over the hottest part of the fire or directly over the heat elements and grill, turning once, until pink and just opaque at the center, 2–3 minutes on each side.

BY GRILL PAN: Using tongs, place the shrimp on the grill pan and grill, turning once, until pink and just opaque at the center, 2–3 minutes on each side.

Arrange the shrimp on a warmed platter and serve at once.

1 lb (500 g) large shrimp (prawns), peeled and deveined

¼ cup (2 fl oz/60 ml) extra-virgin olive oil

2 tablespoons fresh lemon juice

2 tablespoons chopped fresh flat-leaf (Italian) parsley

1 tablespoon minced garlic

Sea salt and freshly ground pepper

MAKES 4 SERVINGS

Zuppa di Pesce

4 lb (2 kg) assorted fish and shellfish such as clams, mussels, snapper, striped bass, cod, haddock, cleaned squid, shrimp (prawns) in the shell, and crabs, in any combination

Sea salt and freshly ground black pepper

¼ cup (2 fl oz/60 ml) olive oil

1 large yellow onion, chopped

3 cloves garlic, 2 minced and 1 halved lengthwise

3 tablespoons chopped fresh flat-leaf (Italian) parsley

1 teaspoon red pepper flakes

1 cup (8 fl oz/250 ml) dry white wine such as Pinot Grigio

3 cups (24 oz/750 g) canned plum (Roma) tomato purée

6 thick slices coarse country bread

MAKES 6 SERVINGS

Along the Tuscan coast, especially around the lively ports of Livorno and Viareggio, *zuppa di pesce,* thick fish stewlike soup ladled over bread, is a popular dish. The ingredients vary according to what is available at the market, so buy what looks best and what your pocketbook can handle. Choose deboned fish fillets if possible.

If using clams, scrub well, discarding any that fail to close to the touch. If using mussels, scrub well, debeard, and discard any that fail to close to the touch. If using fish fillets, cut into large chunks. Clean any whole fish, remove and discard their heads and tails, remove their skin, and cut crosswise into thick slices on the bone. If using squid, cut the body into rings about 1 inch (2.5 cm) wide and the tentacles into medium-sized pieces. Place all the seafood in a bowl of salted cold water and set aside.

In a large saucepan over medium heat, warm the olive oil. Add the onion and sauté until it begins to soften and is fragrant, 3–4 minutes. Add the minced garlic and 2 tablespoons of the parsley and sauté until the garlic is fragrant, 1 minute.

Raise the heat to high, add the red pepper flakes, and pour in the wine. Let the alcohol bubble away for a couple of minutes, then reduce the heat to medium, pour in the tomato purée, and simmer uncovered, stirring occasionally, until the flavors are blended, about 5 minutes.

Begin adding the seafood to the soup, starting with the squid, adding the fish slices after 10 minutes, and ending with the shellfish. After all the seafood is added, reduce the heat to low and cook, uncovered, at a slow simmer for about 15 minutes to cook the seafood and blend the flavors. Season to taste with salt and black pepper.

Meanwhile, toast the bread and rub the surface with the cut sides of the halved garlic. Place 1 bread slice in each warmed soup bowl.

Transfer the soup to a warmed tureen. Sprinkle with the remaining 1 tablespoon parsley. Bring the tureen to the table and ladle a mix of fish and shellfish and some broth onto the toast in each bowl. Serve at once.

Tuna with Garlic, Basil, and Tomato

This Tuscan sauce marries the flavors of the Mediterranean: tomatoes, olives and olive oil, capers, garlic, and basil. It pairs particularly well with fresh tuna, a fish traditionally linked with the Sicilian kitchen, but today enjoyed throughout the country.

In a frying pan over medium heat, warm 3 tablespoons of the olive oil. Add the onion and sauté until it begins to soften, about 3 minutes. Add the minced garlic and sauté until golden, about 2 minutes longer. Stir in the tomatoes, basil, and 2 tablespoons parsley and cook uncovered, stirring occasionally, until thickened, about 15 minutes. Remove from the heat and pass through a food mill fitted with the medium disk held over a bowl. Set aside.

Lightly season the tuna steaks on both sides with salt and pepper. In a frying pan large enough to hold the fish in a single layer, warm the remaining 3 tablespoons olive oil over medium heat. Add the crushed garlic and cook, stirring often, until golden, about 2 minutes. Remove and discard the garlic clove. Add the tuna steaks to the pan, raise the heat to medium-high, and cook, turning once, until lightly browned on both sides, about 2 minutes on each side. Pour the reserved sauce directly over the fish, reduce the heat to low, add the olives and capers, and cook until the sauce thickens, about 5 minutes.

Transfer the tuna steaks and sauce to warmed plates and sprinkle with parsley. Serve at once.

6 tablespoons (3 fl oz/90 ml) olive oil

1 large yellow onion, chopped

3 cloves garlic, 2 minced and 1 crushed

1 lb (500 g) fresh tomatoes, peeled, seeded, and chopped, or 1 can (15 oz/470 g) plum (Roma) tomatoes, drained and chopped

8 fresh basil leaves

2 tablespoons chopped fresh flat-leaf (Italian) parsley, plus more for garnish

4 tuna steaks, each about 1/2 lb (250 g)

Sea salt and freshly ground pepper

1 cup (5 oz/155 g) pitted brine-cured black olives

4 teaspoons capers, rinsed

MAKES 4 SERVINGS

Roasted Branzino with Fennel

1 branzino (sea bass),
1½–2 lb (750 g–1 kg),
cleaned with head and
tail intact

2 tablespoons chopped fresh
flat-leaf (Italian) parsley

1 tablespoon chopped fresh
marjoram or oregano

7 tablespoons (3½ fl oz/
105 ml) olive oil

2 tablespoons fresh lemon
juice

Sea salt and freshly ground
pepper

4 lemon slices

2 lb (1 kg) boiling potatoes

2 small fennel bulbs

½ cup (2½ oz/75 g) Gaeta
or other Mediterranean-style
black olives

MAKES 4 SERVINGS

Preheat an oven to 450°F (230°C). Rinse the fish and pat dry with paper towels. Using a sharp, heavy knife, make slashes on both sides of the fish, cutting down to the bone. In a small bowl, stir together the parsley, marjoram, 4 tablespoons (2 fl oz/60 ml) of the olive oil, and the lemon juice, and season with salt and pepper. Rub the mixture inside the cavity and over the outside of the fish. Tuck the lemon slices inside. Cover and let stand while you prepare the potatoes and fennel.

Peel and slice the potatoes, rinse under cold running water, and pat dry. Place in a bowl. Cut off the stems and feathery leaves from the fennel bulbs and reserve for another use or discard. Cut away and discard any discolored areas of the bulbs. Halve each bulb lengthwise and cut away the tough core. Cut the halves crosswise into thin slices. Add the fennel slices to the potato slices along with the remaining 3 tablespoons olive oil. Season with salt and pepper, toss well, and then spread the vegetables in a roasting pan large enough to hold the slices in a shallow layer.

Bake until the potatoes and fennel begin to brown, 25–30 minutes. Turn the potatoes, stir in the olives, and place the fish on top. Continue to bake until the flesh is opaque when cut near the bone and the potatoes and fennel are tender, 20–30 minutes longer.

Transfer the fish to a warmed platter. Surround with the potatoes, fennel, and olives. Serve at once.

Ligurians feel that if you have a nice fresh fish, you should honor it with a simple preparation and not try to make it look, or taste, like anything else. The absence of sauces and condiments may take some getting used to, but the reward is the subtle flavor and texture of the fish. Here, *branzino*, or sea bass, is roasted, but striped bass and red snapper are also good prepared this way. Marjoram is typical of Ligurian cooking, but other herbs, such as oregano or rosemary, can be substituted.

Halibut with Salsa Verde

Salsa verde, or "green sauce," is served with many different types of meat and fish, including *bollito misto*, an assortment of sliced simmered meats and poultry popular in Piedmont and Emilia-Romagna. Here, the sauce is served with grilled halibut but it is also good with tuna, swordfish, or other flavorful fish steaks. You can make the sauce up to a day in advance and refrigerate it. Bring it to room temperature before serving.

To make the sauce, in a food processor, combine the parsley, garlic, bread cubes, anchovies, and capers. Process until finely chopped. With the motor running, slowly drizzle in the olive oil in a thin, steady stream and process until combined. Transfer to a bowl, add the lemon juice and salt to taste, and let stand at room temperature for 1 hour.

Prepare a charcoal or gas grill for direct grilling over medium-high heat. Generously oil the grill rack. Or, preheat a stove-top grill pan over medium-high heat and brush generously with oil. Rub the fish steaks on both sides with the olive oil, and then sprinkle both sides with salt and pepper

BY GRILL: Arrange the fish steaks over the hottest part of the fire or directly over the heat elements. Cook the fish, turning once, until it is opaque throughout when tested with a knife, 5–7 minutes on each side.

BY GRILL PAN: Arrange the fish steaks on the grill pan and cook, turning once, until opaque throughout when tested with a knife, 5–7 minutes on each side.

Transfer the fish to warmed plates and serve at once, accompanied with the sauce and lemon wedges.

For the sauce

2 cups (2 oz/60 g) firmly packed fresh flat-leaf (Italian) parsley leaves

1 clove garlic

¼ cup (½ oz/15 g) crustless coarse country bread cubes

4 olive oil–packed anchovy fillets

2 tablespoons capers, rinsed and drained

⅔ cup (5 fl oz/160 ml) extra-virgin olive oil

1–2 tablespoons fresh lemon juice

Sea salt

4 halibut fillets, each about 1 inch (2.5 cm) thick

2 tablespoons olive oil

Sea salt and freshly ground pepper

Lemon wedges

MAKES 4 SERVINGS

Pollo alla Diavola

¼ cup (2 fl oz/60 ml) fresh lemon juice

¼ cup (2 fl oz/60 ml) olive oil

1 teaspoon red pepper flakes, or to taste

Sea salt and freshly ground black pepper

1 chicken, about 3 lb (1.5 kg), preferably free range

MAKES 4 SERVINGS

In a large, shallow baking dish, whisk together the lemon juice, olive oil, red pepper flakes, 1 teaspoon salt, and ½ teaspoon black pepper.

Split the chicken along the breastbone, so that it can be opened like a book. Once split, turn the chicken over, skin side up, and, using the heel of your hand, crack the backbone to flatten it. With a meat pounder, pound the chicken gently to flatten it as much as possible. Place the chicken in the lemon juice mixture, and turn to coat well on both sides. Cover and let stand at room temperature for at least 1 hour or for up to 24 hours in the refrigerator.

Prepare a charcoal or gas grill for direct grilling over medium-high heat. Oil the grill rack. Or, preheat a stove-top grill pan or griddle over medium-high heat and brush with oil. Line the bottom of a heavy roasting pan with aluminum foil. Place a heavy object such as a brick in the pan.

BY GRILL: Remove the chicken from the marinade, and place it, skin side down, over the hottest part of the fire or directly over the heat elements. Place the foil-covered pan on top to keep the chicken flat against the grill. Cook the chicken, removing the weight occasionally and turning the chicken over to be sure it does not burn. It is done when the juices run clear when a thigh is pierced with a knife, about 30 minutes. It may be necessary to move the chicken to a cooler part of the grill to prevent burning.

BY GRILL PAN OR GRIDDLE: Remove the chicken from the marinade, and place it, skin side down, on the grill pan or griddle. Place the foil-covered pan on top to keep the chicken flat against the hot surface. Cook the chicken, removing the weight occasionally and turning the chicken over to be sure it does not burn. It is done when the juices run clear when a thigh is pierced with a knife, about 30 minutes. It may be necessary to reduce the heat under the grill or griddle to prevent the chicken from burning.

Transfer the chicken to a serving platter, cut into serving pieces, and serve hot or at room temperature.

The name of this recipe translates to "deviled chicken," a reference to its spiciness. In Tuscany, as the chicken cooks, it is weighted down with a *mattone* (brick), a heavy, glazed terra-cotta disk that looks like a flat pot lid. It ensures the skin of the bird turns out crisp and the meat is evenly cooked. You can find a *mattone* at some cookware shops and online sources outside Italy, or you can use a heavy roasting pan weighted with a brick with good results.

Braised Rabbit Cacciatora

Cacciatora means "hunter's style," and this dish, found on tables throughout Tuscany, is an old-fashioned preparation that once relied on the hunter bringing home a rabbit for his wife to cook. Nowadays, of course, rabbits are more often bought at the local butcher shop, though hunting remains popular in rural Tuscany. Creamy polenta is the typical accompaniment in the region's mountain areas. A cut-up chicken can be substituted and prepared in the same way.

Pat the rabbit pieces dry with paper towels and sprinkle with salt. In a large frying pan over medium heat, warm 3 tablespoons of the olive oil. Add the rabbit pieces and cook, turning as needed, until browned on both sides, about 10 minutes total. Transfer to a plate.

Add the remaining 1 tablespoon oil to the same pan over medium heat, add the onion, and sauté until it begins to soften, about 3 minutes. Add the garlic, carrots, and celery and sauté until tender, about 8 minutes.

Raise the heat to high, pour in the wine, bring to a boil, and deglaze the pan, scraping up any browned bits from the pan bottom. Cook until reduced by half, about 5 minutes. Add the tomatoes, rosemary, sage, and bay leaf and bring the mixture to a boil. Reduce the heat to low and return the rabbit pieces to the pan. Spoon the sauce over the rabbit, cover the pan, and cook gently, stirring and turning the pieces occasionally, until the meat is tender when tested with a knife, about 45 minutes longer.

Transfer the meat to a warmed serving platter and cover loosely with aluminum foil. Cook the sauce in the pan over high heat until it thickens, 5–7 minutes.

Remove and discard the bay leaf and rosemary sprig, then stir in the olives. Season to taste with salt and pepper. Pour the sauce over the rabbit and serve at once.

1 rabbit, 3 lb (1.5 kg), cut into 12 serving pieces

Sea salt and freshly ground pepper

4 tablespoons (2 fl oz/60 ml) olive oil

1 yellow onion, halved and sliced

2 cloves garlic, minced

2 large carrots, diced

1 large celery stalk, diced

½ cup (4 fl oz/125 ml) dry white wine such as Pinot Grigio

1 can (28 oz/875 g) plum (Roma) tomatoes, crushed, with juice

1 fresh rosemary sprig

2 tablespoons chopped fresh sage

1 bay leaf

1 cup (5 oz/155 g) pitted brine-cured black olives

MAKES 4 SERVINGS

Roast Chicken with Lemon and Thyme

1 chicken, about 3½ lb (1.75 kg), preferably free range

2 tablespoons olive oil

Sea salt and freshly ground pepper

1 tablespoon fresh thyme leaves

1 large or 2 small lemons

MAKES 6 SERVINGS

As with any simple dish, the quality of the ingredients for this classic Tuscan supper must be as superb as possible. Serve this chicken with simple *contorno* such as Garlic Roasted Potatoes (page 223) and braised greens. Pour a young red wine, such as Rosso di Montepulciano, or a crisp white, such as Tuscan Chardonnay.

Pat the chicken dry with paper towels. Rub the outside of the chicken with the olive oil, then sprinkle the skin and cavity generously with salt and pepper. Sprinkle the outside of the chicken with the thyme. Place the lemon in the cavity. Tuck the wings behind the back.

Position a rack in the middle of the oven and preheat to 450°F (230°C). Lightly oil a cast iron pan or small roasting pan just large enough to hold the chicken comfortably. Place the chicken, breast side up, in the pan and roast, basting occasionally with the juices, for 30 minutes. Reduce the heat to 400°F (200°C) and continue roasting until it is deep golden brown and the juices run clear when a thigh is pierced with a knife, about 30 minutes longer. An instant-read thermometer inserted into the thickest part of a thigh away from bone should register 170°F (77°C).

Transfer the chicken to a carving board and set the pan aside. Remove the lemon from the cavity and set aside. Loosely tent the chicken with aluminum foil and let rest for 10 minutes.

Using a large spoon, spoon off as much of the fat from the pan juices as possible. When the lemon is cool enough to handle, cut it in half, squeeze the juice into the pan, and discard the spent halves. Add 3 tablespoons water to the pan, place over high heat, bring to a boil, and deglaze the pan, stirring to scrape up the browned bits from the pan bottom. Cook until reduced by about one-third, about 2 minutes.

Carve the chicken and arrange the pieces on a warmed platter. Spoon the pan juices over the top and serve at once.

Balsamic Braised Chicken

Balsamic vinegar, a specialty of Modena and Reggio Emilia, and red wine color this chicken a deep mahogany as it simmers gently on the stove top. Use a medium-bodied dry red, such as a Barbera from Emilia-Romagna or a Chianti from nearby Tuscany, for the most flavorful result.

Pat the chicken pieces dry with paper towels and sprinkle with salt and pepper. In a large frying pan over medium-high heat, warm the olive oil. Add the chicken and garlic and cook the chicken, turning as needed, until well browned on both sides, about 20 minutes total. Adjust the heat as needed to prevent the garlic from burning.

Tip the pan and spoon off the excess fat. Add the rosemary sprig, wine, and vinegar and bring to a simmer. Reduce the heat to medium, cover, and cook, turning the chicken pieces occasionally, until the chicken is opaque throughout when tested with a knife, about 15 minutes. Transfer the chicken pieces to a warmed platter, cover, and keep warm.

Raise the heat to high, bring the liquid to a boil, and cook until the liquid is reduced and has thickened, creating a flavorful pan sauce. Remove and discard the garlic cloves and the rosemary sprig. Taste and adjust the seasoning.

Spoon the sauce over the chicken and serve at once.

1 chicken, about 3 lb (1.5 kg), preferably free range, cut into 8 serving pieces

Sea salt and freshly ground pepper

2 tablespoons olive oil

2 cloves garlic, unpeeled

1 fresh rosemary sprig, 3 inches (7.5 cm) long

1 cup (8 fl oz/250 ml) dry red wine such as Barbera

¼ cup (2 fl oz/60 ml) balsamic vinegar

MAKES 4 SERVINGS

Braised Pork Chops

4 pork loin chops, each about 1 inch (2.5 cm) thick

Sea salt and freshly ground pepper

2 tablespoons olive oil

½ cup (4 fl oz/125 ml) dry Marsala wine

½ cup (4 fl oz/125 ml) fresh orange juice

Grated zest of 1 orange

MAKES 6 SERVINGS

Marsala, traditionally produced in western Sicily, is generally thought of as a fine dessert wine, but it is also excellent for cooking. A blended wine with a rich amber color, it comes in three basic styles: dry, or *secco*; semidry, or *semisecco*; and sweet, or *dolce*. Sweet Marsala is best used in or as an accompaniment to desserts, while young, dry Marsala makes a superb kitchen wine for savory dishes, as in this quick and easy *secondo*.

Pat the pork chops dry with paper towels. Sprinkle the chops with salt and pepper. In a large frying pan over medium heat, warm the olive oil. Add the chops and cook, turning once, until browned on both sides, about 10 minutes total. Reduce the heat to medium-low and continue to cook until the chops are tender but still pale pink and juicy when cut into the center with a knife, about 15 minutes. Transfer to a plate and keep warm.

Add the Marsala to the pan and raise the heat to medium-high. Cook, stirring, until the wine is reduced and slightly thickened, about 2 minutes. Add the orange juice and bring to a simmer. Return the chops to the pan and sprinkle with the orange zest. Cook, basting the chops with the pan juices, for 2 minutes.

Transfer the chops to a warmed platter or warmed plates, spoon the sauce over the top, and serve.

Meatballs in Sugo

This recipe makes a generous amount of *sugo,* or "sauce," so you will have plenty left over to serve with pasta as a *primo* or to save for another meal. Meatballs, known variously as *polpette* and *polpettine,* depending on their size, or as *purpette* in Calabrian dialect, are prepared this way throughout southern Italy.

In a small bowl, mix the crumbled bread and milk and let stand for 10 minutes.

In a large bowl, combine the beef, veal, pork, eggs, Parmigiano-Reggiano, parsley, garlic, 1½ teaspoons salt, and a few grinds of pepper. Squeeze the bread with your hands to remove the excess moisture and discard the liquid. Add the bread to the meat mixture and mix gently until combined.

Rinse your hands with water but do not dry them. Shape the meat into 2-inch (5-cm) balls, rolling them lightly between your moistened palms. As the balls are made, set them aside on a large platter or tray.

In a frying pan large enough to hold all of the meatballs in a single layer, warm the olive oil over medium-high heat. Add the meatballs and cook, turning them occasionally, until crisp and browned on all sides, about 15 minutes. Transfer the meatballs to a plate and drain off all but 2 tablespoons of the fat from the pan.

To make the sauce, return the pan to medium heat, add the onion, and sauté until softened and golden, about 5 minutes. Stir in the garlic and sauté until fragrant, about 30 seconds. Add the crushed tomatoes and their juice, stir well, and deglaze the pan, scraping up any brown bits from the pan bottom. Season with salt and pepper and bring to a simmer. Cook until the sauce thickens, about 20 minutes. Stir in the basil.

Return the meatballs to the pan and cook, basting them often with the sauce, until hot and cooked through, about 10 minutes. Transfer the meatballs to a warmed platter and spoon some of the sauce over them; reserve the remaining sauce for another use. Serve at once.

3 or 4 slices coarse country bread, crusts removed and crumbled (about 1½ cups/ 3 oz/90 g)

½ cup (4 fl oz/125 ml) whole milk

1 pound (500 g) ground (minced) beef chuck

½ pound (250 g) ground (minced) veal

½ pound (250 g) ground (minced) pork

2 large eggs, lightly beaten

1 cup (4 oz/125 g) grated Parmigiano-Reggiano cheese

¼ cup (⅓ oz/10 g) finely chopped fresh flat-leaf (Italian) parsley

1 clove garlic, minced

Sea salt and freshly ground pepper

2 tablespoons olive oil

For the sauce

1 small yellow onion, finely chopped

1 clove garlic, minced

2 cans (28 oz/875 g each) plum (Roma) tomatoes, crushed

Sea salt and freshly ground pepper

3 or 4 fresh basil leaves, torn into small pieces

MAKES 6–8 SERVINGS

Herb-Roasted Pork Loin

4 large cloves garlic

2 tablespoons fresh rosemary leaves

2 tablespoons fresh sage leaves

2 teaspoons crushed fennel seeds

Sea salt and freshly ground pepper

1 bone-in pork loin roast, about 5 lb (2.5 kg)

4 tablespoons (2 fl oz/60 ml) olive oil

1 yellow onion, halved and sliced

1 cup (8 fl oz/250 ml) dry white wine such as Pinot Grigio

MAKES 8 SERVINGS

Preheat the oven to 325°F (165°C).

Using a chef's knife, very finely chop together the garlic, rosemary, and sage. Transfer to a small bowl, add the fennel seeds, season with salt and pepper, and mix well. Make slits ¹/₂ inch (12 mm) deep all over the pork roast and insert some of the mixture into each slit. Rub the roast with the remaining seasoning, then rub with 2 tablespoons of the olive oil. Place the meat in a roasting pan just large enough to hold it.

Roast the meat for 1 hour. In a bowl, toss the onion slices with the remaining 2 tablespoons olive oil and scatter them around the meat. Continue to roast until an instant-read thermometer inserted into the thickest part of the roast away from the bone registers 155°F (68°C), or the meat is pale pink when cut into at the center, about 1¹/₄ hours longer. Transfer to a warmed platter and cover loosely with aluminum foil to keep warm. Let rest for 15 minutes before carving.

Meanwhile, pour off most of the fat in the roasting pan and place the pan over medium-low heat. Add the wine and deglaze the pan, stirring to scrape up any browned bits from the pan bottom. Simmer until the sauce is slightly reduced.

Carve the roast and arrange on a warmed platter. Spoon the pan sauce over the pork and serve at once.

In Tuscany, the word *arista* is used for a pork roast seasoned with rosemary, fennel, and/or other herbs and garlic. According to legend, the pork roast received its name in the fifteenth century, when it was served to a group of visiting Greek bishops who declared it *aristos*—"the best." But most food scholars dismiss that story, pointing out that the fourteenth-century Italian author Franco Sacchetti referred to pork roast as *arista* in one of his novels.

Sausages with Greens and Garlic

Sea salt

1 lb (500 g) broccoli rabe, trimmed

1 lb (500 g) Italian sweet fennel sausages

4 large cloves garlic, thinly sliced

Pinch of red pepper flakes

MAKES 4 SERVINGS

Bring a large pot three-fourths full of water to a rolling boil and add about 1 tablespoon salt. Add the broccoli rabe and cook, testing often, until the stems are softened but not fully cooked, about 5 minutes. Drain and cool under cold running water, then drain again. Set aside.

In a large frying pan over medium heat, combine the sausages and ½ cup (4 fl oz/125 ml) water. Cover the pan and bring the water to a simmer. Cook until the water evaporates and the sausages begin to sizzle and turn brown, about 10 minutes. Uncover the pan and continue to cook, turning the sausages as needed, until lightly browned on all sides, about 5 minutes longer. Transfer the sausages to a plate and cover to keep warm.

Add the garlic and red pepper flakes to the pan drippings and sauté over medium heat until the garlic is lightly golden and fragrant, 1–2 minutes. Add the broccoli rabe and stir well. Return the sausages to the pan, cover, and cook until the broccoli rabe is tender and the sausages are cooked through, about 5 minutes.

Transfer the sausages and greens to a warmed platter and serve at once.

Salsicce e verdure, "sausages and greens," is a favorite combination not only in Campania but throughout southern Italy. Pork sausages seasoned with fennel seeds are the most popular fresh sausages in Campania, but you can substitute the fiery-hot pork sausages of neighboring Calabria or another fresh sausage for some or all of the fennel sausages.

Pork Loin Braised in Milk

In this recipe, known as *maiale al latte*, a boneless pork loin is slowly braised in milk until the meat is tender and the milk is reduced to a rich, flavorful, dense sauce. Similar preparations are popular in the Veneto, Tuscany, and Piedmont. Serve the pork with Garlic Roasted Potatoes (page 223).

Pat the pork dry with paper towels. Sprinkle the pork generously on all sides with salt and pepper. In a Dutch oven or other large, heavy pot over medium heat, melt the butter. Add the pork and cook, turning as needed, until well browned on all sides, about 15 minutes total. Watch carefully to make sure the butter does not burn, adjusting the heat as necessary.

Add the milk and bring to a simmer. Cover the pot, reduce the heat to medium-low, and cook until the pork is very tender when pierced with a fork, 1$\frac{1}{2}$ to 2 hours. Transfer the pork to a warmed platter and cover to keep warm.

Bring the liquid to a boil over high heat, reduce the heat to medium, and simmer until thickened slightly and lightly browned, about 5 minutes. Using a large spoon, skim off the fat from the surface.

Slice the pork and arrange the slices on the platter, spooning the sauce over the slices or passing it at the table. Serve at once.

1 boneless pork loin roast, about 3 lb (1.5 kg)

Sea salt and freshly ground pepper

2 tablespoons unsalted butter

2 cups (16 fl oz/500 ml) whole milk

MAKES 6 SERVINGS

TUSCANY

Bistecca alla Fiorentina

This famed Florentine steak is the exception to the general rule that although Tuscans eat meat often, the portions are relatively small. These steaks are gargantuan—each one large enough for two generous portions. Traditionally, the meat came from the now-dwindling herds of Chianina cattle that graze in Val di Chiana, between Arezzo and Florence. Today, any high-quality beef is used, but the cooking of the meat is still subject to a few easy, but stringent, rules. Each steak, for two people, must weigh between 1¼ and 1¾ pounds (625 and 875 g), be about an inch (2.5 cm) thick, and contain its T-bone, fillet, and tenderloin. You are never asked how you want your meat cooked, for an authentic *bistecca* is always well browned on the outside and rare inside. A fresh juniper branch is usually added to the coals to scent the meat.

Take the meat out of the refrigerator about 2 hours before cooking it. Prepare a charcoal or gas grill for direct grilling over medium-high heat. Oil the grill rack.

Rub the meat on both sides with the olive oil. (Do not add any salt at this point.)

Using tongs, lay the steak directly over the hottest part of the fire or the heat elements about 5 inches (13 cm) above the fire. Cook until browned and juicy on the first side, 5–7 minutes. Turn the steak and sprinkle with salt. Cook on the second side until browned and juicy, 5–7 minutes longer. Then turn the meat over once again and sprinkle with salt

Transfer the steak to a cutting board and season generously with pepper. Garnish with the lemon wedges and arugula and serve at once.

1 T-bone or porterhouse steak, cut from the rib with the bone, 1½ lb (750 g)

2 tablespoons extra-virgin olive oil

Sea salt and freshly ground pepper

Lemon wedges, for garnish

1½ cups (1½ oz/45 g) baby arugula, for garnish

MAKES 2 SERVINGS

Barolo-Braised Pot Roast

1 beef pot roast, about 4 lb (2 kg)

2 cloves garlic, thinly sliced

2 oz (60 g) thick-cut pancetta, chopped

3 tablespoons olive oil

Sea salt and freshly ground pepper

1 cup (8 fl oz/250 ml) Barolo or other dry red wine

6 red onions, thinly sliced

2 carrots, chopped

1 celery stalk, sliced

2 tablespoons chopped fresh flat-leaf (Italian) parsley

2 cups (16 fl oz/500 ml) beef stock (page 273)

2 cups (12 oz/375 g) canned plum (Roma) tomato purée

MAKES 8 SERVINGS

Make small slits about ¹/₂ inch (12 mm) deep all over the roast. Insert some of the garlic and pancetta into each slit.

In a Dutch oven or other large, heavy pot over medium heat, warm the olive oil. Add the beef and brown well on all sides, about 15 minutes. Using a large spoon, spoon off as much fat as possible, then season the beef with salt and pepper.

Add the wine and cook over medium heat until most of the liquid evaporates, about 2 minutes.

Add the onions, carrots, celery, parsley, stock, and tomato purée, cover partially, and bring to a simmer. Reduce the heat to low and cook the meat, turning occasionally, until tender, about 3 hours.

Transfer the meat to a warmed plate and cover to keep warm. Using a slotted spoon, lift out the solids from the pot juices and place in a food processor or blender. Purée until smooth. Return the purée to the liquid in the pot and reheat gently. If the gravy is too thin, raise the heat and boil to reduce it slightly. Taste and adjust the seasoning.

Slice the beef and arrange on a warmed platter. Spoon some of the sauce on top, and pass the remaining sauce at the table. Serve at once.

In Piedmont, pot roast tender enough to cut with a fork is a common cool-weather dish. The plentiful onion gravy in which the beef simmers is also excellent over soft polenta or mashed potatoes. Use a fine Barolo for cooking, and serve the same wine with the meal. A similar dish is served in Tuscany, where a Chianti or Brunello di Montalcino is used.

Braciole

Braciole, rolled slices of beef or veal, are an inventive way to make the most of a small amount of meat. Filled with a savory stuffing and slowly simmered in a tasty tomato sauce, thin slices of a less-than-tender cut take on a substantial appearance. The sauce, flavored with the meat juices, is often tossed with pasta, such as ziti or rigatoni, and served as a first course before the meat is served.

One at a time, place the beef slices between 2 sheets of plastic wrap and pound gently with a meat pounder until 1/4 inch (6 mm) thick. Sprinkle the pounded slices on both sides with salt and pepper. Lay a slice of prosciutto and a piece of cheese on each beef slice. Sprinkle evenly with the pine nuts, raisins, and garlic. Roll up the slices, tucking in the ends, then tie the rolls at 1-inch (2.5-cm) intervals with kitchen string.

In a large frying pan over medium heat, warm the olive oil. Add the beef rolls and cook, turning as needed, until browned on all sides, about 15 minutes total. Add the onion and sauté until tender, about 5 minutes longer. Pour in the wine and deglaze the pan, stirring to scrape up any browned bits from the pan bottom, about 2 minutes.

Add the stock and tomatoes and season with salt and pepper. Reduce the heat to low, cover, and simmer, turning the rolls occasionally, until the beef is tender when pierced with a knife, 1 1/2–2 hours. Check from time to time to see if the sauce is becoming too dry and add water if needed.

Uncover, scatter the parsley and basil evenly over the rolls, and cook for 2 minutes longer. Transfer the rolls to a cutting board and cut into thick slices, removing and discarding the kitchen string. Transfer the slices to warmed plates, spoon the sauce over the top, and serve at once.

1 lb (500 g) boneless beef top round, cut into 4 thin slices each about 1/3 inch (9 mm) thick

Sea salt and freshly ground pepper

4 slices prosciutto

1 thick slice provolone cheese, about 2 oz (60 g), cut into 4 equal pieces

2 tablespoons pine nuts

2 tablespoons raisins

1 clove garlic, minced

1/4 cup (2 fl oz/60 ml) olive oil

1 yellow onion, chopped

1 cup (8 fl oz/250 ml) dry red wine such as Barolo

1 cup (8 fl oz/250 ml) beef stock (page 273)

4 large fresh tomatoes, peeled, seeded, and chopped, or 1 can (15 oz/470 g) plum (Roma) tomatoes, chopped with juice

1 tablespoon chopped fresh flat-leaf (Italian) parsley

3 or 4 fresh basil leaves, torn into small pieces

MAKES 4 SERVINGS

Braised Short Ribs

8 beef short ribs, about 10 oz (315 g) each

Sea salt and freshly ground pepper

2 tablespoons olive oil

2 yellow onions, chopped

2 carrots, chopped

2 celery stalks, chopped

2 cups (16 fl oz/500 ml) dry red wine such as Barolo

1 can (28 oz/875 g) plum (Roma) tomatoes, chopped, with juice

2 cups (16 fl oz/500 ml) beef stock (page 273) or chicken stock (page 274)

2 fresh rosemary sprigs

MAKES 8 SERVINGS

Pat the ribs dry with paper towels and sprinkle generously with salt and pepper. In a Dutch oven or other large, heavy pot over medium-high heat, warm the olive oil. Add as many ribs as will fit in a single layer and cook, turning as needed, until well browned on all sides, about 10 minutes total. Transfer the browned ribs to a bowl, and brown the remaining ribs in the same way. Spoon off all but 2 tablespoons of the fat from the pot.

Add the onions, carrots, and celery to the pot and sauté until tender, about 10 minutes. Add the wine, bring to a simmer, and deglaze the pot, stirring to scrape up any up any browned bits from the pot bottom. Add the tomatoes, stock, and rosemary sprigs and bring the liquid to a simmer. Return the ribs to the pot and bring the liquid back to a simmer. Reduce the heat to low, cover, and cook the ribs, turning them occasionally, until the meat is very tender and falling off the bone, about 2$\frac{1}{2}$ hours. Transfer to a warmed bowl and serve at once.

Short ribs are not a cut you will find in Italy, but this method of slowly braising beef in red wine is typical, especially in the north, where beef is more commonly eaten. The ribs can be cooked and refrigerated for up to 2 days before serving them. This makes a big batch. If you have leftover ribs and sauce, you can bone the ribs, shred the meat, and serve the meat and sauce over pasta or creamy polenta.

Osso Buco with Gremolata

In this classic Lombardian recipe, veal shanks are slowly braised to a melting tenderness. The rich marrow of the bones is as delectable as the meat itself. Pass out small spoons at the table so diners can scoop out every delicious bit. The traditional accompaniments are *gremolata*, a parsley and lemon relish that provides a welcome counterpoint to so much richness, and golden risotto perfumed with saffron (page 144).

Put the flour in a wide, shallow dish and season with salt and pepper. Pat the veal shanks dry with paper towels. Lightly dust the veal shanks with the seasoned flour, shaking off the excess. In a large, heavy frying pan over medium-high heat, warm 1/2 cup (4 fl oz/120 ml) of the olive oil. Working in batches if necessary to avoid crowding the pan, add the shanks to the pan and cook, turning once, until well browned on both sides, about 8 minutes total. Transfer the shanks to a plate.

Return the pan to medium heat, add the onion, carrot, celery, and garlic, and sauté until softened, 3–4 minutes. Add the wine and deglaze the pan, stirring to scrape up the browned bits from the pan bottom. Raise the heat to high and cook until the liquid has thickened and is reduced by half, 3–4 minutes. Add the tomatoes and stock and bring to a boil. Reduce the heat to low, return the veal shanks to the pan, cover, and simmer, turning occasionally, for 1 hour. Uncover and cook until the veal is tender, about 30 minutes longer.

While the veal cooks, make the *gremolata*. In a small bowl, stir together the parsley, lemon zest, and garlic.

Divide the veal shanks among individual plates. Spoon the pan sauce over the top, sprinkle with the *gremolata,* and serve at once.

3/4 cup (4 oz/125 g) all-purpose (plain) flour

Sea salt and freshly ground pepper

6 veal shanks, about 6 lb (3 kg) total weight, each about 1 inch (2.5 cm) thick

3/4 cup (6 fl oz/180 ml) extra-virgin olive oil

1 yellow onion, chopped

1 carrot, diced

1 celery stalk, diced

2 cloves garlic, minced

1 1/2 cups (12 fl oz/375 ml) dry red wine such as Barolo

1 cup (6 oz/185 g) peeled, seeded, and chopped fresh or canned tomatoes

5 cups (40 fl oz/l.25 l) beef stock (page 273)

For the gremolata

1/2 cup (3/4 oz/20 g) minced fresh flat-leaf (Italian) parsley

Grated zest of 1 lemon

2 cloves garlic, minced

MAKES 6–8 SERVINGS

LOMBARDY

Veal Chops Milanese

4 thin veal rib chops

Sea salt and freshly ground pepper

2 eggs

1 cup (4 oz/125 g) plain fine dried bread crumbs

4 tablespoons (2 oz/60 g) unsalted butter

2 tablespoons extra-virgin olive oil

2 cups (2 oz/60 g) arugula (rocket), tough stems removed

Lemon wedges for garnish

MAKES 4 SERVINGS

One at a time, place the veal chops between 2 sheets of plastic wrap and pound gently with a meat pounder, avoiding the bones, until about ¼ inch (6 mm) thick. Season the chops on both sides with salt and pepper. In a shallow bowl, beat the eggs until blended. Spread the bread crumbs on a plate. One at a time, dip the chops in the egg, coating completely, and then in the bread crumbs. With your fingertips, pat the crumbs into the chops to help them adhere. Place on a rack to dry for 10 minutes.

In a large frying pan over medium heat, melt the butter with 1 tablespoon oil. Add the chops and cook, turning once, until browned and crisp on the exterior yet still pink at the center when tested with a knife, about 6 minutes total.

Meanwhile, in a bowl, toss the arugula with the remaining 1 tablespoon oil. Season with salt and pepper and toss again. Set aside.

Transfer the chops to warmed plates, divide the arugula among the plates, and garnish with the lemon wedges. Serve at once.

A no-frills salad of peppery arugula dressed with a fruity olive oil is the perfect complement to the buttery, crisp-fried veal chops. If your frying pan is not large enough to hold all of the chops at one time, cook them two at a time, or use two pans. Pork chops are delicious prepared the same way.

Saltimbocca alla Romana

12 veal scallops, about 1 lb (500 g) total weight, each about ¼ inch (6 mm) thick

12 very thin prosciutto slices, about ¼ lb (125 g) total weight

12 fresh sage leaves

All-purpose (plain) flour for dusting

2 tablespoons unsalted butter

Sea salt and freshly ground pepper

½ cup (4 fl oz/125 ml) dry white wine such as Pinot Grigio

MAKES 4 SERVINGS

One at a time, place the veal scallops between 2 sheets of plastic wrap and pound gently with a meat pounder to flatten them somewhat; they do not need to be paper-thin. Trim the prosciutto slices so they are slightly shorter than the veal slices. Lay a slice of prosciutto on top of each slice of veal, and then top with a sage leaf. Secure the layers together with a toothpick.

Spread the flour in a shallow dish. In a large frying pan over medium heat, melt the butter. Lightly dust the veal bundles with the flour, shaking off the excess. Working in batches, place the veal, prosciutto side down, in the melted butter and brown gently, about 1 minute. Turn the veal and brown the other side, about 1 minute. Season with pepper and, if the prosciutto you are using is not very salty, season with salt as well. Reduce the heat to medium-low and cook until the veal is a light golden brown and cooked through, 4–5 minutes. Transfer the veal to a warmed platter and tent loosely with aluminum foil to keep warm. Repeat with the remaining veal bundles.

When all of the veal bundles have been cooked and removed from the pan, raise the heat to medium-high, add the wine, and bring to a boil. Deglaze the pan, scraping up any browned bits from the pan bottom.

Pour the hot pan sauce over the veal and serve at once.

Saltimbocca means "jump in the mouth," a tip-off that this dish is particularly tasty. Elsewhere in Italy, *saltimbocca* can mean other recipes, but qualified by *alla romana*, it refers to thin-sliced veal, prosciutto, and fresh sage, a staple herb of the Roman garden. Some recipes call for folding the layered ingredients in half, while others shape them into small, neat *involtini* (rolls). But the standard procedure, given here, is to secure the sage to the stacked veal and prosciutto with a toothpick. Pour a big-flavored white wine at the table.

Veal Piccata

The term *piccata* refers to a thin veal slice, which is what Lombardian cooks use to prepare this traditional Milanese dish. It is the perfect addition to a spring menu, served with fresh asparagus or English peas as a *contorno*. If you like, add 1 tablespoon capers, rinsed and chopped, to the sauce when you stir in the parsley.

In a wide, shallow dish, stir together the flour, 1 teaspoon salt, and a few grinds of pepper and then spread the seasoned flour in the dish. In a large frying pan over medium-high heat, melt the butter with the olive oil. While the butter is melting, lightly dust as many of the veal scallops with the seasoned flour as will fit in the pan in a single layer, shaking off the excess. Place them in the pan and cook until nicely browned on the first side, about 2 minutes. Turn the veal and brown on the second side, about 1 minute longer. Transfer the veal to a warmed platter and cover to keep warm. Cook the remaining veal in the same way.

When all of the veal slices have been cooked and removed from the pan, raise the heat to medium-high, add the wine and lemon juice, and bring to a boil. Deglaze the pan, scraping up any browned bits from the pan bottom, and cook until the liquid is slightly thickened, about 3 minutes. Stir in the parsley.

Pour the hot pan sauce over the veal and serve at once.

3 tablespoons all-purpose (plain) flour

Sea salt and freshly ground pepper

2 tablespoons unsalted butter

1 tablespoon olive oil

1 lb (500 g) veal scallops, each about ¼ inch (6 mm) thick

⅓ cup (3 fl oz/80 ml) dry white wine such as Pinot Grigio

2 teaspoons fresh lemon juice

1 tablespoon chopped fresh flat-leaf (Italian) parsley

MAKES 4 SERVINGS

Grilled Marinated Lamb Chops

Wandering the winding streets of Umbrian hill towns will lead you to many trattorias where roaring fireplaces are still used to grill steaks, chicken, sausages, and these simple rib chops, bathed with an olive oil and garlic marinade. The crisp, brown chops are best when eaten sizzling hot off the fire, so the Italians call them *scottadito*, or "burned fingers."

In a small bowl, stir together the garlic, rosemary, olive oil, and a few grinds of pepper. Place the lamb chops in a shallow dish and brush them with the olive oil mixture, coating both sides of the chops. Cover and refrigerate for at least 2 hours or up to overnight.

Prepare a charcoal or gas grill for direct grilling over high heat. Oil the grill rack.

Using tongs, place the chops over the hottest part of the fire or directly over the heat elements and grill, turning once, until browned and crisp on the exterior and medium-rare at the center when tested with a knife, 7–10 minutes total.

Transfer the chops to warmed plates and sprinkle with salt. Garnish with the lemon slices, if using, and serve at once.

3 large cloves garlic, minced

2 tablespoons chopped fresh rosemary

¼ cup (2 fl oz/60 ml) olive oil

Sea salt and freshly ground pepper

8–12 lamb rib chops, trimmed of fat

Lemon slices for garnish (optional)

MAKES 4 SERVINGS

Braised Lamb Shanks

6 small lamb shanks, about ³⁄₄ lb (375 g) each

Sea salt and freshly ground pepper

2 tablespoons olive oil

2 cloves garlic, thinly sliced

1 tablespoon chopped fresh rosemary

1 small dried red chile, crushed, or pinch of red pepper flakes

¹⁄₂ cup (4 fl oz/125 ml) dry white wine such as Pinot Grigio

1¹⁄₂ cups (12 fl oz/375 ml) beef stock (page 273)

1 cup (6 oz/185 g) peeled, seeded, and chopped fresh or canned tomatoes

¹⁄₂ cup (2¹⁄₂ oz/75 g) Gaeta or other Mediterranean-style black olives

1 tablespoon chopped fresh flat-leaf (Italian) parsley

MAKES 6 SERVINGS

Pat the lamb shanks dry with paper towels. Season the shanks generously with salt and pepper. In a Dutch oven or other heavy pot large enough to hold the shanks in a single layer, warm the olive oil over medium heat. Add the lamb shanks and cook, turning as needed, until well browned on all sides, about 15 minutes total. Tip the pot and spoon off the fat with a large spoon.

Add the garlic, rosemary, and chile and sauté over medium heat for 1 minute. Add the wine and bring to a simmer. Add the stock and tomatoes, reduce the heat to low, cover, and simmer the shanks, turning them occasionally, until the meat is fork-tender, about 1¹⁄₂ hours.

Stir in the olives and heat through. Divide the lamb among individual plates, spoon the sauce over the lamb, and sprinkle with the parsley. Serve at once.

The Abruzzo is a region on the Adriatic coast of Italy where, for centuries, raising sheep was the primary occupation. Every year, Abruzzese shepherds drove their flocks to the southeast to spend the cold months grazing along a more temperate part of the coast. In the springtime, the migration would occur again, but in reverse. Over time, towns were built along the shepherds' route to accommodate their needs. This is just the sort of dish those shepherds would have enjoyed.

Contorni

About Contorni

The vegetable dishes that accompany the *secondo* are known as *contorni*, or "contours," because they round out and define the menu. Never an afterthought, they are flavorful preparations that reflect the seasonal best of the garden and market, sharing the table with meat, fish, or poultry.

Italians love to grow, buy, and forage for vegetables, from tender field greens and wild mushrooms to zucchini (courgettes), green beans, eggplants (aubergines), artichokes, asparagus, and tomatoes. Home cooks mark the seasons by preparing whatever vegetables are at their peak and serving them as *contorni*. Often only a handful of distinctive flavoring ingredients are used, so that the unique character of the vegetable can be appreciated.

To a non-Italian, many vegetable *contorni*, as they are served in Italy, seem overcooked. For example, the beans in Romano Beans with Tomatoes and Pancetta (page 217) are cooked until they are quite soft, not tender-crisp. Italians prefer not only the soft texture traditional to such preparations, but also the deeply infused flavors that result from relatively long cooking. To this end, many *contorni* are prepared well in advance of the meal, so their flavors can meld as they cool, and they are served at room temperature. If a *contorno* is made with olive oil, the cook will treat the dish to a light drizzle of extra-virgin oil just before serving, for added flavor and visual appeal.

PLANNING THE CONTORNI

Depending on the size of the group, the occasion, and the whim of the cook, a full Italian meal may include a variety of contrasting, yet complementary *contorni*. Each of them is usually presented in a separate bowl or platter for passing family style at the table. These often include a starchy side dish, such as potatoes, polenta, or beans; a simply prepared seasonal vegetable or two; and a salad.

When deciding on which *contorni* to serve, think about the ingredients that were used to prepare the *secondo piatto* they will accompany. While most of the *contorni* in this chapter will complement most *secondi*, you should always try to avoid duplicating flavors, instead choosing side dishes that add contrasting textures and flavors to the plate.

A hearty braised dish that includes tomatoes, such as Meatballs in Sugo (page 185), would pair better with greens, such as Swiss Chard with Raisins and Pine Nuts (page 227), than with Romano Beans with Tomatoes and Pancetta (page 217). Conversely, the Romano bean dish would be an ideal match for roast pork loin or veal chops, the pancetta echoing the meaty flavor of the *secondo*. A simple grilled fish or shellfish *secondo* will pair well with the briny, assertive flavors of Broccolini with Garlic and Anchovies (page 224). With richer, more substantial *secondi*, serve at least one acidic *contorno*, such as Fennel, Orange, and Olive Salad (page 220) or Peperonata (page 218). In general, the best rule of thumb for coming up with a menu is that the heavier and richer the *secondo*, the lighter and more straightforward the *contorno* should be.

Consider the weather and the time of year as well. Visit a local farmers' market or a good produce vendor to get a sense of which vegetables are in season. To round out a hearty fall or winter menu, a *contorno* of Roasted Cauliflower with Lemon and Olives (page 214) would be an ideal choice, as would a baked *contorno*, such as Jerusalem Artichoke Gratin (page 219), Polenta with Gorgonzola (page 228), or simple, satisfying Garlic Roasted Potatoes (page 223). Stuffed Artichokes (page 234) and Asparagus Milanese (page 239) are bright, fresh options for spring meals. In the summer, when zucchini (courgettes) from the market or your garden are at their peak and sweet peppers (capsicums) are abundant and economical, serve Zucchini with Olive Oil, Garlic, and Basil (page 213) or Peperonata (page 218).

MORE THAN SIDE DISHES

Contorni need not be thought of merely as accompaniments. More substantial preparations, such as Fried Polenta with Wild Mushrooms (page 229), Warm Borlotti Bean and Radicchio Salad (page 230), and Stuffed Artichokes (page 234), can be served as first courses or light main courses.

A selection of *contorni*, perhaps augmented with a pasta dish or an assortment of sliced cured meats or cheeses, is ideal for an open house or brunch buffet. Many *contorni* also pack well for picnicking and outdoor entertaining. Such dishes as Zucchini with Olive Oil, Garlic, and Basil; Roasted Cauliflower with Lemon and Olives; Romano Beans with Tomatoes and Pancetta; Peperonata; and Broccolini with Garlic and Anchovies work particularly well. Transport them in a cooler and allow them to come to room temperature before serving.

Most cooked *contorni* keep well in the refrigerator for a day or more. Consider doubling the recipe or preparing a little extra, so you have leftovers to pack for lunch the following day or to serve at another meal.

Zucchini with Olive Oil, Garlic, and Basil

This simple vegetable side dish makes the most of a few essential Italian ingredients: olive oil, garlic, and fresh sweet basil. Mushrooms and zucchini are two of the best candidates for cooking this way. You can substitute fresh flat-leaf (Italian) parsley for the basil.

Trim the stem ends of each zucchini. Cut in half lengthwise and then cut crosswise into slices about 1/2 inch (12 mm) thick.

In a large, heavy frying pan over medium heat, warm the olive oil. Add the garlic and sauté until fragrant and golden, about 2 minutes. Add the zucchini and cook, stirring often, until the zucchini are tender, about 5 minutes. Sprinkle the basil over the zucchini toward the end of the cooking time.

Season to taste with salt and pepper, transfer to a warmed serving dish, and serve at once.

NOTE: These garlicky zucchini not only make a flavorful side dish but double nicely as a pasta sauce. Boil 1 lb (500 g) of pasta, such as penne or rigatoni, according to package directions. Drain and add to the frying pan. Toss with the zucchini. Serve with plenty of grated Parmigiano-Reggiano.

2 lb (1 kg) zucchini (courgettes)

1/3 cup (3 fl oz/80 ml) extra-virgin olive oil

2 cloves garlic, finely chopped

2 tablespoons finely chopped fresh basil

Sea salt and freshly ground pepper

MAKES 4 SERVINGS

Roasted Cauliflower with Lemon and Olives

**1 head cauliflower, about
1½ lb (750 g)**

⅓ cup (3 fl oz/80 ml) olive oil

Zest of 1 lemon

**½ cup (75 g) pitted green
olives, such as Cerignola,
roughly chopped**

**Sea salt and freshly ground
pepper**

MAKES 4 SERVINGS

Trim the cauliflower and cut it into 2-inch (5-cm) florets.

Position a rack in the middle of the oven and preheat to 400°F (200°C). In a shallow roasting pan large enough to hold the cauliflower pieces in a single layer, combine the cauliflower, olive oil, lemon zest, and olives. Season with salt and pepper and toss to mix well. Spread the ingredients in a single layer.

Bake the cauliflower, stirring occasionally, until browned and tender when pierced with a fork, about 15 minutes. Transfer to a warmed serving dish and serve at once.

In this recipe, mild cauliflower is the perfect foil for savory olives and tangy lemon zest. You can substitute Romanesco cauliflower, sometimes called Romanesco broccoli, for the white cauliflower. These eye-catching members of the big cabbage family are a beautiful shade of lime green and have cone-shaped florets that look like exotic seashells. They are slightly sweeter and more tender than white cauliflower. You'll find Romanesco cauliflower in the market from late September through November.

Romano Beans with Tomatoes and Pancetta

Romano beans, long, flat, wide green beans sometimes labeled Italian beans, are the most common variety of snap bean in Italy. If you cannot find them in your market, regular green beans can be substituted.

In a saucepan large enough to hold the beans, cook the pancetta over medium heat, stirring often, until crisp, about 5 minutes. Using a slotted spoon, transfer the pancetta to paper towels to drain.

Add the olive oil to the fat remaining in the pan and heat over medium heat. Add the green onions and sauté until softened, about 3 minutes. Add the tomatoes and simmer, stirring occasionally, until they reduce slightly, about 10 minutes.

Stir in the beans and sprinkle with salt and a few grinds of pepper. Reduce the heat to low, cover, and cook until the beans are tender, about 15 minutes. Check often and add a few tablespoons of hot water if the sauce looks dry. (The dish can be prepared up to this point, cooled, covered, and refrigerated, and then reheated gently the next day. It will taste even better the second day.)

Stir in the pancetta, transfer to a warmed serving dish, and sprinkle with the parsley. Serve at once.

2 oz (60 g) pancetta, chopped

1 tablespoon olive oil

3 green (spring) onions, including tender green tops, thinly sliced

½ lb (250 g) fresh tomatoes, peeled, seeded, and chopped, or 1 can (14 oz/440 g) plum (Roma) tomatoes, coarsely chopped, with juice

1 lb (500 g) romano beans or green beans, ends trimmed

Sea salt and freshly ground pepper

1 tablespoon finely chopped fresh flat-leaf (Italian) parsley

MAKES 6 SERVINGS

Peperonata

¼ cup (2 fl oz/60 ml) extra-virgin olive oil

1 yellow onion, halved and thinly sliced

1 clove garlic, thinly sliced

4 red, yellow, and/or green bell peppers (capsicums), halved, seeded, and thinly sliced crosswise

2 fresh tomatoes, peeled, seeded, and chopped, or 1 cup (6 oz/185 g) seeded and chopped canned plum (Roma) tomatoes

Sea salt and freshly ground pepper

2 tablespoons chopped fresh basil or flat-leaf (Italian) parsley

MAKES 4 SERVINGS

In a large frying pan over medium heat, warm the olive oil. Add the onion and sauté until tender, about 5 minutes. Add the garlic and sauté until fragrant, about 1 minute longer.

Stir in the bell peppers and cook, stirring occasionally, just until they begin to brown, about 10 minutes. Add the tomatoes and cook until the peppers are tender and the sauce has thickened, about 20 minutes longer.

Season with salt and pepper, transfer to a serving dish, and sprinkle with the basil. Serve hot or at room temperature.

NOTE: *Peperonata* also makes an excellent antipasti dish. Serve with plenty of toasted, garlicky crostini.

Peppers are grown all over Italy, including the northern region of Piedmont, where they are roasted for salads, are an important part of *bagna cauda* (page 71), are stuffed and baked, and are preserved in vinegar or olive oil. *Peperonata*, a combination of bell peppers, onions, and tomatoes, is a popular preparation of Piedmontese cooks, though similar dishes are also found in other parts of the country, especially the sunny south.

LAZIO

Jerusalem Artichoke Gratin

Native to North America, Jerusalem artichokes were originally dubbed *girasole*, Italian for "sunflower," by early Europeans, a name that evolved into Jerusalem in the English-speaking world. The moniker is apt, for the tubers come from a type of sunflower that is a close relative of the common garden sunflower. Also known as sunchokes, Jerusalem artichokes have a sweet, nutty flavor reminiscent of artichokes, though the resemblance stops there.

Position a rack in the middle of the oven and preheat to 400°F (200°C). Grease the bottom of an oval gratin dish about 12 inches (30 cm) long with 1 tablespoon of the butter.

Bring a large saucepan three-fourths full of water to a boil. Add 1 tablespoon salt and the Jerusalem artichokes and cook until slightly softened, about 5 minutes. Drain well. When the artichokes are cool enough to handle, cut into slices about 1/4 inch (6 mm) thick.

Arrange the slices in the prepared dish. Sprinkle with salt and pepper. Cut the remaining 2 tablespoons butter into bits and dot the surface evenly. Sprinkle evenly with the cheese.

Bake the gratin until the cheese is golden and begins to melt and the Jerusalem artichokes are piping hot and tender when pierced with a knife, 15–20 minutes. Serve at once directly from the dish.

3 tablespoons unsalted butter

Sea salt and freshly ground pepper

1 lb (500 g) Jerusalem artichokes, peeled

1/2 cup (2 oz/60 g) grated Parmigiano-Reggiano cheese

MAKES 4–6 SERVINGS

Fennel, Orange, and Olive Salad

2 fennel bulbs

2 blood oranges or flavorful regular oranges

2 tablespoons extra-virgin olive oil

Sea salt and white pepper

About 24 Gaeta olives or other Mediterranean-style black olives, pitted

MAKES 4 SERVINGS

Cut off the stems and feathery leaves from the fennel bulbs and reserve for another use or discard. Cut away and discard any discolored areas of the bulbs. Halve each bulb lengthwise and cut away the tough core. Cut the halves crosswise into very thin slices.

Using a sharp knife, cut a slice off both ends of each orange to reveal the flesh. Place the orange upright on the cutting board and, using the knife, cut downward to remove the peel and pith, following the contour of the fruit. Cut the orange in half through the stem end, then slice each half crosswise as thinly as possible. Eliminate any seeds and visible pith.

Divide the fennel slices among 4 plates. Sprinkle the orange slices over the fennel, again dividing evenly, and drizzle the olive oil evenly over the top. Season with salt and white pepper, and scatter about 6 olives on each plate. Let stand for a few minutes before serving, to give the orange slices time to release some of their juice into the fennel.

Fennel, cooked or raw, is a favorite winter vegetable throughout Italy, but the addition of orange slices makes this a Sicilian dish. The small brown-purple olives named for Gaeta, a picturesque port town not far from Rome, are favorites throughout the country, though any good brine-cured Mediterranean-style olives can be used. This refreshing salad can also be offered at the beginning of the meal, as an antipasto. Serve with a dry white wine, such as Pinot Grigio or Verdicchio.

Garlic Roasted Potatoes

Roasted potatoes are one of the most versatile side dishes and can be prepared with almost no effort. You can roast other root vegetables using this same method. Try sweet potatoes or butternut squash, peeled and cut into chunks. You can also roast vegetables such as bell peppers (capsicums), mushrooms, and leeks using this method.

Preheat the oven to 400°F (200°C). Cut the potatoes into 1-inch (2.5-cm) chunks. Brush a rimmed baking sheet with 1 tablespoon of the oil. Scatter the potato chunks and the garlic in a single layer on the prepared pan. Sprinkle with the rosemary. Season with salt and pepper and drizzle with the remaining olive oil. Toss gently to combine the ingredients, then spread them out evenly.

Roast the potatoes, stirring 1 or 2 times, until the skins are crisp and browned and the potatoes are tender when pierced with a knife, about 20 minutes. Remove the pan from the oven and transfer to a serving bowl. Serve at once.

1½ lb (750 g) Yukon gold or other roasting potatoes

3 tablespoons olive oil

3 cloves garlic, thinly sliced

1 tablespoon finely chopped fresh rosemary

Sea salt and freshly ground pepper

MAKES 4–6 SERVINGS

CALABRIA

Broccolini with Garlic and Anchovies

2 bunches *broccolini*, about 10 oz (315 g) each, stem ends trimmed

Sea salt

2 tablespoons olive oil

2 large cloves garlic, thinly sliced

Pinch of red pepper flakes

6 olive oil–packed anchovy fillets

2 tablespoons capers, rinsed and drained

MAKES 6 SERVINGS

Bring a large pot three-fourths full of water to a boil. Add the broccolini and salt to taste and cook for 2 minutes. Drain and rinse under cold running water. Drain again and set side.

In a large frying pan over medium heat, warm the olive oil. Add the garlic and red pepper flakes and sauté until the garlic is lightly golden, about 2 minutes. Add the anchovies and capers and stir until the anchovies dissolve, 1–2 minutes.

Add the *broccolini* and stir gently to coat with the oil. Cover and cook until the *broccolini* is tender, 5–10 minutes.

Transfer the *broccolini* to a warmed platter and serve at once.

Developed by a Japanese seed company, *broccolini*, with its slim stems and small flowering heads, is a relatively new vegetable in the world kitchen. Sometimes marketed under the name *asparation*, it is a cross between Chinese kale and broccoli, has a sweet flavor, and requires only minimal trimming. Here, it is prepared in the style of southern Italy, with garlic, anchovies, and capers. Ordinary broccoli can be used in its place.

Swiss Chard with Raisins and Pine Nuts

Swiss chard and spinach are often used interchangeably in Italy. Both can be prepared this way, though chard is especially good, as its natural sweetness is complemented by the flavors of the raisins and butter.

In a small, dry frying pan over medium heat, toast the pine nuts, shaking the pan often, until golden, about 3 minutes. Pour onto a plate to cool.

Cut the chard crosswise into strips 1 inch (2.5 cm) wide. In a large saucepan over medium heat, combine the chard, $1/2$ cup (4 fl oz/125 ml) water, and about 2 teaspoons salt. Cover and cook, uncovering to stir once or twice, until wilted and tender, about 5 minutes. Drain well in a colander, pressing out any excess moisture with the back of a spoon.

Rinse out the saucepan and return to low heat. Add the butter. When it melts, add the chard and raisins and cook, stirring occasionally, until the chard and raisins are evenly coated with the butter and the flavors are blended, about 5 minutes. Season to taste with salt and pepper.

Transfer to a warmed serving dish and sprinkle with the pine nuts. Serve at once.

2 tablespoons pine nuts

1½ lb (750 g) Swiss chard, tough stems trimmed

Sea salt and freshly ground pepper

2 tablespoons unsalted butter

2 tablespoons raisins

MAKES 4 SERVINGS

Polenta with Gorgonzola

2 cups (16 fl oz/500 ml) whole milk

1 cup (5 oz/155 g) coarse-ground polenta

Sea salt

¼ lb (125 g) Gorgonzola cheese, rind removed and crumbled

2 tablespoons unsalted butter, at room temperature

½ cup (2 oz/60 g) grated Parmigiano-Reggiano cheese

MAKES 8 SERVINGS

Position a rack in the middle of the oven and preheat to 375°F (190°C).

In a 2-qt (2-l) baking dish, whisk together 3 cups (24 fl oz/750 ml) water with the milk, polenta, and 1 teaspoon salt. Bake, uncovered, until the liquid has been absorbed and the polenta is tender, about 1 hour.

Remove the dish from the oven and whisk the polenta until creamy. Stir the Gorgonzola and butter into the polenta, distributing them evenly. Sprinkle the Parmigiano-Reggiano evenly over the top.

Return the dish to the oven and bake until the cheeses are melted and the top is lightly browned, about 10 minutes. Serve at once directly from the dish.

This rich baked polenta, typical of both Lombardy, where Gorgonzola is traditionally made, and neighboring Piedmont, is easier to cook than polenta prepared on the stove top. You need only whisk together the polenta and liquid and let the mixture bake in the oven. Serve as an accompaniment to Braised Short Ribs (page 196) with or without the Gorgonzola.

Fried Polenta with Wild Mushrooms

In Trentino–Alto Adige, in Italy's northeast corner, cooks usually serve polenta rather than rice, including this dish of crisp polenta slices topped with sautéed mushrooms. If possible, use wild mushrooms, such as yellow or black chanterelles, porcini, or hedgehogs, though any type of flavorful fresh mushroom, wild or cultivated, can be used. Serve the polenta as an accompaniment to beef stew or pot roast.

To make the polenta, in a large, heavy saucepan, bring 3 cups (24 fl oz/750 ml) of water to a boil. In a large measuring pitcher, whisk together 1 cup (8 fl oz/250 ml) water, the polenta, and 2 teaspoons salt. Slowly add the polenta mixture to the boiling water while whisking constantly. Then cook, stirring constantly, until the mixture returns to a boil. Reduce the heat to low, cover, and cook, uncovering and stirring occasionally, until the polenta is thick, pulls away from the sides of the pan, and no longer tastes grainy, about 40 minutes. Watch carefully to make sure the polenta does not scorch. If it becomes too thick before it is cooked, stir in a little warm water.

Remove from the heat and pour the polenta onto a rimmed baking sheet. Dip a rubber spatula in cold water and spread the polenta into an even sheet about $1/2$ inch (12 mm) thick. Let cool, cover, and refrigerate until firm, at least 1 hour or for up to overnight.

Cut the polenta into 2-inch (5-cm) squares. Lightly brush a large nonstick frying pan with olive oil and heat over medium-high heat. Pat the polenta squares dry with paper towels. Working in batches, add the polenta squares to the pan in a single layer and cook, turning once, until golden brown on both sides, about 10 minutes.

Meanwhile, cook the mushrooms. In a large frying pan over medium heat, warm the olive oil. Add the mushrooms and sauté until browned, 8–10 minutes. Season with salt and pepper. Push the mushrooms to one side of the pan, and add the garlic and parsley to the uncovered portion. Sauté until the garlic is lightly golden, about 2 minutes. Stir together the mushrooms, garlic, and parsley.

Arrange the polenta squares on a warmed platter. Top with the mushroom mixture and serve at once.

For the polenta

1 cup (5 oz/155 g) coarse-ground polenta

Sea salt

Olive oil for frying

For the mushrooms

3 tablespoons olive oil

1 lb (500 g) assorted fresh wild and/or cultivated mushrooms, brushed clean and sliced

Sea salt and freshly ground pepper

2 large cloves garlic, minced

2 tablespoons chopped fresh flat-leaf (Italian) parsley

MAKES 4 SERVINGS

Warm Borlotti Bean and Radicchio Salad

2 oz (60 g) pancetta, chopped

3 tablespoons extra-virgin olive oil

1 clove garlic, lightly crushed

2-inch (5-cm) sprig fresh rosemary

2 cups (14 oz/440 g) cooked borlotti or cranberry beans (page 275)

Sea salt and freshly ground pepper

1 small head radicchio, about ¼ lb (125 g), trimmed and cut crosswise into narrow strips

1 tablespoon fresh lemon juice

2 tablespoons chopped fresh flat-leaf (Italian) parsley

MAKES 4 SERVINGS

In a saucepan large enough to hold the beans, cook the pancetta over medium heat, stirring often, until crisp, about 5 minutes. Using a slotted spoon, transfer the pancetta to paper towels to drain.

Add 1 tablespoon of the olive oil to the fat in the pan and warm over medium heat. Add the garlic and rosemary and sauté until the garlic is lightly golden, about 2 minutes. Stir in the beans and season with salt and pepper. Reduce the heat to medium-low, cover, and simmer, stirring occasionally, for 5 minutes to blend the flavors.

Remove the beans from the heat and remove and discard the rosemary and garlic. In a serving bowl, toss together the beans, radicchio, and reserved pancetta. Add the remaining 2 tablespoons oil and the lemon juice and toss again.

Taste and adjust the seasoning with salt and pepper, sprinkle with the parsley, and serve at once.

This salad from the Veneto is a study in contrasts: warm, creamy, sweet-tasting beans against crisp, cool, lightly bitter radicchio and salty, crisp pancetta. Cannellini or other white kidney beans can be substituted for the *borlotti* beans. Serve the salad as an accompaniment to grilled tuna or roasted chicken.

Cannellini Beans with Garlic and Sage

In Tuscany, small birds, or *uccelletti*, such as quail and thrushes, are often cooked with tomatoes, garlic, and sage, which is how this simple bean recipe, known as *fagioli all'uccelletto*, got its name. Great Northern or other dried white beans can be substituted for the cannellini beans.

Cook the beans as directed on page 275, then drain, reserving the liquid.

In a large saucepan over medium heat, warm the olive oil. Add the garlic and sage and sauté until the garlic is lightly golden, about 1 minute. Add the beans and tomato and season with salt and pepper. Simmer, stirring occasionally, to blend the flavors, about 20 minutes, adding a little of the reserved liquid if the beans become too dry.

Taste and season with salt and pepper if necessary. Transfer to a serving dish and serve hot or at room temperature.

1 rounded cup (8 oz/250 g) dried cannellini beans

¼ cup (2 fl oz/60 ml) olive oil

3 cloves garlic, minced

4 fresh sage leaves

1 large tomato, peeled, seeded, and chopped

Sea salt and freshly ground pepper

MAKES 6 SERVINGS

Stuffed Artichokes

6 large artichokes

1 lemon, halved

⅔ cup (2½ oz/75 g) plain fine dried bread crumbs

½ cup (2 oz/60 g) freshly grated *pecorino romano* cheese

¼ cup (⅓ oz/10 g) chopped fresh flat-leaf (Italian) parsley

1 clove garlic, minced

Sea salt and freshly ground pepper

About 4 tablespoons (2 fl oz/60 ml) olive oil

MAKES 6 SERVINGS

Working with 1 artichoke at a time, trim the stem even with the artichoke bottom, peel and chop the stem, and set aside. Snap off the small, tough leaves around the base. Cut off the top ¾ inch (2 cm) of the leaves with a serrated knife or chef's knife to remove the prickly tips. Gently pry the center leaves open and, using a small spoon, scoop out the prickly choke and discard. Repeat with the remaining artichokes. Rub the cut sides of each artichoke with a lemon half as you trim them to prevent the artichoke from darkening.

In a bowl, combine the chopped stems, bread crumbs, cheese, parsley, and garlic and season with salt and pepper. Add about 2 tablespoons of the olive oil, or just enough to moisten the mixture. Gently spread open the center and the rows of leaves of an artichoke and push a little of the stuffing mixture between them. Stuff all the artichokes in this way.

Place the artichokes upright in a pot just large enough to hold them. Add water to reach about one-third of the way up the sides of the artichokes. Drizzle the tops of the artichokes with the remaining 2 tablespoons olive oil.

Cover the pot and place over low heat. Bring to a simmer and cook until the artichoke hearts are tender when pierced with a knife and a leaf is easily pulled out, about 45 minutes. Add a little more water if the liquid evaporates too quickly.

Transfer the artichokes to individual plates or bowls and serve warm or at room temperature.

Artichokes lend themselves to stuffing. You'll find them filled with canned tuna in Abruzzo, sausage meat in Calabria, rice in the Veneto, and ricotta and salami in Sicily. This filling, with minor variations, is popular throughout southern Italy.

TUSCANY

Fresh Peas
with Onion and Basil

4 lb (2 kg) English peas in their pods

6 tablespoons (3 fl oz/90 ml) extra-virgin olive oil

1 small yellow onion, finely chopped

Sea salt and freshly ground pepper

Handful of fresh basil leaves

MAKES 4 SERVINGS

Shell the peas into a bowl and set aside. You should have about 4 cups (1¼ lb/ 625 g) shelled peas.

In a heavy-bottomed saucepan over medium heat, warm the olive oil. Add the onion and sauté until translucent and golden, about 10 minutes. Add the peas and stir well. Pour in just enough water to cover the peas, cover the pan, and cook just until soft, 5–7 minutes. Season to taste with salt and pepper, and stir in the basil. Continue cooking until the peas are tender but still firm, about 3 minutes longer. Transfer to a serving dish and serve at once.

In Tuscany, peas are only to be served, and found in the markets, when they are in season, and their season is fleeting. If you catch it perfectly in early spring, you will be rewarded with tiny, tender, sweet vegetables. This recipe celebrates the early spring bounty.

TUSCANY

Braised Fennel
with Parmesan

Fennel, known as *finnochio* in Italian, is a native ingredient of the Mediterranean. Widely used throughout Italy, it is often served thinly sliced and raw, baked, or braised, as here. Its delicate anise flavor lends itself to simple preparations. It is excellent with fish, such as Halibut with Salsa Verde (page 175).

Working with 1 fennel bulb at a time, cut off the stalks and feathery leaves and discard or reserve for another use. Peel away the tough outer layer of the bulb, then cut lengthwise into medium-sized wedges. If the core seems very tough, trim it, but do not cut it away fully or the wedges will fall apart.

In a large frying pan over medium-high heat, warm the olive oil. Add the fennel, sprinkle with salt and pepper, and cook until browned on both sides, about 5 minutes.

Reduce the heat to low. Add the chicken stock, cover, and cook until the fennel is tender, about 10 minutes. Arrange the wedges on a warmed serving dish and sprinkle with the Parmesan. Serve at once.

4 fennel bulbs

⅓ cup (3 fl oz/80 ml) olive oil

Sea salt and freshly ground pepper

½ cup (4 fl oz/125 ml) chicken stock (page 274)

⅓ cup (1½ oz/45 g) shaved Parmigiano-Reggiano

MAKES 4 SERVINGS

Asparagus Milanese

Bunches of bright green asparagus in various thicknesses are one of the first signs in an Italian vegetable market that winter has finally given way to spring. The thinnest spears are gathered wild in the countryside, their scarcity and brief seasonality translating into a relatively high price tag. Wild asparagus is a prized ingredient in frittatas and the occasional pasta sauce. Medium-stalked cultivated asparagus is used for this dish, which, though meatless, is considered substantial enough to be offered as a main course, accompanied with a green salad, in some restaurants.

Bring a large pot three-fourths full of water to a boil. Add the asparagus and cook until crisp-tender, about 4 minutes. Drain and divide the spears evenly among warmed plates.

In a large frying pan over medium heat, melt the butter. Break each egg into the pan, taking care not to puncture the yolk or let the egg whites overlap. Cook for 2 minutes, then season with salt and pepper. Sprinkle 2 tablespoons water into the pan, cover, and cook until the whites are solid but the yolks are still runny, about 2 minutes longer.

Using a spatula, carefully drape 1 fried egg over each serving of asparagus. Sprinkle each serving liberally with the cheese and serve at once.

1 lb (500 g) medium asparagus spears, tough ends removed

2 tablespoons unsalted butter

4 extra-large eggs

Sea salt and freshly ground pepper

½ cup (2 oz/60 g) freshly grated Parmigiano-Reggiano cheese

MAKES 4 SERVINGS

Dolci

About Dolci

Like other Italian courses, the *dolce,* or dessert course, is enjoyed at a leisurely pace. The more elaborate the meal, the more this course becomes a series of individual moments—from fruit to coffee to after-dinner drinks—designed to prolong the pleasures of company around the table.

At the Italian home table, dessert is generally a simple affair: fruit, sometimes cheese, and good, strong coffee. A sweet dessert is not always on the menu, though on special occasions, a homemade pudding, custard, cake, or tart; a confection from a good pastry shop; or a purchased gelato or frozen dessert might also be enjoyed.

THE FRUIT COURSE

Italy's vegetables are rivaled only by its fresh fruits, many of which are grown locally, or brought from south to north in the colder months. To serve a fruit course in the Italian style, put together a platter, bowl, or basket of fresh fruits for passing at the table, and set out a bowlful of cold water for diners to dip their fruit to wash it. Outfit guests with a sharp knife, a dessert fork, and a small plate, so that they can enjoy fruit the Italian way, cutting segments and peeling them as they go.

Fresh fruit is also often enjoyed as *macedonia,* or fruit salad, a mixture of cut-up fruits sprinkled with a little lemon juice, lemon zest, sugar, and perhaps a fruit liqueur, like maraschino or kirsch. Another simple Italian way to serve summer fruits, such as peaches, nectarines, or strawberries, is to cut them into chunks, spoon them into wineglasses, and cover them with red or white wine. Chunks of fruit are also frequently served sprinkled with a little sugar and a drizzle of balsamic vinegar, which enhances their natural flavor. For a richer presentation, serve Summer Fruits with Cannoli Cream (page 251).

THE DESSERT COURSE

Frozen desserts are popular year-round in Italy and make a particularly fitting ending to meals in the warmer months. With excellent gelati and *sorbetti* available in the cafés and *gelaterie* of most Italian cities and towns, these frozen confections are seldom made at home. When served at home, gelato might take the form of Affogato (page 245), in which a scoop of gelato is doused with hot coffee. If you own an ice-cream maker, whipping up authentic-tasting Lemon Sorbetto (page 246) or Gelato alla Crema (page 255), which can also be used a base for making other flavors, is easy and rewarding. The refreshing Espresso Granita (page 250) is even simpler to prepare, requiring no special equipment.

In Italy, custards and puddings are found on the dessert lists of most restaurants and are also enjoyed at home. The Italian favorites in this chapter include delicate yet decadent Panna Cotta with Berries (page 249); Marsala-scented Zabaglione (page 252) served over fresh fruit; a Piedmontese Chocolate-Caramel Custard (page 266); Zuppa Inglese (page 265), Italy's version of the trifle; and Tiramisù (page 270), which, along with gelato, has become Italy's best-known dessert.

Cakes and fruit tarts, such as Peach Crostata (page 259), Olive Oil Cake with Cherry Compote (page 256), and Pistachio Cake (page 269), and Chocolate-Hazelnut Fritters (page 262) are simple, traditional desserts, equally at home at the conclusion of a special meal or with afternoon coffee or tea.

THE CHEESE COURSE

A selection of cheeses makes an easy, savory dessert. The cheese course can accompany or follow the fruit course. Visit a good cheese shop and ask to sample a variety of Italian cheeses. Choose two to four types with contrasting and complementary qualities: fresh versus aged or an assortment of cow's, sheep's, or goat's milk cheeses. You may want to include a rich, soft cheese, such as *crescenza, robiola,* or Taleggio; an Italian blue, such as Gorgonzola; a medium-soft, semiaged cheese, like a Tuscan pecorino; and/or an aged cheese, such as Parmigiano-Reggiano or *grana padano.* Serve the cheese course with thin slices of bread, honey, toasted nuts, and dried fruit. An Italian sparkling or dessert wine makes a good accompaniment.

DESSERT WINES

Sweet Italian wines are often poured after the meal. These include sparkling wines, such as Asti Spumante, as well as still and fortified wines, like Moscato, Malvasia, Marsala, and *vin santo.* Cookies, such as Pine Nut–Orange Biscotti (page 260) and Brutti ma Buoni Cookies (page 261), are often served with wine.

COFFEE AND CORDIALS

Coffee is generally offered after the dessert course and takes the form of a shot of intense espresso. To make Italian-style coffee, use an electric espresso machine or a stove-top espresso pot. If using the latter, heat the pot over medium-high heat until the coffee begins to emerge into the top chamber, then reduce the heat so the coffee seeps out slowly, ensuring a concentrated flavor. Serve in demitasse cups followed by a selection of after-dinner drinks, like grappa, Fernet Branca, Cynar, or limoncello served ice-cold.

Affogato

As with many classic Italian recipes, the beauty of this recipe lies in its utter simplicity, which also makes it important to use only the best-quality ingredients. At its most basic, *affogato*, which means "drowned" (a reference to the ice cream "drowning" in coffee), has only two ingredients. Feel free to experiment with different flavors of gelato.

If the gelato is firm, remove it from the freezer and let stand at room temperature for about 10 minutes prior to serving.

Put one or two scoops of gelato in each individual bowl. Divide the hot espresso among 4 espresso cups. Serve the espresso alongside the bowls of ice cream, inviting diners to pour the espresso over their serving.

Gelato alla Crema (page 255), or 1 pint (16 fl oz/500 ml) vanilla gelato

1 cup (8 fl oz/250 ml) freshly brewed espresso or strong coffee

MAKES 4 SERVINGS

Lemon Sorbetto

²/₃ cup (5 oz/155 g) sugar

1 teaspoon grated lemon zest

¹/₂ cup (4 fl oz/125 ml) fresh lemon juice, strained

MAKES ABOUT 1 QT (1 L),
OR 6 SERVINGS

In a small saucepan over medium heat, combine 1 cup (8 fl oz/250 ml) water and the sugar and bring to a simmer. Reduce the heat to low and simmer, stirring occasionally, until the sugar is dissolved, about 4 minutes.

Pour the sugar syrup into a bowl and let cool. Stir in an additional 2 cups (16 fl oz/500 ml) water, the lemon zest, and the lemon juice, cover, and refrigerate until chilled, about 3 hours or for up to 24 hours.

Pour the mixture into an ice-cream maker and freeze according to the manufacturer's instructions. The *sorbetto* can be served immediately, directly from the ice-cream maker, when it is still soft and very fruity tasting. Or, you can transfer the *sorbetto* to a freezer-safe container, cover, and freeze until firm, at least 3 hours or for up to 2 days, before serving. Let soften slightly before serving.

The Sicilians are the premier *sorbetto* makers of Italy. They turn out the frozen dessert in a wide variety of flavors, from berry to almond to chocolate, and eat it at all times of the day, often sandwiched in a soft brioche roll. This lemon version is the perfect finish to a seafood meal.

Panna Cotta with Berries

Panna cotta, or "cooked cream," is a specialty of Piedmont, where large herds of dairy cows yield an abundance of fresh milk. It has the pure flavor of fresh cream, with a slightly thickened, custardlike consistency, thanks to a touch of gelatin. Using a vanilla bean imbues the cream with a particularly delicate floral aroma, but 1 teaspoon pure vanilla extract can be substituted for the bean, adding it after removing the pan from the heat.

In a large bowl, sprinkle the gelatin over the milk. Let stand for about 2 minutes to soften the gelatin.

In a saucepan over medium heat, stir together the cream and sugar. Using a small, sharp knife, split the vanilla bean in half lengthwise. Using the tip of the knife, scrape the seeds from the vanilla bean into the cream. Add the vanilla bean pod to the cream. Heat, stirring occasionally, until small bubbles appear around the edges of the pan. Remove from the heat and let cool briefly.

Remove the vanilla bean. Slowly add the warm cream to the gelatin mixture, stirring constantly until completely dissolved. Pour the mixture into four ³/₄-cup (6–fl oz/180-ml) ramekins or custard cups, dividing it evenly. Cover and refrigerate for at least 4 hours or for up to overnight.

When ready to serve, run a small knife blade around the inside of each ramekin to loosen the panna cotta, and then invert each ramekin onto a dessert plate. Arrange the berries around each panna cotta and serve at once.

2¹/₂ teaspoons (1 package) unflavored gelatin

¹/₄ cup (2 fl oz/60 ml) whole milk

2 cups (16 fl oz/500 ml) heavy (double) cream

¹/₄ cup (2 oz/60 g) sugar

1 vanilla bean

4 cups (1 lb/500 g) berries such as blackberries, sliced strawberries, blueberries, and/or raspberries, in any combination

MAKES 4 SERVINGS

Espresso Granita

3 cups (24 fl oz/750 ml) hot freshly brewed espresso

½ cup (4 oz/125 g) sugar

MAKES 6 SERVINGS

In a bowl, combine the espresso and sugar and stir until the sugar is completely dissolved, about 3 minutes. Let cool to room temperature, about 30 minutes.

Pour the mixture into a 9-inch (23-cm) round or square metal pan. Place in the freezer and freeze until the mixture begins to harden around the edges and a thin layer of ice forms on the surface, about 30 minutes. Remove the pan from the freezer and, using a fork, break up any frozen areas into shards and mix the shards back into the liquid. Return the pan to the freezer, freeze for about 20 minutes, and repeat the scraping. Continue to freeze, stirring the mixture every 20 minutes, until the mixture forms flakes and is icy throughout, about 1 hour total.

Serve the granita shortly after making for the best texture, spooning it into chilled dessert glasses.

Almost nothing is simpler than making a granita. This one calls for just coffee and sugar, frozen together with only occasional stirring, but it makes an elegant finish to a meal and rolls dessert and coffee into a single portion. For a more elaborate presentation, layer the granita with whipped cream in tall parfait glasses.

Summer Fruits with Cannoli Cream

The sweetened ricotta cheese used to fill cannoli is also a delightful partner to fresh fruit. Ricotta cheese, traditionally made from whey left over from cheese making, is fresh and relatively light, which allows the summer fruits to shine. In autumn and winter, you can pair this same topping with dried fruits, such as figs and apricots simmered in brandy and sweetened with honey. For the best results, seek out a freshly made artisanal ricotta.

In a bowl, using a whisk or wooden spoon, beat the ricotta cheese until smooth and creamy. Beat in the confectioners' sugar, vanilla, lemon zest, and cinnamon until blended.

In a small bowl, combine the apricots, plums, cherries, granulated sugar, and liqueur. Toss well, being careful not to bruise the fruits. Scatter the raspberries over the top.

Spoon the fruits into goblets or other attractive serving vessels. Top each serving with an equal amount of the ricotta mixture. Sprinkle with the chocolate and serve at once.

2 cups (1 lb/500 g) whole-milk ricotta cheese

¼ cup (1 oz/30 g) confectioners' (icing) sugar

1 teaspoon pure vanilla extract

½ teaspoon finely grated lemon zest

Pinch of ground cinnamon

6 apricots, pitted and sliced

6 plums, pitted and sliced

1 cup (4 oz/125 g) cherries, pitted and halved

2 tablespoons granulated sugar

2 tablespoons cherry or raspberry liqueur

1 cup (4 oz/125 g) raspberries

3 tablespoons chopped semisweet (plain) chocolate

MAKES 8 SERVINGS

Zabaglione

½ cup (4 oz/125 g) sugar

7 large egg yolks

1 cup (8 fl oz/250 ml) sweet Marsala

2–3 cups (8–12 oz/250–375 g) strawberries, hulled and sliced, or fresh figs, stemmed and quartered

MAKES 6 SERVINGS

This light and foamy custard is traditionally flavored with Marsala, but other sweet wines, such as *vin santo* or tawny port, can be used. Be sure the water is simmering very gently as you cook the custard, or the egg yolks will curdle.

Select a heatproof bowl that fits snugly in the rim of a saucepan. Pour water to a depth of about 2 inches (5 cm) into the saucepan and bring to a very gentle simmer. Meanwhile, in the heatproof bowl, whisk together the sugar and egg yolks until the sugar has dissolved and the mixture is pale yellow, thick, and creamy, 2–3 minutes. Continuing to whisk, gradually add the Marsala.

Place the bowl over, not touching, the simmering water in the pan, and cook, whisking constantly, until the mixture is thick and frothy, and has tripled in volume, about 10 minutes.

Divide the fruit among dessert bowls, and top with the zabaglione, dividing it evenly. Serve at once.

Gelato alla Crema

The only flavors in this smooth, rich gelato, other than a hint of orange, are sweet cream, sugar, and egg yolks. Serve it as an accompaniment to Peach Crostata (page 259) or Pistachio Cake (page 269), or as the base for Affogato (page 245). You can use it as the base for other gelatos, too, by adding chunks of chocolate, bits of fruit, or nuts during the last minute or so of freezing.

In a saucepan over medium heat, combine the milk, cream, and orange zest and heat, stirring occasionally, until small bubbles appear around the edges of the pan. Remove the pan from the heat.

Meanwhile, in a large bowl, whisk together the egg yolks and sugar until pale and creamy, about 3 minutes. When the milk mixture is ready, slowly add it to the egg mixture while whisking constantly. Return the mixture to the same saucepan and cook over medium-low heat, stirring continuously with a wooden spoon, until the custard has thickened enough to coat the back of the spoon, about 5 minutes. Do not allow the mixture to come to a simmer.

Immediately remove from the heat and pour through a fine-mesh sieve placed over a bowl. Let cool, cover, and refrigerate until chilled, about 1 hour.

Pour the mixture into an ice-cream maker and freeze according to the manufacturer's instructions. The gelato can be served immediately, directly from the ice-cream maker, when it is still soft. Or, you can transfer the gelato to a freezer-safe container, cover, and freeze until firm, at least 3 hours or for up to 2 days, before serving.

2 cups (16 fl oz/500 ml) whole milk

1 cup (8 fl oz/250 ml) heavy (double) cream

1 orange zest strip, 3 inches (7.5 cm) long

6 large egg yolks

²⁄₃ cup (5 oz/155 g) sugar

MAKES ABOUT 5 CUPS (40 FL OZ/ 1.25 L), OR 8 SERVINGS

Olive Oil Cake with Cherry Compote

For the compote

½ cup (4 oz/125 g) sugar

1 lb (500 g) fresh or thawed frozen cherries, pitted

1 lemon zest strip

2 teaspoons cornstarch (cornflour)

For the cake

1½ cups (6 oz/185 g) cake (soft-wheat) flour

1½ teaspoons baking powder

½ teaspoon salt

3 large eggs, at room temperature

1 cup (8 oz/250 g) sugar

⅓ cup (3 fl oz/80 ml) olive oil

1 teaspoon pure vanilla extract

2 tablespoons fresh lemon juice

1 teaspoon grated lemon zest

MAKES ONE 9-INCH (23-CM) CAKE

To make the compote, in a saucepan over medium heat, combine the sugar and ½ cup (4 fl oz/125 ml) water. Bring to a simmer and cook, stirring, until the sugar is dissolved, about 3 minutes. Add the cherries and the lemon zest strip, bring the liquid back to a simmer, and cook until the cherries are tender but still firm, about 2 minutes.

In a small bowl or cup, stir together 2 tablespoons water and the cornstarch until the cornstarch is dissolved. Stir the cornstarch mixture into the simmering cherries and cook, stirring gently, until the liquid is clear and slightly thickened, about 1 minute. Transfer the compote to a bowl, remove and discard the lemon zest strip, and let the compote cool to room temperature.

Position a rack in the middle of the oven and preheat to 350°F (180°C). Butter a 9-inch (23-cm) springform pan.

To make the cake, in a bowl, sift together the flour, baking powder, and salt.

In a large bowl, using an electric mixer on medium speed, beat the eggs until thick and pale yellow, about 3 minutes. While continuing to beat, slowly add the granulated sugar in a thin, steady stream until fully combined. Then add the oil in a thin, steady stream, continuing to beat constantly. Beat in the vanilla and the lemon juice and zest.

Using a rubber spatula, gently fold the flour mixture into the egg mixture in 3 batches. Do not overmix. Scrape the batter into the prepared pan.

Bake the cake until it is golden brown and springs back when pressed in the center, 35–40 minutes. Remove from oven, place the pan on a wire rack, and let cool for about 10 minutes. Run a small knife around the inside edge of the pan to loosen the cake, then release and remove the pan sides. Transfer the cake to serving plate. Accompany each slice with the compote.

In this recipe, olive oil imparts richness and moisture to a simple sponge cake. The flavor of the oil is subtle and slightly fruity, and your guests may never guess your secret ingredient. The ruby red cherry compote delivers a wonderful splash of color and sweet-tart flavor.

Peach Crostata

Fresh, juicy peaches in a crisp, tender pastry shell are a classic Italian summer dessert. Plums, apricots, or cherries can be used in place of the peaches. Serve the *crostata* the same day that you make it, while the crust is crisp and warm.

To make the pastry, in a large bowl, combine the flour, granulated sugar, baking powder, salt, and lemon zest and stir to mix. Scatter the butter pieces over the flour mixture. Using a pastry blender or 2 knives, cut in the butter until the mixture forms large, coarse crumbs the size of peas.

In a small bowl, whisk together the whole egg, the egg yolk, and the vanilla until well blended. Pour the egg mixture over the flour mixture and stir until the dough is evenly moist and begins to come together. If the mixture seems dry, add a teaspoon or so of cold water. Transfer the dough to a work surface and divide into 2 disks, one slightly larger than the other. Wrap separately in plastic wrap, and refrigerate for at least 30 minutes or for up to overnight.

Position a rack in the lower third of the oven and preheat to 375°F (190°C). To make the filling, in a bowl, toss together the peach slices, granulated sugar, and flour. Set aside.

On a lightly floured work surface, roll out the larger dough disk into a 12-inch (30-cm) round. Carefully roll the dough around the pin, position the pin over a 10-inch (25-cm) tart pan with a removable bottom, and unroll the dough, pressing it gently but firmly against the bottom and sides of the pan. Trim the edges of the dough, leaving a ¹/₂-inch (12-mm) overhang. Fold the overhang over against the inside of the rim of the pan. Pour the peaches into the pastry-lined tart pan, spreading them into an even layer.

Roll out the second dough disk into a 10-inch (25-cm) round. Using a pastry wheel or a knife, cut the dough round into 10 strips each ¹/₂ inch (12 mm) wide. Arrange half of the strips across the top of the tart, spacing them evenly. Give the pan a quarter turn and place the remaining dough strips across the top to form a lattice pattern. If the strips break, patch them together with a drop of water. Press the ends of the strips against the sides of the tart shell to seal.

To make the topping, in a bowl, whisk together the egg and 1 tablespoon water. Using a pastry brush, gently brush the dough strips with the egg mixture. Sprinkle the strips generously with the coarse sugar. Bake until the pastry is golden brown, about 45 minutes. Transfer to a wire rack, let cool for 10 minutes, then remove the outer ring and cool until warm or room temperature. Cut into wedges to serve.

For the pastry

2³/₄ cups (14 oz/440 g) all-purpose (plain) flour

¹/₂ cup (4 oz/125 g) granulated sugar

1¹/₂ teaspoons baking powder

¹/₂ teaspoon salt

Grated zest of 1 lemon

³/₄ cup (6 oz/185 g) chilled unsalted butter, cut into small pieces

1 large whole egg, plus 1 large egg yolk

1 teaspoon pure vanilla extract

For the filling

2 cups (12 oz/375 g) peeled, pitted, and sliced peaches

¹/₂ cup (4 oz/125 g) granulated sugar

2 tablespoon all-purpose (plain) flour

For the topping

I large egg

Demerara, turbinado, or other coarse sugar for sprinkling

MAKES ONE 9-INCH (23-CM) TART

Pine Nut–Orange Biscotti

2 cups (10 oz/315 g) pine nuts

3 large eggs

1¹⁄₂ cups (12 oz/375 g) sugar

6 tablespoons (3 oz/90 g) unsalted butter, melted and cooled

Grated zest of 1 orange

3 cups (15 oz/470 g) all-purpose (plain) flour

¹⁄₈ teaspoon salt

MAKES ABOUT 4 DOZEN BISCOTTI

Position a rack in the middle of the oven and preheat to 325°F (165°C). Spread the pine nuts in a single layer on a rimmed baking sheet and toast in the oven, shaking the pan every 2–3 minutes, until the nuts are golden, about 8 minutes. Pour them out onto a plate to cool. Put one-third of the cooled nuts into a food processor and pulse to chop finely; do not grind to a paste. Set aside. Raise the oven temperature to 350°F (180°C).

In a large bowl, whisk together the eggs and sugar until well blended. Stir in the butter until combined. Add the finely chopped nuts and the orange zest and mix well. Add the flour and salt and mix well. Finally, add the whole pine nuts and stir to distribute them evenly. At this point, the dough will be very stiff.

Line 2 rimmed baking sheets with parchment (baking) paper. Transfer the dough to a floured work surface. Divide the dough into 4 equal portions. Form each portion into a log about ³⁄₄ inch (2 cm) thick, 2 inches (5 cm) wide, and 6 inches (15 cm) long. Using a long spatula, transfer the logs to the prepared baking sheets, spacing them about 2 inches (5 cm) apart.

Bake the logs, watching to make sure the bottoms do not get too brown, until the top of each is firm to the touch, about 30 minutes. Remove from the oven and, using the spatula, transfer the logs to a cutting board. Let cool slightly, then, using a large serrated knife, cut each log on the diagonal into slices ¹⁄₂ inch (12 mm) thick. Place the slices, with a cut side down, on the baking sheets (if all the slices won't fit, bake them in 2 batches).

Bake the biscotti until they color slightly and are quite firm to the touch, about 20 minutes longer. Transfer the biscotti to a wire rack and let cool completely. Store in an airtight container at room temperature for up to 2 weeks.

Biscotti means "twice cooked:" first baked in a log and then cut into slices and baked again until crisp. The resulting cookies are designed for dunking. They are excellent with espresso or coffee, and are equally delicious with a sweet after-dinner wine such as *vin santo* or orange muscat.

Brutti ma Buoni Cookies

Despite the name, which means "ugly but good," these little meringue cookies are not really ugly, but they are exceptionally good. They are often made with almonds, but here they are flavored with chocolate and hazelnuts, a favorite flavor combination of Piedmontese bakers.

Position a rack in the middle of the oven and preheat to 325°F (165°C). Spread the hazelnuts in a single layer on a rimmed baking sheet and toast in the oven, stirring once or twice, until fragrant, the color deepens, and the skins begin to crack and loosen, about 10 minutes. Transfer the nuts to a towel and rub firmly to remove the skins. Not all of the skins will come off. Let the nuts cool, and then chop them coarsely.

Line the baking sheet with parchment (baking) paper. In a large bowl, using an electric mixer on medium speed, beat together the egg whites and salt until foamy. Increase the speed to high and gradually add the sugar, beating until soft peaks form when the beaters are lifted. Reduce the speed to low and beat in the cocoa and hazelnuts.

Transfer the mixture to a large, heavy saucepan and place over medium heat. Cook, stirring constantly with a wooden spoon, until the mixture is shiny and smooth, about 5 minutes. Watch carefully to make sure it does not scorch. Remove from the heat.

Drop the mixture by tablespoons onto the prepared baking sheet, spacing the cookies about 2 inches (5 cm) apart.

Bake the cookies until firm and slightly cracked on the surface, about 30 minutes. Transfer the cookies to a wire rack and let cool completely. Store in a airtight container at room temperature for up to 3 days.

1½ cups (7½ oz/235 g) hazelnuts (filberts)

3 large egg whites, at room temperature

Pinch of salt

1½ cups (12 oz/375 g) sugar

1 cup (3 oz/90 g) Dutch-process cocoa powder

MAKES ABOUT 2 DOZEN COOKIES

Chocolate-Hazelnut Fritters

12 hazelnuts (filberts)

1³/₄ cups (9 oz/280 g) all-purpose (plain) flour

2 teaspoons baking powder

¹/₂ teaspoon salt

1 large egg

¹/₃ cup (3 oz/90 g) granulated sugar

¹/₃ cup (3 fl oz/80 ml) whole milk

2 tablespoons unsalted butter, melted and cooled

Canola oil for deep-frying

2 oz (60 g) milk chocolate, cut into 12 chunks

Confectioners' (icing) sugar for dusting

MAKES 12 FRITTERS

Position a rack in the middle of the oven and preheat to 325°F (165°C). Spread the hazelnuts in a single layer in a small baking pan and toast in the oven, stirring once or twice, until fragrant, the color deepens, and the skins begin to crack and loosen, about 10 minutes. Transfer the nuts to a towel and rub firmly to remove the skins. Not all of the skins will come off. Set the nuts aside to cool.

In a large bowl, whisk together the flour, baking powder, and salt. In a separate bowl, whisk together the egg and granulated sugar until thick and creamy. Beat in the milk and butter until combined. Pour the liquid ingredients over the flour mixture and stir with a wooden spoon just until blended.

Pour the oil to a depth of 3 inches (7.5 cm) into a deep, heavy frying pan and heat to 370°F (188°C) on a deep-frying thermometer. Line a platter with paper towels and set it next to the stove.

When the oil is ready, scoop up a rounded tablespoonful of the dough and press a piece of the chocolate and a hazelnut into the center. Then, with a second spoon, shape the dough over the filling to enclose it completely. Push the dough off the spoon into the hot oil, being careful it doesn't splash. Repeat to make a few more fritters, being careful not to crowd the pan. Fry the fritters, turning them once, until nicely browned, about 2 minutes. Using a slotted spoon, transfer the fritters to the towel-lined platter to drain. Shape and fry the remaining fritters in the same way.

Transfer the fritters to a platter. Using a fine-mesh sieve, dust the fritters generously with confectioners' sugar. Serve warm.

Sweet fritters, called *zeppole*, are found all over Italy, from cream-filled pastry puffs in Lazio to pine-nut spheres in Emilia-Romagna to brandy-flavored rounds in Abruzzo. Here, a chunk of chocolate and a hazelnut are enclosed in each doughnutlike puff. For a special treat, serve the fritters with hot chocolate on a cold day.

Zuppa Inglese

Explanations vary as to the meaning behind this dessert's name, which translates as "English soup." Some say it refers to its similarity to the English dessert called a trifle. Others believe it is a corruption of the verb *inzuppare*, "to sop." One of the key ingredients, *alchermes*, is a bright red liqueur that gets its color from *kermes*, an insect-based dye. Because *alchermes* may be hard to find, another red liqueur, such as Chambord, can be substituted.

To make the sponge cake, position a rack in the middle of the oven and preheat to 375°F (190°C). Butter an 8-inch (20-cm) round cake pan, dust with flour, and tap out the excess. In a bowl, using an electric mixer on medium speed, beat together the 4 egg yolks and granulated sugar until thick and pale yellow, about 5 minutes. In a separate bowl, using the mixer with clean beaters, beat the 4 egg whites on medium speed until frothy. Add the salt and beat on medium-high speed until stiff, glossy peaks form. In a small bowl, whisk together the flour and baking powder. Using a rubber spatula, gradually fold the flour mixture into the yolk mixture. Stir about one-third of the whites into the yolk mixture, and then gently fold in the remaining whites just until no white streaks remain. Pour the batter into the prepared pan. Bake the cake until a toothpick inserted into the center comes out clean, about 30 minutes. Transfer to a wire rack, let cool for about 10 minutes, and then turn the cake out onto the rack.

While the cake is baking, make the custard: In a saucepan over medium heat, combine the milk and lemon zest strip and heat until small bubbles appear around the edges of the pan. Remove from the heat, let cool slightly, and then remove and discard the lemon zest. Meanwhile, in a bowl, whisk together the whole egg, 3 egg yolks, and granulated sugar until well blended. Whisk in the flour 1 tablespoon at a time, and then continue whisking until the mixture is thick and pale yellow, about 5 minutes. Slowly pour the hot milk into the egg mixture while stirring constantly. Then pour the contents of the bowl into the saucepan, place over low heat, and heat gently, stirring constantly, until the mixture is thick enough to coat the back of a spoon, about 7 minutes. Remove from the heat and pour through a fine-mesh sieve into a bowl. Stir in the sambuca. Let cool to room temperature, stirring from time to time to prevent a skin from forming.

To assemble, using a serrated knife, cut the cake into slices about 2 by 3 inches (5 by 7.5 cm) and 1/4 inch (6 mm) thick. Line the bottom of glass serving bowls with some of the cake slices. Sprinkle the cake slices with some of the rum and some of the *alchermes*. Spread half of the custard over the cake slices. Top with another layer of cake slices, sprinkle with the rum and *alchermes,* and spread the remaining custard over the top. Repeat to make a final layer of cake, rum, and *alchermes*. Cover and refrigerate for several hours, or preferably overnight, before serving.

In a bowl, combine the cream and confectioners' sugar, and beat with a balloon whisk until medium-stiff peaks form. Spoon an equal amount of the cream on top of each bowl and sprinkle with the chocolate. Serve at once.

For the sponge cake

4 large eggs, separated

1/3 cup (3 oz/90 g) granulated sugar

Pinch of salt

1/3 cup (1 1/2 oz/45 g) cake (soft–wheat) flour

1 teaspoon baking powder

For the custard

2 cups (16 fl oz/500 ml) whole milk

1 large lemon zest strip

1 large whole egg, plus 3 large egg yolks

1/3 cup (3 oz/90 g) granulated sugar

1/4 cup (1 1/2 oz/45 g) all–purpose (plain) flour

1 teaspoon *sambuca*

1/4 cup (2 fl oz/60 ml) rum, or more to taste (optional)

1/4 cup (2 fl oz/60 ml) *alchermes* (see note), Chambord, or framboise

1/2 cup (4 fl oz/125 ml) heavy (double) cream

2 teaspoons confectioners' (icing) sugar

About 2 tablespoons grated bittersweet chocolate

MAKES 6 SERVINGS

Chocolate-Caramel Custard

2 cups (1 lb/500 g) sugar

3 cups (24 fl oz/750 ml) whole milk

4 large eggs

1 cup (3 oz/90 g) Dutch-process cocoa powder

12 amaretti, finely crushed (about ¾ cup/2½ oz/75 g)

1 tablespoon rum

1 teaspoon pure vanilla extract

MAKES 8 SERVINGS

Have ready an 8-inch (20-cm) round ceramic or glass baking dish. In a small saucepan over medium heat, combine 1 cup (8 oz/250 g) of the sugar and ¼ cup (2 fl oz/60 ml) water and cook, stirring occasionally, until the sugar is completely dissolved, about 3 minutes. As soon as the sugar dissolves, stop stirring and wash down any sugar crystals from the sides of the pan with a pastry brush dipped in water. Continue to cook until the mixture boils and begins to turn brown around the edges, then gently swirl the pan over the heat until the syrup is an even golden brown. This will take about 5 minutes. Immediately pour the caramel into the reserved dish and swirl to coat the bottom evenly. Set aside; the caramel will cool and harden.

Position a rack in the middle of the oven and preheat to 325°F (165°C).

In a large saucepan over medium heat, heat the milk, stirring occasionally, until small bubbles appear around the edges of the pan. Remove from the heat.

In a large bowl, whisk the eggs with the remaining 1 cup sugar until blended. Stir in the cocoa, crushed amaretti, rum, and vanilla until combined. Gradually pour in the hot milk while whisking constantly.

Strain the mixture through a fine-mesh sieve into the caramel-lined dish. Place the dish in the center of a large shallow baking pan, and carefully pour very hot water into the pan to reach about halfway up the side of the dish.

Bake the custard until the top is set but the center is still soft and jiggly when the dish is shaken, about 50 minutes. Carefully transfer the dish to a rack and let cool slightly. Cover and refrigerate until chilled, at least 4 hours or up to overnight.

To serve, run a small knife around the inside edge of the dish. Invert a flat serving plate on top of the dish, and then invert them together. Lift off the dish and serve at once, cut into wedges.

This creamy custard dessert was originally baked in a bowl, chilled, and then unmolded before serving. The Piedmontese call the rich, chocolaty custard *bonèt*, which means small, round cap in the local dialect.

Pistachio Cake

Sicily is known for its flavorful pistachios, particularly those from around Bronte, on the eastern side of the island. Cooks use them to make gelato, biscotti, and this orange-scented cake. Accompany each slice with a scoop of Gelato alla Crema (page 255).

Position a rack in the middle of an oven and preheat to 325°F (165°C). Spread the pistachios in a single layer on a rimmed baking sheet and toast in the oven, shaking the pan every few minutes, until fragrant and lightly toasted, 5–8 minutes. Pour onto a plate to cool.

Raise the oven temperature to 350°F (180°C). Butter a 9-inch (23-cm) springform pan. Line the bottom with parchment (baking) paper cut to fit. Butter the paper.

In a food processor, coarsely chop half of the toasted nuts, then remove and set aside. Add the remaining toasted nuts and $^1/_2$ cup (4 oz/125 g) of the granulated sugar to the food processor and process until the nuts are finely chopped. Add the flour and orange zest and pulse to blend.

In a large bowl, using an electric mixer on medium speed, beat together the egg whites and salt until foamy. Increase the speed to high and gradually add the remaining $^3/_4$ cup (6 oz/185 g) granulated sugar and the vanilla, beating until soft peaks form.

Sprinkle the flour mixture on top of the whites and fold in gently with a rubber spatula. Add the butter and reserved coarsely chopped nuts and fold in gently. Scrape the batter into the prepared pan.

Bake the cake until a toothpick inserted into the center comes out clean, about 40 minutes. Transfer to a wire rack and let cool for 10 minutes. Run a thin knife around the inside edge of the pan to loosen the cake, then release the pan sides and lift off. Using the knife, slide the cake off of the parchment and pan bottom and onto the rack. Let the cake cool completely.

To serve, place the cake on a serving plate. Using a fine-mesh sieve, dust the top of the cake with the confectioners' sugar, if desired. Serve in wedges.

2 cups (8 oz/250 g) shelled pistachio nuts

1¼ cups (10 oz/315 g) granulated sugar

1 cup (5 oz/155 g) all-purpose (plain) flour

½ teaspoon grated orange zest

6 large egg whites, at room temperature

⅛ teaspoon salt

1 teaspoon pure vanilla extract

6 tablespoons (3 oz/90 g) unsalted butter, melted and cooled

Confectioners' (icing) sugar for dusting (optional)

MAKES ONE 9-INCH (23-CM) CAKE

Tiramisù

½ cup (4 oz/125 g) sugar

2 cups (16 fl oz/500 ml) freshly brewed espresso

¼ cup (2 fl oz/60 ml) dark rum

45 ladyfingers or *savoiardi* (see note)

For the filling

⅓ cup (3 oz/90 g) sugar

6 large egg yolks

½ cup (4 fl oz/125 ml) heavy (double) cream

1½ cups (12 oz/375 g) mascarpone cheese

1½ teaspoons pure vanilla extract

Unsweetened cocoa powder for dusting

MAKES 8 SERVINGS

In a small saucepan over medium heat, combine the ½ cup sugar and ½ cup (4 fl oz/125 ml) water. Bring to a simmer and cook, stirring, until the sugar is dissolved, about 3 minutes. Remove from the heat, stir in the espresso, and let cool to room temperature. Stir the rum into the cooled espresso mixture.

Pour the espresso mixture into a wide, shallow bowl. Working in batches, briefly immerse the ladyfingers in the liquid, then transfer the ladyfingers to a plate. Set aside.

To make the filling, select a heatproof bowl that fits snugly in the rim of a saucepan. Pour water to a depth of about 2 inches (5 cm) into the saucepan and bring to a very gentle simmer. Meanwhile, in the heatproof bowl, whisk together the ⅓ cup sugar and egg yolks until the sugar has dissolved and the mixture is pale yellow and creamy, about 2 minutes. Place the bowl over, not touching, the simmering water in the pan. Using a handheld mixer on medium speed, beat the yolk mixture until very thick and tripled in volume, about 6 minutes. Remove the bowl from the heat and set the yolk mixture aside to cool completely, stirring frequently.

Meanwhile, in a bowl, using the mixer on medium-high speed, beat the cream until stiff peaks form.

Add the mascarpone and vanilla to the cooled yolk mixture. Beat with the mixer on medium speed just until smooth and well blended. Using a large rubber spatula, fold in the whipped cream just until combined.

To assemble, carefully transfer 15 soaked ladyfingers to a 9-inch (23-cm) square cake pan. Arrange them in a single layer in the bottom of the pan. Using the rubber spatula, evenly spread one-third of the filling over the ladyfingers. Place another layer of 15 ladyfingers over the filling in the pan and evenly spread with half of the remaining filling. Top with the remaining ladyfingers and filling, again spreading evenly.

Gently tap the pan against the counter to settle the ingredients. Cover with plastic wrap and refrigerate for at least 6 hours or for up to overnight.

Run a small knife around the inside edge of the pan to loosen the sides. Using a fine-mesh sieve, dust the top with the cocoa powder. Cut into slices and serve directly from the pan.

Various stories surround the origin of tiramisù, some of them off-color. Everyone agrees, however, that these ladyfingers soaked in espresso (hence the name, which means "pick-me-up") and rum, layered in mascarpone cheese and cream, and dusted with cocoa are as decadent as dessert can get. Ladyfingers—slender little sponge cakes that are as long as a finger—are available in many bakeries. *Savoiardi*, the Italian version, are sold in specialty-food stores and by mail order.

Basic Recipes

This collection of classic Italian sauces, from summery tomato sauce to slow-simmered Bolognese to fresh pesto, can be used to expand your Italian repertoire beyond the recipes in this book. There are also recipes for homemade stock, pasta, and doughs as well as tips for cooking beans.

Classic Tomato Sauce

4 tablespoons (2 oz/60 g) unsalted butter

2 carrots, finely chopped

1 small celery stalk, finely chopped

1 small yellow onion, finely chopped

2 lb (1 kg) fresh plum (Roma) tomatoes, peeled, seeded, and chopped, or 1 can (28 oz/875 g) plum (Roma) tomatoes, drained and chopped

Sea salt and freshly ground pepper

In a large frying pan over medium heat, melt the butter. Add the carrots, celery, and onion and cook, stirring occasionally, until the onion is translucent and the carrots and celery are very tender, about 15 minutes. If necessary, reduce the heat slightly to prevent the from browning.

Add the tomatoes, 1 teaspoon salt, and a pinch of pepper and cook until the sauce begins to bubble. Reduce the heat to the lowest setting and cook, stirring occasionally, until the sauce has thickened and the tomato juices have evaporated, about 1 hour.

Taste and adjust the seasoning. For a chunkier sauce, remove from the heat and use as is; for a smoother sauce, use an immersion blender or transfer the sauce to a food processor to purée the sauce to the desired consistency.

Use immediately, or let cool, cover, and refrigerate in an airtight container for up to 5 days or freeze for up to 2 months.

Makes about 4 cups (32 fl oz/2 l)

Tomato Cream Sauce

After the sauce has simmered for about 1 hour and is nicely thickened, use an immersion blender to purée the sauce to a fairly smooth consistency. Stir in $1/2$ cup (4 fl oz/125 ml) heavy (double) cream. Simmer for 5 minutes longer, then taste and adjust the seasoning.

Fresh Tomato Sauce

$1/4$ cup (2 fl oz/60 ml) olive oil

2 large cloves garlic, minced

2 lb (1 kg) plum (Roma) tomatoes, peeled, seeded, and chopped

Sea salt and freshly ground pepper

Pinch of dried oregano

About 6 fresh basil leaves, torn into small pieces

In a large frying pan over medium heat, warm the olive oil. Add the garlic and sauté until fragrant, about 30 seconds. Add the tomatoes and their juice, bring to a simmer, and season with salt, pepper, and oregano. Cook, crushing the tomatoes with the back of a wooden spoon and stirring occasionally, until thick and rich, 20–25 minutes. Remove from the heat and stir in the basil.

Use immediately, or let cool, cover, and refrigerate in an airtight container for up to 5 days or freeze for up to 2 months.

Makes about 4 cups (32 fl oz/2 l)

Bolognese Sauce

2 tablespoons unsalted butter

2 small carrots, chopped

1 celery stalk, chopped

1 yellow onion, chopped

2 oz (60 g) thick-cut pancetta, chopped

$1/2$ lb (250 g) ground (minced) pork

$1/2$ lb (250 g) ground (minced) beef chuck

$1/2$ cup (4 fl oz/125 ml) dry red wine such as Barbera

1 cup (6 oz/185 g) drained, chopped canned plum (Roma) tomatoes

1–2 tablespoons tomato paste

2 cups (16 fl oz/500 ml) beef stock (page 273), plus more as needed

1 cup (8 fl oz/250 ml) whole milk

Sea salt and freshly ground pepper

$1/8$ teaspoon freshly grated nutmeg

In a Dutch oven or other large, heavy pot over medium-low heat, melt the butter. Add the carrots, celery, onion, and pancetta and cook, stirring occasionally, until the ingredients are tender and rich golden brown, about 30 minutes. If the ingredients are beginning to brown too much, reduce the heat slightly and stir in a spoonful or two of warm water.

Add the ground pork and beef to the pot and stir well. Raise the heat to medium and cook, stirring often and breaking up the meats with a wooden spoon, until the meats are lightly browned and crumbly and their juices have evaporated, about 20 minutes.

Add the wine and deglaze the pot, scraping up the browned bits from the pot bottom. Cook until the wine evaporates, about 2 minutes. Stir in the tomatoes, 1 tablespoon of the tomato paste, the 2 cups stock, the milk, 1 teaspoon salt, $1/4$ teaspoon pepper, and the nutmeg. Heat the mixture until it just begins to simmer, then reduce the heat to very low and continue to cook, uncovered, stirring occasionally, for about 1 hour. If the sauce seems to be getting too thick or it threatens to scorch, add a little more stock.

Partially cover the pot and continue cooking the sauce on the lowest heat setting until it is thick and dark brown, 1–1½ hours longer. When the sauce is ready, use a large spoon to skim off and discard any fat that floats on the surface.

Use immediately, or let cool, cover, and refrigerate in an airtight container for up to 5 days or freeze for up to 2 months.

Makes about 4 cups (32 fl oz/2 l)

Pesto

1½ cups (1½ oz/45 g) lightly packed fresh basil leaves

3 tablespoons pine nuts

1 clove garlic, coarsely chopped

Sea salt

⅓ cup (3 fl oz/80 ml) extra-virgin olive oil

¼ lb (125 g) Parmigiano-Reggiano cheese, grated

In a large mortar, combine the basil, pine nuts, garlic, and about ½ teaspoon salt. Using a pestle, and working in a circular motion, grind the ingredients together until a dense, thick green paste forms. This can take several minutes. Slowly drizzle in the olive oil while stirring continuously with the pestle until a thick, flowing sauce forms. Transfer to a bowl and stir in the cheese. Taste and adjust the seasoning.

Alternatively, in a food processor or blender, combine the basil, pine nuts, garlic, and about ½ teaspoon salt and process until finely chopped. Then, with the motor running, pour in the oil in a slow, steady stream and process until a smooth, flowing sauce forms. Transfer

to a bowl and stir in the cheese. Taste and adjust the seasoning.

Use at once, or refrigerate in an airtight container for up to 2 days or freeze for up to 2 months.

Makes about 1 cup (8 fl oz/250 ml)

White Sauce

3 cups (24 fl oz/750 ml) whole milk

6 tablespoons (3 oz/90 g) unsalted butter

6 tablespoons (2 oz/60 g) all-purpose (plain) flour

Sea salt

In a saucepan over medium heat, heat the milk until small bubbles appear around the edges of the pan, about 5 minutes. Remove from the heat.

Meanwhile, in a heavy, nonstick saucepan over medium-low heat, melt the butter. Using a wooden spoon, stir in the flour and cook, stirring constantly, until a thick, smooth paste forms, 3–4 minutes. Remove from the heat.

Slowly drizzle 1–2 tablespoons of the hot milk into the flour paste while whisking constantly. The mixture will immediately become thick and lumpy. Continuing to whisk vigorously, add the milk about 2 tablespoons at a time. The sauce will gradually become smooth. After adding about ½ cup (4 fl oz/125 ml) of the milk, slowly add the remaining milk in a thin, steady stream while whisking constantly.

Stir in ½ teaspoon salt, return the pan to medium heat, and cook, stirring constantly, until the sauce is smooth and thick enough to coat the back of the spoon, about 1 minute.

Use immediately, or let cool, cover, and refrigerate in an airtight container for up to 2 days. Reheat over low heat, stirring constantly and adding a little hot water or milk to thin, if necessary.

Makes about 2 cups (16 fl oz/500 ml)

Beef Stock

6 lb (3 kg) meaty beef and veal shanks

2 yellow onions, coarsely chopped

1 leek, including about 6 inches (15 cm) of the green tops, coarsely chopped

2 carrots, coarsely chopped

1 celery stalk, coarsely chopped

6 cloves garlic

4 fresh flat-leaf (Italian) parsley sprigs

3 fresh thyme sprigs

2 small bay leaves

10 whole peppercorns

In a stockpot, combine the beef and veal shanks, and add cold water to cover. Place the pot over medium-high heat and slowly bring almost to a boil. Using a large spoon, skim off any scum and froth from the surface. Reduce the heat to low and simmer uncovered, skimming the surface as needed and adding more water if necessary to keep the shanks immersed, for 2 hours.

Add the onions, leek, carrots, celery, garlic, parsley, thyme, bay leaves, and peppercorns and continue to simmer over low heat, uncovered, until the meat begins to fall from the bones and the stock is very flavorful, about 2 hours longer.

Remove from the heat and let stand until the liquid is almost room temperature, about 1 hour. Using a slotted spoon, lift out the meat and reserve for another use. Pour the stock through a fine-mesh sieve into a large vessel, then discard the solids. Line the sieve with cheesecloth (muslin) and strain again, pouring it into 1 or 2 containers with a tight-fitting lid.

Let the stock cool to room temperature, then cover and refrigerate until fully chilled. Using a spoon, lift off the congealed layer of fat on top and discard. Store the stock in the refrigerator for up to 5 days or in the freezer for up to 2 months.

Makes 4–5 qt (4–5 l)

Chicken Stock

5 lb (2.5 kg) chicken backs and necks

1 leek, including about 6 inches (15 cm) of the green tops, coarsely chopped

2 carrots, coarsely chopped

1 celery stalk, coarsely chopped

12 fresh flat-leaf (Italian) parsley stems

1 fresh thyme sprig

8–10 black peppercorns

In a stockpot, combine the chicken parts, leek, carrots, celery, parsley, thyme, and peppercorns. Add cold water to cover by 1 inch (2.5 cm). Place the pot over medium-high heat and slowly bring almost to a boil. Using a large spoon, skim off any scum and froth from the surface. Reduce the heat to low and simmer uncovered, skimming the surface as needed and adding more water if necessary to keep the ingredients immersed, until the meat has fallen off the bones and the stock is fragrant and flavorful, about 3 hours.

Remove from the heat and let stand until the liquid is almost room temperature, about 1 hour. Using a slotted spoon or skimmer, lift out the large solids and discard. Pour the stock through a fine-mesh sieve into a storage container with a tight-fitting lid, and discard the solids from the sieve.

Let the stock cool to room temperature, then cover and refrigerate until fully chilled. Using a spoon, lift off the congealed layer of fat on top and discard. Store the stock in the refrigerator for up to 5 days or in the freezer for up to 2 months.

Makes about 3 qt (3 l)

VARIATION

To make brown chicken stock, brown the chicken parts and vegetables in the stockpot for about 15 minutes over high heat. Deglaze with 1 cup (8 fl oz/250 ml) dry white wine. Proceed with the recipe.

Fresh Egg Pasta Dough

2½ cups (12½ oz/390 g) unbleached all-purpose (plain) flour, plus more for dusting

4 large eggs

2 teaspoons extra-virgin olive oil

Place 2 cups (10 oz/315 g) of the flour in a food processor. Add the eggs and olive oil and process until the flour is evenly moistened and crumbly, about 10 seconds. If the dough is very sticky, add some of the remaining ½ cup (2½ oz/ 75 g) flour, 1 tablespoon at a time, processing until the flour is incorporated; you may not need all of it. After about 30 seconds of processing, the dough should come together and form a loose ball on top of the blade, and feel moist but not sticky when pinched.

Dust a work surface with flour, and place the ball of dough on it. To knead the dough, use the heel of one hand to push it away from you. Lift it from the far side, fold it back toward you, and then rotate the dough a quarter turn. Again, push the dough away with the heel of one hand, pull it back, and rotate a quarter turn. Stop kneading the dough when it feels damp without being sticky and is an even yellow with no streaks of flour. This will take only a minute or two. You will continue kneading with the pasta machine.

Shape the dough into a ball, cover with a large overturned bowl, and let rest for 30 minutes. The dough is now ready to use.

Makes about 1 lb (500 g)

VARIATIONS

■ For black pepper pasta, add 1 teaspoon freshly ground pepper to the eggs.

■ For fresh herb pasta, add 1 tablespoon finely chopped herbs such as basil, marjoram, oregano, parsley, thyme, chives, or a mixture to the eggs.

■ For saffron pasta, add a pinch of crushed saffron threads to the olive oil.

Fresh Spinach Pasta Dough

1 bunch spinach, about 10 oz (315 g), stemmed

3 large eggs

2½ cups (12½ oz/390 g) unbleached all-purpose (plain) flour, plus more for dusting

In a large pot over medium heat, combine the spinach and ¼ cup (2 fl oz/60 ml) water, cover, and cook, stirring occasionally, until tender, 3–4 minutes. Drain the spinach and let cool. Place in a kitchen towel and squeeze to extract the excess liquid. Finely chop the spinach. You should have about ½ cup (3½ oz/105 g).

In a food processor, combine the spinach and eggs and process until the mixture is smooth and well blended. Add 2 cups (10 oz/315 g) of the flour and process until the flour is evenly moistened and crumbly, about 10 seconds. If the dough is very sticky, add some of the remaining ½ cup (2½ oz/75 g) flour, 1 tablespoon at a time, processing until the flour is incorporated; you may not need all of it. After 30 seconds of processing, the dough should come together and form a loose ball on top of the blade, and feel moist but not sticky when pinched.

Dust a work surface with flour, and place the ball of dough on it. To knead the dough, use the heel of one hand to push it away from you. Lift it from the far side, fold it back toward you, and then rotate the dough a quarter turn. Again, push the dough away with the heel of one hand, pull it back, and rotate a quarter turn. Stop kneading the dough when it feels damp without being sticky and is an even green with no streaks of flour. This will take only a minute or two. You will continue kneading with the pasta machine.

Shape the dough into a ball, cover with a large overturned bowl, and let rest for 30 minutes. The dough is now ready to use.

Makes about 18 oz (560 g)

Focaccia

**2 packages active dry yeast
(about 3 teaspoons)**

1 teaspoon sugar

³/₄ cup (6 fl oz/180 ml) extra-virgin olive oil

**5 cups (25 oz/780 g) all-purpose (plain) flour,
plus more for kneading**

2 teaspoons fine sea salt

1 teaspoon coarse sea salt (optional)

To make by hand, in a large bowl, dissolve the yeast in 1³/₄ cups (14 fl oz/430 ml) warm water and let stand until foamy, about 5 minutes. Add the sugar, ¹/₂ cup (4 fl oz/120 ml) of the olive oil, the flour, and the fine sea salt and stir with your hand or a wooden spoon until a rough ball forms. Transfer the dough to a floured work surface and knead the dough until smooth and elastic, 5–7 minutes. Add up to ¹/₂ cup (2¹/₂ oz/75 g) flour to the work surface while kneading to prevent the dough from sticking.

To make in a stand mixer, dissolve the yeast in the warm water in the 5-qt (5-l) bowl and let stand until foamy, about 5 minutes. Add the sugar, ¹/₂ cup (4 fl oz/120 ml) of the olive oil, the flour, and the fine sea salt. Place the bowl on the mixer, attach the dough hook, and knead on low speed until the dough is smooth and elastic, 5–7 minutes. Add up to ¹/₂ cup (2¹/₂ oz/75 g) flour while kneading to prevent the dough from sticking. Remove the dough from the bowl.

Form the dough into a ball, transfer it to a lightly oiled bowl, and cover the bowl with plastic wrap. Let the dough rise in a warm, draft-free spot until doubled in bulk, 1–1¹/₂ hours. For a more flavorful bread, make the dough up to this point, punch it down, cover the bowl with plastic wrap, and refrigerate overnight. Let the dough come to room temperature before shaping.

Pour the remaining ¹/₄ cup (2 fl oz/60 ml) olive oil into a rimmed baking sheet (about 11 by 17 inches/28 by 43 cm), coating it evenly. Turn the dough out into the pan and press it evenly over the bottom. If it is too elastic to spread without springing back, let it rest for 5 minutes. Cover the pan loosely with a dry kitchen towel and let the dough rise in a warm, draft-free spot until doubled in size, 1 hour.

Position a rack in the lower third of the oven and preheat to 450°F (230°C). Dimple the dough by pressing your fingertips all the way into it at 1-inch (2.5-cm) intervals over the entire surface. Sprinkle the surface with the coarse salt, if using.

Bake the focaccia until golden brown, about 25 minutes. Transfer to a wire rack and let cool in the pan. Cut into squares and serve warm or at room temperature. Store tightly wrapped in aluminum foil at room temperature for up to 1 day or freeze for up to 2 weeks. Reheat at 375°F (190°C) for 10 minutes.

Makes 1 large flatbread

Pizza Dough

**2 packages active dry yeast
(about 3 teaspoons)**

**4–4¹/₂ cups (20–22¹/₂ oz/625–705 g)
all-purpose (plain) flour, plus more for dusting**

2 teaspoons salt

Olive oil

Semolina flour for dusting

Pour 1¹/₂ cups (12 fl oz/350 ml) lukewarm water (100°–110°F/30°–43°C) into the bowl of a stand mixer. Sprinkle the yeast over the top and let stand until foamy, 5 minutes. Place the bowl on the mixer fitted with the dough hook. Add ¹/₂ cup (2¹/₂ oz/75 g) of the flour and the salt; mix until combined. Add the remaining flour, about ¹/₂ cup at a time, continuing to mix until all of the flour is incorporated, scraping down the sides of the bowl if necessary. Knead with the dough hook until the dough is smooth but not sticky, about 10 minutes. Transfer the dough to a lightly floured work surface, divide into 4 portions, then shape each into a ball. Rub each ball with oil, and lightly oil a baking sheet. Place the balls on the baking sheet and cover loosely with plastic wrap. Set aside in a warm place and let rise until doubled in bulk, 2 hours. Use as directed in the recipe. Alternatively, shape the dough into a large round, coat with oil, then place in a zippered plastic bag. Place in the refrigerator overnight. Remove the dough from the refrigerator and divide into 4 equal balls. Transfer the balls to a baking sheet and allow to come to room temperature, about 1 hour. Use as directed in the recipe.

Makes four 12-inch (30-cm) pizzas

Cooking Dried Beans

1 cup (7 oz/220 g) dried beans

Salt and freshly ground pepper

Pick over the beans and discard any misshapen beans or stones, then rinse the beans under cold running water and drain. Place in a large bowl with cold water to cover by about 3 inches (7.5 cm) and let soak for at least 4 hours or for up to overnight. Alternatively, transfer the rinsed beans to a large pot, add water to cover by 3 inches, bring to a boil, remove from the heat, and let stand for 1–2 hours.

Drain the beans, place in saucepan with water to cover by about 4 inches (10 cm), and bring to a boil over high heat, skimming off the foam that rises to the surface. Reduce the heat to low, cover partially, and simmer until the beans are tender, 1¹/₂–2¹/₂ hours. The timing will depend on the variety and age of the beans. Use immediately, or refrigerate in an airtight container for up to 1 week.

Makes 2¹/₂–3 cups (18–21 oz/560–655 g) beans

Glossary

AL DENTE Literally "to the tooth," this Italian phrase refers to pasta or rice that has been cooked until tender but is still firm at the center, thus offering some resistance to the bite.

ANCHOVIES Blended into a sauce or draped over a pizza, tiny anchovies, also called *acciughe* or *alici,* appear widely in Italian cooking. They are available preserved two ways, as whole anchovies layered with salt and as fillets packed in oil. To use salt-packed anchovies, rinse them under cold water, scrape away the skin with the tip of a knife, and cut away the dorsal fin. Press the anchovy open, lift away the backbone, and cut the fish into 2 fillets. Rinse again and dry on paper towels before using. If purchasing oil-packed fillets, look for higher-quality anchovies in glass jars, rather than cans, and make sure the oil is olive oil. Oil-packed fillets can be used directly from the container without rinsing.

ARTICHOKES These Mediterranean natives, called *carciofi,* are cultivated for their thistlelike flowers, which are harvested before they bloom. The bud has thick, green, thorn-tipped leaves enclosing a tender heart. Artichokes available in Italy range from *mamme,* large globe artichokes, to *morellini,* small green-and-purple specimens.

ARUGULA A member of the mustard family, this slender, leafy green, also known as rocket, grows wild in the Italian countryside, and both wild and cultivated arugula is sold in local markets. It is used in salads, in quickly cooked dishes, as a topping for pizza, and alongside meat in recipes such as *bistecca alla fiorentina* (page 191). Tender, young arugula leaves have a pleasing delicacy, while older specimens have a more peppery, slightly bitter taste.

BALSAMIC VINEGAR *Aceto balsamico tradizionale,* or "traditional balsamic vinegar," comes from the area around Reggio Emilia and Modena in Emilia-Romagna and is made from the cooked must of Trebbiano and Lambrusco grapes. The finest examples are aged for at least 12 years in a series of barrels constructed of a variety of aromatic woods. The final product is slightly thick and syrupy, with a sweet, mellow taste, and is used sparingly as a condiment on finished dishes. Less expensive versions of varying quality are widely available and can be used in vinaigrettes, marinades, and other preparations. *See also* vinegar entry.

BAROLO One of Italy's most prized red wines, Barolo is made from Nebbiolo grapes and is produced in Piedmont.

BEANS Italians often call protein-rich beans the poor man's meat. Look for dried beans imported from Italy in Italian markets. Good-quality canned beans are a convenient alternative to cooking dried beans, especially in dishes that do not require long cooking. For every 2/3 cup (4 1/2 oz/140 g) dried beans or 2 cups (14 oz/440 g) cooked beans in a recipe, substitute one 15-oz (470-g) can. Rinse the beans well with cold water and drain before using.

Borlotti These popular, mild-flavored Italian beans sport an attractive pink-beige background speckled with maroon. They typically appear in soups, particularly *pasta e fagioli* (page 97) and minestrone (page 104).

Cannellini Ivory-colored beans of moderate size with a fluffy texture when cooked, cannellini are the signature beans of Tuscany. They are often served warm, drizzled with extra-virgin olive oil, either as a topping for bruschetta or as a popular *contorno*. White kidney beans or Great Northern beans can be used in their place.

Chickpeas Also known as garbanzo beans and in Italy as *ceci,* these round, beige beans have a rich, nutty flavor, a firm texture, and hold their shape well during cooking.

Cranberry Similar to *borlotti* beans, cranberry beans are cream colored with small red speckles. They can be used in any recipe that calls for *borlotti* beans.

Fava Pale green fava (broad) beans resemble lima beans but have a slightly bitter flavor. Tuscans call them *baccelli* and in spring, when the beans are at their tender best, they slip them from their pods and serve them raw with young pecorino cheese (page 58). Fresh and dried fava beans are different in flavor and should not be substituted for each other in recipes.

Romano Also called Italian beans, these edible-pod beans are similar to green beans but have broader, more flattened pods and a more robust flavor and texture.

BELL PEPPERS Sweet-fleshed, bell-shaped members of the pepper family, bell peppers *(peperoni)* are also known as sweet peppers or capsicums. Green bell peppers are usually more sharply flavored than red ones, the latter being simply a sweeter and more mature stage of the former. Orange and yellow bell peppers are separate varieties. Peppers traveled to Italy after Columbus's voyages to America and were at first cultivated for decorative purposes only, their edibility regarded with suspicion.

BESCIAMELLA The Italian version of French béchamel, *salsa besciamella* is a thick white sauce made by creating a roux of butter and flour and then adding milk and heating until thickened.

BISCOTTI This term is most commonly used for dry cookies that are baked twice, first in a loaf and then as slices. Each Italian region flavors its biscotti with different spices and studs them with different nuts.

BRACIOLE   Thin slices of meat that are sometimes rolled around a stuffing before cooking (page 195). Braciole appear as both *primi* and *secondi.*

BRANZINO   Firm, white-fleshed fish caught off the coast of Italy. Also known as *spigola* in southern Italy and as sea bass in North America, it is prepared in a variety of ways, from roasted and grilled to poached.

BRESAOLA   This salt-cured, air-dried beef is considered a specialty of the Valtellina, an alpine valley in Lombardy. It is usually served thinly sliced like prosciutto, though it is less salty and has a firmer texture. Often paired with arugula (rocket) and shaved Parmigiano-Reggiano, it is served as both an antipasto and a light *secondo.*

BROCCOLI RABE   A relative of turnip greens, broccoli rabe, also known as broccoli raab, *rapini,* and *rape,* has leafy, dark green stems topped by clusters of broccoli-like florets. Be sure to remove any of the tough stems and wilted leaves before cooking. If the skin on the lower part of the stalks is fibrous, peel it with a vegetable peeler.

CAPERS   The preserved, unopened flower buds of a wild shrub, *capperi* have a piquant flavor enjoyed throughout the Mediterranean. Capers packed in sea salt retain their intense floral flavor and firm texture better than brined capers, but the latter are more commonly available. Rinse salted and brined capers before using.

CAVOLO NERO   Literally "black cabbage," *cavolo nero* is not black but an extraordinarily deep, dark green. The plume-shaped, crinkled leaves, which have a pleasant bitterness much like kale, a closely related green, are an essential ingredient in the hearty Tuscan soup *ribollita* (page 103). In Tuscany, *cavolo nero* is harvested after the first frost, which softens the heavy texture of the leaves. It can be difficult to find

outside Italy, but dinosaur kale and regular kale are good substitutes.

CHEESE   Italians have long savored their instinctive regional cheeses, making them in a variety of ways from the milk of different domesticated animals and enjoying them on their own or as part of cooked dishes.

Asiago   An Italian cow's milk cheese that comes in several forms: the ordinary semifirm variety has a medium sharpness, while young Asiago, also semifirm, is milder. Both types melt well. Aged Asiago is a hard grating cheese with a full, sharp flavor.

Fontina   Originating in the Valle d'Aosta region that borders Piedmont, this rich, firm, earthy cheese is made from the milk of cows that graze on subalpine slopes. It is excellent for melting. For more information, see page 32.

Mascarpone   A fresh double-cream cow's milk cheese with a spreadable consistency and an edge of tangy acidity. This specialty of Lombardy is used in both savory and sweet recipes.

Mozzarella   Many consider the best mozzarella to be *mozzarella di bufala,* made fresh from the milk of water buffalo that graze in Campania. Sold floating in watery whey, the cheese has a delicate, tangy flavor and a pleasantly stringy texture. The more common cow's milk mozzarella is known as *fior di latte.* For more information, see page 21.

Parmigiano-Reggiano   The pride of Italian cheese makers, Parmigiano-Reggiano is produced according to a long-codified process. Partially skimmed cow's milk is molded into large wheels and aged for a minimum of one year to develop a complex, nutty flavor and firm texture. Its dry, granular character makes it ideal for grating over pasta or shaving over antipasti and salads. *Grana padano,* another hard grating

cheese, resembles Parmigiano-Reggiano and is often used in its place.

Pecorino Romano   A sharp, hard grating cheese made from the milk of ewes, this was originally produced only in the countryside surrounding Rome. Today, the area of production, defined by law, has been expanded to include Sardinia. Younger pecorino is also popular for cooking and eating. Similar pecorino cheeses are produced in other regions, including Sicily and Tuscany.

Provolone   Made from cow's milk, provolone is sold in young and aged versions. Both are smooth, dense, and lightly salty, and have a buttery essence; the latter has a spicier, sharper taste, is harder, and is used for grating.

Ricotta   The name of this cheese means "recooked," which describes the process by which it is produced. The whey left over from the making of pecorino and other cheeses, including mozzarella, is recooked, resulting in a fresh white cheese with a fluffy texture and a mild, sweet, nutty taste, ideal for pasta fillings and desserts. Cow's milk ricotta is common outside Italy, but traditional Italian ricotta comes from the milk of sheep, goats, or water buffalo. Whole-milk ricotta is richer than commercial varieties made from reduced-fat milk.

Ricotta Salata   This variation of ricotta cheese is a rindless, dense, supple sheep's milk cheese made by pressing lightly salted curds and then drying them for 3 months. It is grated, shaved, crumbled, or diced for adding to savory dishes.

Scamorza   This *pasta filata* (spun or pulled) cheese is slightly drier, chewier, and more sharply flavored than fresh mozzarella. It is sometimes smoked.

CHILES   In Italy, small hot red chiles are known as *peperoncini.* Cooks, primarily in southern Italy, add the fiery whole chiles to everything from pasta sauce to sautéed vegetables, and remove them before serving. (For milder fire, remove the seeds before using.) *Peperoncini* are available in well-stocked supermarkets and Italian or specialty markets. Any small dried red chile or red pepper flakes (use $^1/_2$ teaspoon for each chile) can be substituted.

CRESPELLE Italian-style crepes typically rolled around a sweet or savory filling. In Emilia-Romagna, the term *crespelle* is also used for fried dough strips dusted with sugar.

CROSTINI A Tuscan specialty, crostini are small, thin bread slices (toasted or untoasted) topped with a paste of chicken livers, greens, or other ingredients and served as an antipasto.

EGGPLANT In Italian kitchens, eggplants, also called aubergines, are grilled; rolled with a filling and then baked; or used in pasta sauces. The most familiar variety is the globe eggplant, which is usually large and pear shaped, and has a thin, shiny, deep purple skin. Many markets also carry more elongated Italian eggplants, which are smaller and also deep purple.

ESPRESSO Made by forcing steam through finely ground dark-roast coffee, espresso is more intensely flavored and has a thicker consistency than regular coffee. Properly brewed espresso always includes what is called the *crema,* a layer of reddish brown foam floating on top.

FARRO One of the world's oldest grains, *farro,* also called emmer wheat, is high in protein and has a deliciously nutty, wheatlike flavor. It is used in soups and salads or cooked like risotto. It is grown in only small pockets of Italy, most famously in the hills of the Garfagnana above the town of Lucca, where it thrives in poor soil otherwise unsuitable for planting. Look for pearled *farro,* which is partly hulled and cooks more quickly than whole-grain *farro.*

FENNEL With its bright green, feathery leaves, aniselike flavor, and ribbed aromatic seeds, wild fennel is one of the Mediterranean's oldest herbs. The seeds are an essential ingredient in many *salumi* (cured meats) and fresh sausages, in some biscotti, and in other preparations. The creamy-colored cultivated bulb, known as *finocchio,* is eaten either raw or cooked.

FIGS The ancient Romans believed figs, or *fichi,* imported from Greece were superior to those grown on local trees, but today Italians are happy with their own harvests, eating the plump, rich fruits with prosciutto, baking them into breads, or mixing them with nuts and honey for cookies. Figs both are cultivated and grow wild, and many varieties yield two harvests each year. In Rome, the small, sweet green or black figs of early autumn are called *settembrini* (little Septembers).

FLOUR Flour provides the body and substance of pasta, pizza, and bread doughs and many desserts. Italians classify their flour as 1, 0, or 00, which refers to how finely milled the flour is and how much of the husk and grain of the wheat have been removed. Since Italian flour is difficult to locate outside Italy, other, more readily available types can be used.

All-purpose Also known as plain flour, all-purpose flour is made from a mixture of soft and hard wheats. It can be used for making some pizza and pasta doughs.

Cake Low in protein, high in starch, and finely textured, cake flour, also known as soft-wheat flour, is milled from soft wheat and is used primarily for delicately crumbed cakes. It is similar to the standard flour used in Italy for both savory and sweet recipes.

Semolina This somewhat coarse flour is milled from high-protein durum wheat. It is typically used in the manufacture of dried pastas and is called for in some pizza and bread doughs.

GNOCCHI Little dumplings that are cooked in water or baked. Many versions exist all over Italy: in Liguria and the Piedmont they are usually made from potatoes, in Sicily from semolina flour, in Friuli from stale bread, and in Lombardy, puréed pumpkin is added to the dough, to name only a handful of possibilities.

GREMOLATA A mixture of chopped garlic, lemon zest, and parsley traditionally sprinkled over osso buco just before serving.

HERBS Italian cooks make the most of a variety of herbs that they gather in the wild, raise in home gardens, or buy fresh at the market. Among the most commonly used are:

Basil A member of the mint family, this iconic Mediterranean herb adds a highly aromatic flavor to foods. It is traditionally paired with tomatoes, is the base of Liguria's signature pesto sauce (page 273), is combined with tomatoes and mozzarella on pizza Margherita (page 156), and is used in countless other classic Italian dishes. Always use fresh basil.

Bay Leaf Strong and spicy, the whole glossy leaves of the bay laurel tree are indispensable in long-simmered savory preparations such as *ragù.* European bay leaves have a milder, more pleasant taste than the California-grown variety. The leaves are almost always sold dried and should be removed from a dish before serving.

Marjoram A close cousin of oregano, marjoram has a delicate floral flavor that complements tomato-based dishes. If possible, always use fresh, rather than dried, marjoram.

Nepitella Known as calamint in English, mint-scented *nepitella* is an Italian herb whose earthy flavor partners perfectly with porcini mushrooms.

Although it is closely related to mint, thyme is the best substitute. Before adding it to a recipe, rub it between your fingers to release its flavor.

Oregano Unlike most herbs, strongly scented oregano gains flavor when dried. Related to mint and thyme, it is often added to sauces, especially those based on tomatoes or other vegetables. Before using dried oregano, or any dried herb, crush the leaves to release the herb's aromatic oils, the source of its flavor.

Parsley, Flat-Leaf This flat-leafed, dark green variety of the popular Mediterranean herb has a more complex, peppery flavor than curly-leaf parsley. It is commonly used as both a seasoning and a garnish. Always use fresh parsley.

Rosemary Taking its name from the Latin for "dew of the sea," reflecting its relationship to oceanside climates, this Mediterranean native contributes a powerful but pleasantly aromatic flavor to lamb, veal, chicken, and other foods. It can be used fresh or dried.

Sage An ancient healing herb that takes its name from the Latin *salvus,* meaning "safe," this strong, heady, slightly musty-tasting herb is used either fresh or dried to season meats, poultry, vegetables, beans, and brown butter sauces.

Thyme Highly aromatic and yet subtle in flavor, this ancient Mediterranean herb is included in many slow-cooked dishes and is especially useful for the digestive properties it contributes to dishes featuring fat-rich meat or poultry.

MARSALA An amber-colored fortified wine made in the area around the Sicilian city of the same name. Available in sweet and dry forms, it is enjoyed as a dessert wine and is used as a flavoring in savory and sweet dishes.

MUSHROOMS The popularity of all types of mushrooms has resulted in the successful farming of many different varieties, blurring the distinction between cultivated and wild. A few species have resisted cultivation and are truly still wild, requiring foraging.

Cremini These common brown mushrooms are closely related to the all-purpose white mushrooms sold in grocery stores, but they have a firmer texture and fuller flavor. When mature, they become large, dark brown portobellos. Cremini can be substituted in recipes that call for fresh porcini.

Porcini Prized throughout Italy, these woodland mushrooms emerge in the spring and autumn, when the weather is warm and damp. Porcini, "little pigs" in Italian, are plump and have a firm texture and full, earthy flavor. Their large, smooth, pale brown caps resemble those of cremini, but their stems are thick and bulbous. Porcini, also known as cèpes, ceps, or *boletes,* are difficult to find fresh outside Europe. They are among the best drying mushrooms, however, and the dried form is widely available. Fresh shiitake, cremini, or other full-flavored mushrooms can be used in recipes that call for fresh porcini.

NUTS Cooks in Italy make use of many locally grown nuts in both sweet and savory dishes.

Hazelnuts Also known as filberts, and called *nocciole* in Italian, hazelnuts grow in abundance in northern Lazio and find their way into everything from biscotti to gelato. The grape-sized nuts have hard shells that come to a point like an acorn, cream-colored flesh, and a sweet, rich, buttery flavor. They are usually sold shelled.

Pine Nuts These long, slender nuts, the seeds of umbrella-shaped stone pines that grow all over the Mediterranean, are high in oil and have a delicate flavor. Called *pinoli* or *pignoli,* pine nuts are used in both savory and sweet recipes, including pastas, meat sauces, biscotti, and Liguria's classic pesto sauce (page 273).

Pistachios Grown in the warm climate of Sicily, pistachios have a thin, hard, rounded, creamy tan shell. As the nut ripens, its shell cracks to reveal a light green kernel inside. The nuts are used in pastas, rice dishes, gelati, biscotti, and pastries and as a garnish.

OLIVE OIL Perhaps no ingredient is more essential to Italian cuisine than the country's olive oil. Extra-virgin olive oil, with its fine, fruity flavor, is made from the first press of the olives without the use of heat or chemicals. It is used on salads, for drizzling on finished hot dishes such as soups, and in some cooked dishes. Olive oils labeled "pure," "virgin," or simply "olive oil" are the product of subsequent pressings and are good, less-expensive cooking oils that add subtle flavor. Store olive oils away from heat and light.

OLIVES The fruit of the olive tree is enjoyed throughout Italy, whether picked when unripe and green, partially ripe and purple-black, or fully ripened and deep black; cured in brine or salt; and preserved in oil, vinegar, or brine. Among the most popular varieties are the plump, sharp-flavored green olives of Sicily and the black olives produced near the coastal town of Gaeta on the Tyrrhenian Sea.

ONIONS Onions, in many varieties, are used to flavor numerous Italian dishes.

Green Although often used interchangeably with spring onions, green and spring onions are actually slightly different. The former are slim all the way from their dark green leaves down to the light green and white root, while the latter's white root swells into a small rounded shape. Only spring onions are found in Italy, but the white and light green parts of the green onion can be substituted.

Red Also called Bermuda onions or Italian onions, red onions are purplish and sweet.

Shallots A small member of the onion family, shallots, called *scalogni,* look like large garlic cloves covered with papery bronze or reddish skin. They have white flesh lightly streaked with purple, a crisp texture, and a flavor subtler than that of an onion.

Sweet One variety of Italian onion that has recently gained popularity abroad is the red *cipolla di Tropea,* named for a seaside town in Calabria. Medium sized and shaped like a top, they are almost always eaten raw, rather than cooked. Crisp, sweet Vidalia, Maui, or Walla Walla onions, which are in season from spring into fall, can be substituted.

White Although more pungent than a red onion, the all-purpose white onion is milder and less sweet than the yellow onion.

Yellow This all-purpose onion has parchmentlike golden brown skin and pale yellow flesh. Usually too strongly flavored to eat raw, it becomes rich and sweet when cooked.

PANCETTA The name of this flavorful unsmoked bacon is derived from *pancia,* Italian for "belly." This flat cut of belly pork is first cured with salt and perhaps a selection of spices that may include black pepper, cinnamon, clove, nutmeg, or juniper berries, and is then rolled into a tight cylinder for air drying. When the cylinder is cut, the slices display a distinctive spiral of lean, satiny meat and pure, white fat.

PASTA Scores of different fresh and dried pasta shapes are enjoyed throughout Italy. All of them should be cooked only until al dente (see page 276), still firm and slightly chewy. To prevent overcooking, begin to taste the pasta as the end of the cooking time indicated on the package

nears. Each brand and shape can have a slightly different cooking time. Dried pasta, or *pasta secca,* is made from a dough of semolina flour and water and is traditionally eaten with tomato- and oil-based sauces. Fresh pasta, or *pasta fresca,* is generally made from egg-and-flour dough and is best suited to sauces featuring butter, cream, and/or cheese. For more information on types of pasta and on pairing pastas and sauces, see pages 30–31. Some of the most common pasta shapes called for in this book include:

Bucatini Hollow, spaghettilike strands.

Fettuccine Usually fresh pasta ribbons, the width varies slightly from region to region.

Linguine "Small tongues," describing long, thin strands of dried or fresh pasta.

Orecchiette Small, concave ear shapes of dried or fresh pasta.

Pappardelle Fresh, wide ribbons about 1 inch (2.5 cm) wide.

Penne Dried pasta tubes with angle-cut ends resembling quill pens.

Spaghetti Classic long, round strands of pasta.

Tagliatelle Fresh pasta ribbons, similar to fettuccine, about $1/4$ inch (6 mm) wide.

Trenette Flat, thin linguinelike strands.

PIZZA PEEL Cooks, especially professional bakers, place garnished pizzas on this wide, flat tool to transfer them to and from the oven safely and with ease. Peels are typically made from wood, or sometimes metal, and measure 24 inches (60 cm) or more in diameter. They have a thin edge and a long handle. A large upside-down baking sheet can be substituted.

PIZZA STONE Also called a baking stone or baking tile, this square, rectangular, or round slab of unglazed stoneware creates the effect of a wood-fired brick oven in a home oven. The stone should be preheated in the oven for at least 45 minutes or up to 1 hour before anything is put on it to cook. Unglazed terra-cotta tiles can be substituted for the stone. Use the tiles to line the bottom of your oven. A pizza peel is used to slide the pizza or bread onto the hot stone.

POLENTA The term refers to both uncooked cornmeal and the thick, porridgelike dish made from it. Soft polenta is an excellent base for a hearty sauce and also makes a good accompaniment to roast meat or poultry. Amended with a swirl of Gorgonzola cheese, it can be a simple meal on its own. It can also be allowed to cool and then cut into pieces and fried or grilled. For the best results, seek out a coarse-ground polenta imported from Italy.

PROSCIUTTO This famed Italian ham made from the rear leg of the pig is lightly seasoned, cured with salt, and then air dried. Celebrated for its subtle but intense flavor, prosciutto is eaten raw or is cooked as a flavoring agent. It is almost always used in paper-thin slices. For information on *prosciutto di San Daniele*, see page 14.

RABBIT While some Italians have access to wild rabbit, most cooks use farm-raised rabbits for such classic recipes as rabbit stewed with wine, olives, and pine nuts or prepared *cacciatora* style (page 177). Farm-raised *conigli* have fine, lean white flesh that is less gamy than the flesh of wild rabbits. Smaller rabbits, weighing 2 to $2^1/2$ pounds (1 to 1.25 kg), are tender enough to be used in any recipe for chicken. Rabbit is more common in European markets than outside the continent, but quality butcher shops can special-order rabbit and cut it into the serving pieces called for in recipes.

RADICCHIO Pleasantly astringent, bitter, and crisp, this prized member of the chicory family is found in various varieties in Italy. The most familiar types are compact, round heads of white-ribbed burgundy leaves, such as *radicchio di Chioggia* and *radicchio di Verona.* They are best used raw in salads. In autumn, the less bitter *radicchio di Treviso* appears in markets. The long, narrow leaves, sometimes red with white ribs or light green with red tips, are enjoyed raw in salads as well, but are also well suited to cooked dishes, such as risotto.

RED PEPPER FLAKES Flakes and seeds of *peperoncini,* small dried red chiles, are a popular seasoning and table condiment in central and southern Italy. Just a pinch or two add heat to many dishes. *Olio piccante,* olive oil infused with the flakes, is a fiery condiment for drizzling over pizza. The chiles may be bought already crushed or may be purchased whole and crushed in a heavy-duty plastic bag with a rolling pin.

RICE Three main types of rice are used in Italy to cook risotto. Best known is Arborio rice, preferred in the kitchens of Lombardy, Emilia-Romagna, and Piedmont. Its plump, oval grains are rich in the surface starch that produces risotto's distinctive creamy character. The best Arborio is grown in the Po River valley. Vialone Nano rice, a favorite in the Veneto for its smaller grains, has less surface starch and yields firmer-textured, less creamy risotto. The more costly Carnaroli variety is a hyrbrid of Vialone Nano and a Japanese rice and combines the creaminess of Arborio with the firm texture of Vialone Nano.

SAFFRON The stigmas of a type of crocus, saffron is used in many regions of Italy to add a subtle, distinctive flavor and appealing yellow color to a variety of dishes, including risottos, pastas, and stews. For the best flavor, buy saffron in whole "threads," and check the date on the package to make sure the saffron has not been on the shelf too long.

SALT COD Known as *baccalà* in Italy, salt cod is an important ingredient throughout the country, especially during Lent. It must be soaked in water to remove some of the salt and reconsitute it before using. Salt cod has a robust flavor and firm texture that many Italians prefer over fresh cod. Available filleted and unfilleted, with or without skin, salt cod is sold in bulk and in small wooden boxes. Look for white flesh with a silvery sheen that has not discolored from age.

SARDINES These small saltwater fish are a particularly popular ingredient in Sicily, but they are enjoyed elsewhere throughout Italy as well. When purchased fresh, they are generally fried, grilled, or baked. They are also available preserved in olive oil.

SFORMATO A sweet or savory egg-based mixture that is molded in a ring mold and usually cooked in a water bath.

SQUID Many seafood merchants sell squid already cleaned and ready to cook. If you need to clean squid yourself, begin by cutting off the tentacles just above the eyes. Grab the tentacles at their base and squeeze to pop out the squid's beak, discarding it. Rinse the tentacles well under cold running water. With your finger, pull out and discard the clear quill (rudimentary shell) from the body, then rinse the body well, discarding all the entrails.

TOMATOES During summer, vine-ripened tomatoes are in ample supply throughout Italy. At other times of the year, fresh plum, or Roma, tomatoes, which are small and have a plump pear shape, offer the best quality. Canned plum tomatoes are a good choice year-round. The finest variety of plum tomato is San Marzano, cultivated in southern Italy. These prized tomatoes are canned and shipped to markets inside and outside Italy.

TRUFFLES The area around Alba, in Piedmont, is the home of the white truffle. Harvested from autumn into winter with the help of specially trained dogs, the truffles are found around the roots of oaks, poplars, willows, and other trees. The fungi are shaved raw to add intense aroma and flavor to pasta, risotto, and other savory recipes. Slightly milder but still strong and earthy, black truffles are found primarily in Umbria around the towns of Spoleto and Norcia.

VINEGAR The term *vinegar* refers to any alcoholic liquid caused to ferment a second time by certain strains of yeast, turning it highly acidic. Vinegars highlight the qualities of the liquid from which they are made. Red wine vinegar, for example, has a more robust flavor than vinegar produced from white wine. Both varieties are indispensable to the Italian pantry.

ZUCCHINI In general, small zucchini (courgettes) are preferred for their fewer seeds and fuller flavor, and are often sold with their flowers still attached as an indication of freshness. The versatile squashes are cut into chunks, strips, or rounds, and deep-fried, sautéed, steamed, stewed, marinated, stuffed, grilled, or baked.

ZUCCHINI BLOSSOMS The large, golden blossoms of the prolific zucchini (courgette) vine serve as tasty vessels for a wide variety of meat and cheese fillings. Italians enjoy them battered and fried, stirred into a frittata, or tossed with pasta and fava (broad) beans. Female flowers often come attached to tiny zucchini, but the larger male flowers are better for stuffing.

Index

OXMOOR HOUSE INC.

Oxmoor
House.

Oxmoor House books are distributed by Sunset Books
80 Willow Road, Menlo Park, CA 94025
Telephone: 650-321-3600 Fax: 650-324-1532
VP and Associate Publisher Jim Childs
Director of Sales Brad Moses

Oxmoor House and Sunset Books are divisions of
Southern Progress Corporation

WILLIAMS-SONOMA, INC.
Founder & Vice-Chairman Chuck Williams

WELDON OWEN INC.
CEO, Weldon Owen Group John Owen
CEO and President Terry Newell
Chief Financial Officer Simon Fraser
VP Sales and New Business Development Amy Kaneko
VP and Creative Director Gaye Allen
VP and Publisher Hannah Rahill
Senior Art Director Kyrie Panton
Senior Editor Kim Goodfriend
Photo Director Marisa Kwek
Designer Rachel Lopez Metzger
Associate Editor Donita Boles
Production Director Chris Hemesath
Color Manager Teri Bell
Production Manager Michelle Duggan
Photographer Bill Bettencourt
Photographer's Assistant Angelica Cao
Food Stylist Jen Straus
Food Stylist's Assistant Alexa Hyman
Text Writer Steve Siegelman

ACKNOWLEDGMENTS
Weldon Owen would like to thank the following people for their
generous support in producing this book:
Carrie Bradley, Cathy Burgett, Erica de Mane, Ken DellaPenta,
Lori De Mori, Judith Dunham, Maureen B. Fant, Laurie Loftus,
Stephanie Rosenbaum, Pamela Sheldon Johns, and Sharon Silva.

THE ESSENTIALS SERIES
Conceived and produced by
WELDON OWEN INC.
814 Montgomery Street, San Francisco, CA 94133
Telephone: 415-291-0100 Fax: 415-291-8841

In Collaboration with Williams-Sonoma, Inc.
3250 Van Ness Avenue, San Francisco, CA 94109

A WELDON OWEN PRODUCTION
Copyright © 2007 Weldon Owen Inc.
and Williams-Sonoma, Inc.

First printed in 2007
10 9 8 7 6 5 4 3 2

ISBN 13: 978-0-8487-3120-5
ISBN 10: 0-8487-3120-4

Printed by Midas Printing Limited
Printed in China